DISCARDED

DISCARDED

EAGLES OF
THE ANDES
South American Struggles for Independence

/\./\./\./\./\./\./\./\./\

By Carleton Beals

The Southlands

Eagles of the Andes
Nomads and Empire Builders
Lands of the Dawning Morrow
Rio Grande to Cape Horn
Pan America: A Program for the Western Hemisphere
The Coming Struggle for Latin America
America South
What the South Americans Think of Us (a symposium)

The Nations

Fire on the Andes
The Crime of Cuba
The Long Land: Chile
Mexican Maze
Mexico: an Interpretation
Rome or Death: The Story of Fascism

Personal Experience

House in Mexico
The Great Circle
Glass Houses: Ten Years of Free-Lancing
Banana Gold
Brimstone and Chili

Biography

Cyclone Carry: The Story of Carry Nation
John Eliot: The Man Who Loved the Indians
Adventure of the Western Sea: The Story of Robert Gray
Stephen F. Austin: The Father of Texas
The Story of Huey P. Long
Porfirio Diaz: Dictator of Mexico

Americana

Brass-Knuckle Crusade: The Great Know-Nothing Conspiracy
American Earth: The Biography of a Nation
Our Yankee Heritage: The Making of Bristol
Our Yankee Heritage: The Making of Greater New Haven
Our Yankee Heritage: New England's Contribution to American
Civilization

Novels

Taste of Glory
Dawn Over the Amazon
The Stones Awake
Black River
Destroying Victor

EAGLES OF
THE ANDES

South American Struggles for Independence

By CARLETON BEALS

/\/\/\/\/\/\/\/\/\/\/\/\/\/\/\/\

CHILTON BOOKS

A DIVISION OF CHILTON COMPANY

Publishers

Philadelphia   New York

Upsala College
Library
East Orange, N. J.

980.02
B366a

Copyright © 1963 by Carleton Beals
First Edition
All Rights Reserved
Published in Philadelphia by Chilton Company,
and simultaneously in Toronto, Canada,
by Ambassador Books, Ltd.
Library of Congress Catalogue Card Number 63-17559
Second printing, January 1965

To ERNESTINE EVANS

With affection and gratitude

108014

Designed by William E. Lickfield
Manufactured in the United States of America by
Quinn & Boden Company, Inc., Rahway, N. J.

Preface

/\/\/\ The armies of Latin American independence crossed and recrossed the Andes, the second highest mountain ranges on earth, through snow and ice. They marched across the thousands of miles of the Pampa and the llanos of Venezuela. They traversed blazing deserts, fought their way for weeks through vast swamps. They endured tropic deluges and hurricanes and found the mighty rivers, among the largest on the globe, no obstacle to their determination to drive out the Spanish and destroy the largest, most powerful empire in all history. The battles raged from California and Texas to the Straits of Magellan, over an area sixteen and a half times that of the original thirteen seaboard colonies of North America. Up until World War II, it was the most far-flung colossal conflict ever waged by man.

Toward the end of those eighteen years of sacrifice and struggle and death, Bolívar turned his army over to that noblest of all the independence leaders, the Ecuadorean General José Antonio de Sucre; and, perhaps remembering the tens of thousands of miles he had led his men across the continent, advised him, with a hint of weariness, "Maneuver for one big successful battle, then all other battles will be easy. Above all, avoid marching too much. Feet spared Peru, feet saved Peru, and feet can lose Peru again. We cannot fly to our enemies; we must conserve our energies . . . Sooner or later they will stop running, and we shall defeat them."

Soon after, up among the clouds of the Andes, the crucial battle of Ayacucho was fought, the final important engagement of the many campaigns, which sealed the fate of the Spanish. Three centuries of Conquest absolutism had come to an end. A continent and a half had been liberated from colonialism; or so people believed. Except for the Guianas, the European imperialists had been swept out of all South

America and the basis laid for the ten republics (eleven if Panama is included).

The parallel to our present era of continental liberation and the creation of new nations commands our attention.

What is even more pertinent in the case of South America is that the present struggles there for human liberation—again building up to continental proportions—are in many respects merely a continuation of the earlier independence movement which won national independence but failed to create economic and political freedom. This unremitting battle for human rights has gone on ever since the Spaniards were driven out, in repeated sporadic outbursts in which the people have been betrayed over and over again. Thus the present upsurge cannot be understood unless its beginnings of a century and a half ago are understood, unless the aspirations of the South American people are properly appreciated.

For Independence was not merely a nationalistic enterprise; it was a many pronged affair in which all the races and classes sought to improve their lot, to throw off the yoke of military and political and ecclesiastical tyranny and become free men. How badly they were betrayed soon after their victory, and how badly they have been betrayed ever since, can be verified by the most casual visit to Peru, Ecuador, Colombia and elsewhere; or even to Argentina, once more under the military boot. Except for the generals and politicians, a few urban traders and owners of large haciendas, the people of Peru are worse off today under so-called republican rule than they were four centuries ago under the Incas. There is even less land under cultivation.

The original Spanish Conquest was part of the Spanish counter-revolution and Spanish nationalism, which not only drove the most skillful farmers and artisans out of Spain, the Moors and the Jews, but also sought to shut out the Renaissance, the Reformation and the modern enlightenment of Europe. For three centuries they maintained the harsh feudalism and exploitation of the New World peoples and kept them in a cage of isolation, trying to shut out all new ideas, to keep the people in total ignorance of the rest of the world.

Even before the Independence movement was well under way, in many places control was taken over by the wealthier Creoles, not to free the people but to perpetuate the Conquest feudal structure and prevent the liberating ideas of the French revolution from reaching them. It was, in many respects, merely a counter-revolution. And where that was not the case, the counter-revolution came soon after, so that all South America—from that day to this—has been held to a Conquest feudal system.

The new countries were also soon taken over by what their historians call the "Second Colonialism"; that is, the intrusion of the great European powers and the United States, rushing in to gain possession of their resources, to take over control of their raw materials, and to secure commercial advantages. Inevitably the newcomers, known as the "New Creoles," allied themselves with the ruling South American military, ecclesiastic and land-holding aristocrats, became for all practical purposes, then as now, part of the feudal Conquest system.

Now, as the long-delayed industrial revolution knocks with powerful iron fists on the doors of the under continent, the struggle, which began with the Independence wars and is now building to a new climax, has taken on new aspects. As is the case with all political struggles, the conflict has deepened to economic goals, without the achievement of which, neither democracy and capitalism, nor communism, nor any other system can succeed; without which the original independence will remain truncated and mutilated, without which no sort of peace can come to the South American continent. The matter is urgent now. Furthermore, by the end of this century Latin America will have 600,000,000 people. Another China? Marching feet lost Peru, marching feet saved Peru; and for Peru read the entire South American continent. The feet are on the march again. The Independence struggle still goes on. Here in this book I have tried to put down some of the story of how, why and when this long, never-halted march toward human freedom began.

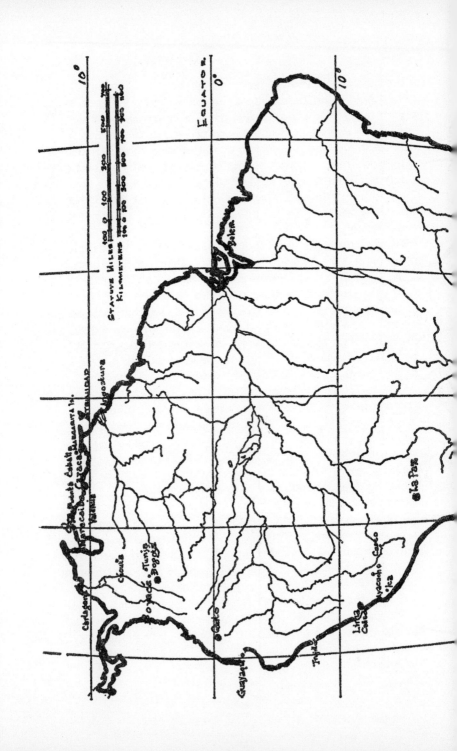

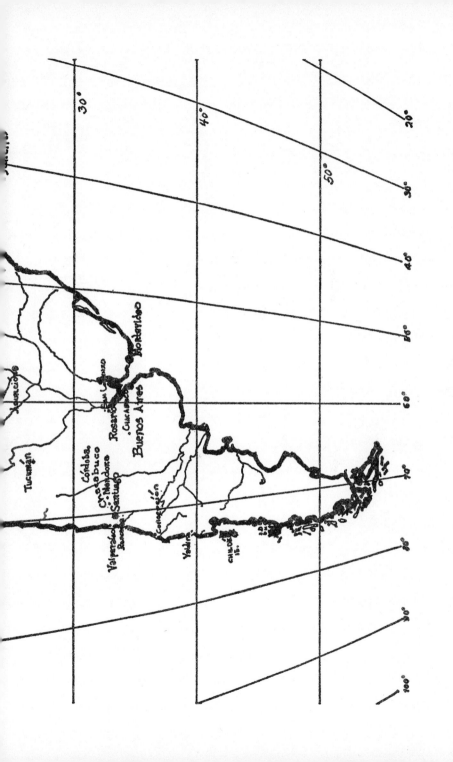

Contents

xi

EAGLES OF
THE ANDES
South American Struggles for Independence

1

Francisco de Miranda: Precursor

⋀⋁⋀ The chief human link between the independence of the thirteen American colonies and the independence struggle of Hispanic America was the Venezuelan Creole dandy and aristocrat, Francisco de Miranda. He is also a direct link with the French Revolution, in which, briefly, he was an active participant; his name is among those of the distinguished generals of the French revolution inscribed on the Arc de Triomphe in Paris.

Miranda visited the United States in 1783 when he was in his early thirties, a month after the final peace treaty was ratified. His way was well paved by letters of introduction from the Governor of Cuba, Juan Manuel Cagigal, and by his own exploits while the revolutionary struggle was going on. Two years earlier he had been a lieutenant colonel with an expedition that had driven the British out of Baton Rouge, Natchez, Mobile, and Pensacola, the last with the aid of North American patriots. He spent most of his time rummaging through the Pensacola bookshops, but was able, also, to get funds for the French Admiral Count de Grasse to take his fleet on to Chesapeake Bay, thereby forcing Cornwallis' surrender at Yorktown. As a member of another expedition, Miranda negotiated for the British surrender of the Bahamas.

In the United States he met everyone of importance, including General George Washington. He was faintly disgusted by the hysterical admiration accorded the American hero, which he found peculiar when so many other capable men in the Colonies went almost unnoticed, and on dining with him was repelled by his stiff taciturn reserve, but Washington's "suave manner and great moderation made it endurable."

It was in New York, after a dinner at the Cincinnati Society where he met Alexander Hamilton and General Henry Knox, that his dream of freeing the Latin American countries crystallized.

"In the year 1784 in the city of New York, I formed a project for the liberty and independence of the entire Spanish-American continent." A few weeks later, he and Knox were busily working out a project for an expedition to Venezuela: the needed arms, men, and money. Miranda considered Knox to be the only colonial leader with a command of military science.

Miranda knew that knowledge was the most important ingredient in the art of war, as in all other undertakings, that war itself was also politics, and that success depended on a complete awareness of all factors in the social order. Thus he visited every battlefield and fortification in the colonies from South Carolina to Massachusetts, talked with the participants, studied the operations, and filed everything away on paper and in his mind for possible use in his own grandiose schemes. He also studied farms and factories and schools, looked over art, and read what American literature there was.

Charles Willson Peale's portraits of the patriots aroused his admiration. Cotton Mather's *Magnalia Christi Americana* he considered "one of the most curious and authentic documents of fanaticism imaginable." Nor did he neglect early scientists: he saw David Rittenhouse, astronomer and clock and instrument maker; Benjamin Rush, studying diseases of the mind, the forerunner of American psychiatrists and psychoanalysts.

Hamilton, with whom he discussed his plans in detail, gave

him the *Letters from Phocion,* with a dedication: "the influence of our example" has "penetrated the gloomy regions of despotism" and "pointed the way to inquiries which may shake its deepest foundations."

Miranda found Yale under Dr. Ezra Stiles—probably the greatest scholar in the colonies—a fine, progressive institution. He attended Stiles' Hebrew classes and listened to professorial and student discourses in Latin. Stiles wrote in his own *Diary* about his admiration for Miranda—his extensive travels and experiences, his command of languages, his wide knowledge in all fields of learning. "A learned man and a flaming son of liberty," he concluded.

In contrast, Miranda found Harvard a narrow, provincial institution concerned chiefly with theological doctrine and devoid of curiosity about modern life and thought.

If sometimes repelled by the crudeness of American life and distressed by the swarms of insects and the loudness of the bullfrogs at night, Miranda was impressed by its democratic spirit. A few days after he landed in New Bern, North Carolina, he was invited to a barbecue where all classes rubbed shoulders, illustrating "all that Grecian poets and historians have told us about similar celebrations among the free peoples of Greece." But New England democracy went too far for his fastidiousness. He rode horseback with a servant from New Haven to Boston and, at the inns where workers, coach drivers, grooms, and workmen ate at the same table, he had considerable difficulty in having his servant fed apart.

Miranda's "amorous adventures with American ladies" were not inconsiderable. The only person in the United States whom he utterly detested was the Marquis de Lafayette, a "mediocrity," a cheap little man, treacherous to boot, running about with his tongue hanging out for popular applause.

He met wealthy merchants and easily convinced them that his proposals were practical and that they would reap large commercial rewards. Some aided him then, and a quarter of a century later, with considerable sums.

It had been 80 years ago in Cádiz also. When Miranda was a young officer in the Spanish army, he had so captivated wealthy British merchant John Turnbull that the latter aided him with money the rest of his life and participated in his many efforts. This was a great help, because Turnbull was close to William Pitt and other high British officials.

Above all, on his trip to the United States he met two men: Thomas Paine, who later helped save his life in France, and Colonel William S. Smith, who as much as anybody else made possible the clandestine departure of his later expedition from New York. Smith, soon to become an attaché at the U.S. Embassy in London, accompanied Miranda on a trip half across Europe and then gave him money to continue alone to Hungary, Italy, Greece, and Turkey.

ii

Miranda knew all about the philosophy behind the French Revolution long before it happened. As a young military officer, he had read the Encyclopedists—Diderot, Voltaire, and, above all, Rousseau—works proscribed inside the Spanish Empire. The bent of his youthful mind had been revealed when the Inquisition had discovered he was reading Grotius, Helvétius, Montesquieu, and the works of other banned French philosophers. These and other books had been seized and burned, and he had been threatened with arrest.

He had already been arrested twice on false charges of defalcation of money and army supplies—a Creole officer had to pay high to get a commission (in Miranda's case 8,000 pesos) and was never safe from discrimination, contempt, and jealousy—but he had been allowed to join an Aragón regiment bound for Martinique in the West Indies.

Later, in Cuba, he had again been threatened with arrest—despite a remarkable job of espionage and arranging for the exchange of prisoners in Jamaica—for alleged involvement in smuggling. This he claimed had been the payoff—he had in no way profited—for obtaining precise information about British armaments, fortifications, and shipping in the West Indies. But he had slipped out of Havana before dawn on January 1, 1783, on a U.S. vessel, the sloop *Prudent*.

Quite likely Miranda knew the Spanish authorities were aware he had been in contact with seditious elements in Venezuela, including three prisoners, one the brother of Simón Bolívar, the later liberator; while he was in the United States, the Spanish government put out circulars throughout the colonies, calling him "a perfidious man, an intriguer, and without any religion."

On Miranda's tour of Europe with Smith, he looked over battlefields and witnessed Prussian troop maneuvers. In Switzerland, he visited the shrines of Voltaire and Rousseau. In Italy, he secured names of Jesuits expelled from the New World who might become allies in a rebellion for independence.

With an Austrian passport, as "Count Miranda," he crossed the Black Sea and went up the Dnieper River to Kherson, where he presented himself at the mansion of Russia's commander in chief, the one-eyed Ukrainian, Grigory Potemkin, Prince of Tauris, paramour of Empress Catherine the Great, who invited Miranda to accompany him to the front. Soon Miranda was a pet of Catherine; she became a strong believer in New World independence and for years gave him money and protected him in many countries, until she grew frightened by the French Revolution.

After incredible adventures to avoid the police in various countries, Miranda settled in England in June, 1789, taking lodgings in Mr. Barlow's house, 47 Jermyn Street, London, at a rent of 100 guineas a year. He asked to be made a member of the Russian Legation staff, so he could not be molested or deported to Spain, and at once sought to interest high British officials in backing an armed expedition against the Spanish possessions. He had numerous conferences with Prime Minister William Pitt who, cautious and vacillating, ever

Machiavellian, blew hot and cold. Time and again, he seemed on the brink of acting, then always drew back. After years of disappointment, Miranda wrote Pitt a furious letter, accusing him of stealing his plans and being a crude double-crosser and adding that it was neither "just [n]or reasonable to appropriate what belongs to another and to fail in the engagements and promises . . . made in the name of your nation. . . . My compatriots do not lack the means to thwart your sinister views." This letter was sent on March 9, 1792, just as Miranda was embarking for revolutionary France with the hope of interesting the "free" government of Paris in backing his efforts.

Following the fall of the Bastille on July 14, 1789, the National Assembly had made its famous "Declaration of the Rights of Man," which was to become the cornerstone of the revolution. The month after Miranda's arrival, the Girondists (moderates) and Feuillants (a rightist splinter faction of the Jacobin extremists) gained control of the Assembly and forced Louis XVI to declare war on Austria and Prussia. This was favored by all parties: the monarchists, because they hoped to restore absolutism; the radicals, in the hope of stirring up revolution in all of Europe and establishing a republic.

Miranda promptly made friends with the highest Girondist officials. He lived through stirring days. Early in August, as news came of the smashing defeat of the French army under Lafayette and invasion of French soil by enemy troops was rumored, a mob raged through the Paris streets, killed thousands of royalists, massacred hundreds of prisoners in their jail cells, and forced the Assembly to suspend the king. Georges Jacques Danton and Maximilien Robespierre set up a popular commune in Paris, and Danton became Minister of Justice in the national government. A call was made for a new, popularly elected constitutional convention. General Charles Dumouriez was rushed to the front to take over the army and stem the enemy advance.

Under the stress of such urgent events, Miranda's pleas for aid in freeing America were shunted aside. Instead, on September 1, he was appointed—somewhat against his wishes—a major general and sent at once to the Belgian front.

He got there in time to participate in the inspiring French victory at Valmy on September 20, which threw back the Prussian army, and was congratulated by the mayor of Paris for having borne himself "as an experienced officer and an excellent citizen."

The following day, September 21, the new National Convention deposed the king and established the First French Republic. For Miranda, still at the front, this move was a preview of political and military processes similar to those that eventually would overthrow Spanish rule and set up the countries of the New World as republics.

Even while campaigning, Miranda continued to press for an appointment to a West Indian post and to get backing for a liberating expedition, either from France or its colonies. Meanwhile, he was winning important victories: he had become an intimate friend of Dumouriez, who called him "dear comrade . . . my friend, my brother," and was rapidly raised to division general and then army general. He entered Antwerp in triumph, one of the signal victories of the war. There he showed himself more interested in art, history, and books, and in talking with famous scholars, than in military and political duties.

After several more minor victories, Miranda had to lift the siege of Maastricht when the main French army was routed. By this time he was in a difficult political position. The extremists and Jacobins led by Danton, Robespierre, and Jean Paul Marat, were fighting for control of the Convention. Over the protests of the Girondists, they ordered the execution of Louis XVI (carried out January 21, 1793), and set up a Revolutionary Tribunal. Soon Miranda's friends, leading Girondists, were being ousted or thrust into prison.

Miranda had counted on the friendship of Dumouriez, but Marat attacked the Commander in Chief virulently, accusing him of plotting to betray the Revolution and restore the monarchy. Miranda became aware that it was only too true, and friendship cooled.

Against Miranda's advice, Dumouriez pushed his forces into the hastily improvised battle of Neerwinden. The Austrians launched their main attack against the left flank, commanded by Miranda, and it crumpled. The French army was badly crushed, and Miranda was charged with abandoning his troops and hiding out. In any event, to cover up his own ineptitude and traitorous plotting, Dumouriez threw the Venezuelan to the wolves.

Army General Francisco de Miranda found himself in Conciergerie Prison, charged with military misconduct, cowardice, and betraying the Revolution. He was a pawn in the fierce political battle between the Girondists and the Mountain, the Jacobin extremists. His position brightened when the Girondists rallied in the Convention and threw Marat into prison, but the Revolutionary Tribunal acquitted Marat on April 24, and he stormed back into the Convention with the people at his back.

Miranda's trial before the Revolutionary Tribunal began on May 12 and revealed his courage and brilliance in a moment of extreme adversity. The nasty bitterness of his denouncers was apparent; the testimony of one was thrown out entirely because of flagrant bias. Among those who defended him was none other than Thomas Paine, at this time a member of the all-powerful National Convention. "The destiny of the French Revolution was always intimately related to the favorite object of his heart, namely, the deliverance of Spanish America, a design for which he had been hunted by the Spanish court during the greater part of his life."

Another valiant defender was Joel Barlow, poet and patriot (later minister to France), who the year before had published such a strong defense of the French Revolution, *Advice to the Privileged Orders,* that it had been suppressed by the British government. "Taking Nature as his guide," Barlow told the court, "[Miranda] discovered that he was a man, that all men are equal, that it was his duty to teach this lesson, to overthrow tyrants and liberate his native land."

But Miranda's own passionate eloquence most influenced the court. His handsome bearing, his flashing eyes, his words, rushing out in a torrent of counter accusation and burning defense of the rights of man, swept all before him.

His close friend, English poetess Helen Maria Williams, wrote that Miranda "pleaded his cause . . . with . . . sublime energy." His "powers as an orator were not inferior to his talents as a general. He covered himself with glory and his enemies with confusion."

His legal counselor, the brilliant Claude F. Lagarde, declared, "One cannot imagine more grandeur in character, more elevation in ideas, or more true love for all the virtues."

Miranda was acquitted unanimously, and the cheering courtroom crowd carried him out on their shoulders in triumph and crowned him.

He was fortunate, for by the end of the month an insurrection purged all Girondists from the Convention. The Jacobins were in full power and in possession of the new Committee of Safety.

iii

On July 9, Miranda was thrust into La Force Prison. However, on July 13, he was allowed to address the Convention. "There is oppression against society when even one citizen is oppressed. . . . Yes, Citizen Legislators, I am oppressed—I, who have always been the strongest supporter of Liberty."

The Convention cheered, but that night Marat was stabbed in his bathtub by the young girl, Charlotte Corday, and more violent men came into power. Miranda was kept in jail, his fate uncertain, for Robespierre began openly attacking the Venezuelan as a Girondist, as heinous a word for the Jacobins as Trotskyite is today for a Communist. Poetess Williams wrote that Robespierre's persecution of Miranda was really

due to his hatred "towards all men of talents," not merely
Miranda. But it was more than that. He was trying to whip
up the passions of the mob by sharpening his spurs on Miranda
and others.

On April 5, 1794, Danton was sent to the guillotine, scorn-
fully defiant until his last breath. The terror grew worse. Before Robespierre's three-months' rule was over, 1285 victims
perished.

Robespierre ordered the Venezuelan to be put to trial on
July 30, 1794—Thermidor XII—eighteen months after his arrest. By then, trials consisted merely of denunciations, with no
right of defense. Miranda provided himself with poison, having no intention of going to the guillotine, and spent the inter-
vening months reading history and science.

But Robespierre himself was arrested by the Convention on
July 27—ironically, because he advocated mitigation of the
terror—amid cries of "Down with the tyrant!" The mob and
the militia of the Paris Commune rescued him, but the Convention sent troops to the Hotel de Ville to rearrest him. A
young gendarme shot the dictator in the jaw. The following
day, suffering great agony, he was tried and rushed to the
guillotine along with twenty-one of his adherents. Miranda
was saved by two days!

He was not released until mid-January, 1795. The Committee of Public Safety made some amends by ordering that he
be paid his back officer's salary and compensation for injuries—
35,002 livres in cash and 21,104 livres in assignats, or Treasury
orders. More than 10,000 livres of this was never paid over,
and the value of the assignats depreciated greatly, but Miranda
had enough to set up a princely sort of life and plunged into
an affair with Madame Delphine de Cudine, wife of a fellow
prisoner. He entertained lavishly. Young officer Napoleon
Bonaparte, invited to one large dinner party, commented, "He
lodges on the third floor, and it is furnished for a satrap. In
the midst of this luxury, he complains of poverty, then gives
dinners prepared by Meó and served on silver dishes." But

men of great importance were present, and Napoleon added, "He is a Don Quixote . . . but not mad. He has a sacred fire in his soul."

In July, 1795, Miranda brought out a pamphlet criticizing the structure of the Revolutionary government and its territorial expansion and made suggestions for a policy to liberate Spanish America. Moves were made by friends, as had been done when he was campaigning, to have him named governor of Santo Domingo and be provided with troops against the Spanish.

But in November he was thrust into Plessis Prison and presently was ordered deported to Switzerland. Allowed to go under guard to dine at the home of Poetess Williams, he calmly walked out the back door and hid out. The police soon located him on the Rue St. Florentine with his "maid and mistress," but, except for searching his quarters several times (about which he protested vehemently to high authorities), merely kept him under surveillance.

Miranda now conducted a worldwide correspondence to promote the cause closest to his heart (many letters to Madame de Stael date from this period) and lived on in this precarious twilight through 1796 and 1797. In September of the latter year, he was listed for deportation to French Guiana, so he laid low and fixed up his fences through Turnbull and others in order to return to England; a Cuban revolutionist, Pedro J. Caro (later to become a Spanish secret agent), was very helpful in making arrangements. Pitt, observing the way Spain and France were drawing together (England was at war with Spain), wanted to probe again into the possibilities of provoking uprisings in South America, and on January 3, 1798, disguised in a wig and spectacles, Miranda slipped out of Paris.

He would have been dismayed could he have foreseen the long years of frustrations that lay ahead and had he fully realized the prolonged cat-and-mouse game the British government would continue to play with him to further, not the freedom of the New World peoples, but the crassest designs of imperi-

alistic aggrandizement. For years he had been hounded by the
Spanish government and driven from end to end of Europe,
but this was to seem a small penalty compared to the humiliations and anxieties he was to suffer in England.

iv

When John Turnbull informed Pitt of Miranda's arrival,
the Prime Minister invited him to come to his residence in
Hollwood as soon as he reached London.

Pitt was friendly (no mention was made of Miranda's huffy
letter) but he wanted to know what was Miranda's authorization to act. The Venezuelan promptly produced instructions
"granted by the commissioners, deputies, and representatives
of the Spanish-American colonies." He was the direct representative of the "Junta of Deputies" of Mexico, Peru, Chile,
La Plata, Venezuela, and New Granada (Colombia). Among
the signers were exiled Jesuits.

What would be needed, inquired the English minister?
Miranda was "authorized" to ask for 27 vessels of the line,
8,000 soldiers, 2,000 cavalry, in return for granting England
commercial privileges in the freed countries and an eventual
payment of 30,000,000 pounds.

Pitt seemed fully agreeable, but he expressed great fears of
the French revolutionary system. What kind of governments
would be set up?

"I assure you," replied Miranda emphatically, "we should
prefer to see the Spanish Americans continue for a century
under the oppressive rule of the King of Spain rather than see
them submerged in the calamities of the abominable French
system." Miranda's proposal was for a limited monarchy with
an "Inca king" on the throne; in short, a near replica of the
British system. Naturally this pleased Pitt. Whether it would
please Hispanic Americans scarcely entered into these plans
for intervention.

Miranda next called upon the United States ambassador,

Rufus King, who had always been friendly, and proposed an alliance between England and the United States against Spain and France (only yesterday the staunch friend of U.S. freedom) to free the Spanish colonies. The aiding nations, Miranda said, would be charged lower tolls and tariffs across the Isthmus of Panama. He suggested that the United States and England divide the West Indies between themselves to compensate for their aid.

King was impressed enough to inform his government. But Lord Grenville, Pitt's cousin, a cabinet minister who previously had advocated helping Miranda, had cooled off and told King the time was not ripe; Miranda should be kept on tap with a salary until France actually invaded Spain.

In March, Miranda wrote Pitt anxiously that, unless a prompt invasion were undertaken, New World convulsions would soon occur which would lead to the adoption of "the anarchic and subversive French regime." He believed that revolutionary fervor was now so great he could do with only 6 or 8 ships and 4,000 or 5,000 recruits, and he sent emissaries to consult with Alexander Hamilton, now in the United States cabinet.

Hamilton's interest had declined, and his attitude toward Miranda had changed greatly since his own political ascension, and he wrote, on one letter from Miranda, "an intriguing adventurer." But by April, the United States was embroiled with France over the XYZ correspondence and the demand by French officials for bribes from United States emissaries. Congress, outraged, was preparing to arm and ordered a war vessel sent to France to bring back the U.S. envoys.

Rufus King wrote Hamilton that if war came with France, "the destiny of the New World would . . . be placed in our hands." He sent an enthusiastic letter to Miranda about the new possibilities and also pushed the matter with Downing Street. In October he informed Miranda that England would cooperate as desired.

Hamilton hurriedly shifted ground and wrote that the

United States (not England) should "furnish the whole land force necessary. The command . . . would naturally fall upon me." He wrote Miranda that he would back no emancipation of Spanish America unless the effort was *wholly* patronized by the United States. On that basis, the government might cooperate. England, however, could provide the ships, and a government would be set up satisfactory to both countries. Again, no mention of the people. Apparently, imperialism was born with the establishment of the American republic.

Miranda, sure that the local populations would rise en masse as soon as an armed expedition appeared on the horizon, urged a simultaneous attack on Buenos Aires by two expeditions. "There is no doubt the spirit of Independence will soon spread from one end of South America to the other." Mexico, he said, was also ripe but should be left to the last, for it was close enough to the United States, which could handle the Spaniards there at any time.

But the British government was now worried about a possible Napoleonic invasion of England and did not want to be caught in any far-flung enterprise requiring men, ships, and money. Realizing he was getting the same sort of runaround—promises, half promises, rejections—that he had suffered at British hands for more than ten years, Miranda determined to go to Trinidad, hoping that there, near the scene, he could get together an invasion force. But he was denied permission to leave England. The Minister of War said, "General Miranda has recently become an object of suspicion to the government."

"Behold," retorted Miranda, "how despotism always seeks to arm itself in . . . calumny . . . against the blameless!"

By mid-1799 he was utterly furious. All he had won from England was "the dreadful alternative of contracting debts or soliciting alms." He redoubled his efforts to obtain a passport to the West Indies or the United States. Rufus King interceded in his behalf, but the response was negative. Miranda actually took passage in the *Washington* for America but was not permitted to leave.

Angrily, he now took the position that no foreign power should be allowed to interfere in the management of a free Venezuela. "We have two grand examples before our eyes: The American Revolution and the French Revolution."

Through the rest of 1799 and on into 1800, his hopes for action waned and ebbed or flared into new life. At one point things seemed so promising he wrote to a fellow conspirator in Trinidad to begin recruiting West Indian sympathizers; the hour to strike was almost at hand.

Miranda's home became the rendezvous for all exiled Spanish Americans. One who came under his spell was the Chilean student, Don Bernardo Riquelme, the illegitimate son of Captain General of Chile—and, more recently, Viceroy of Peru—Irish ex-peddler Ambrosio O'Higgins. The youth had been sent secretly to England to study so as to conceal his existence from the Spanish colonial office, lest Ambrosio's career be hampered.

Young Bernardo O'Higgins looked upon Miranda as another Washington, threw himself wholeheartedly into the Liberator's arms, and was duly initiated into Miranda's new secret revolutionary order, the Lautaro Lodge (the Great American Reunion), taking an oath to dedicate his life to Latin-American freedom.

"Behold in me, sir," he told the Venezuelan, "the melancholy remains of my countryman, Lautaro [an early Araucanian revolter]. In my breast burns the same spirit as that which liberated my native land Arauco from its oppressors!" The Spaniards had never been able to subdue the southern Araucanos. (Not long after Miranda had gone to his death, O'Higgins would be striding across the Andean snow passes, with San Martín, to free his own land.)

When young O'Higgins prepared to leave England for Spain after completing his studies, Miranda gave him much advice:

how to operate, how to conduct himself, what books to study. "You should not forget for a single instant that outside of this country there is in all the world only one other nation in which you can discuss politics except in the tested heart of a friend. That country is the United States. Choose, therefore, such a friend, but choose with the greatest care, for if you blunder you are lost."

To Spain, O'Higgins carried with him Miranda's plans for liberation and worked with the Lautaro underground, which met secretly at the Pillars of Hercules outside Cádiz. San Martín, then a young Spanish officer, likely also became a member of the group.

v

For five more years, Miranda tried to push his project in England. For five years his overtures were received warmly, or he was given the cold shoulder. At one time, the government agreed to provide supplies and money and did put up part of what it promised. With the help of British merchants, ships were hired and outfitted. But again a shift in continental affairs caused the Prime Minister to call a halt.

Miranda had already advised his followers abroad, even as to the exact date the expedition would set out. The sudden change meant failure and possible death for his comrades, and it cast a shadow on his own leadership. He could endure no more of this shabby treatment and determined to slip away to the United States. He could not begin to cover his debts— one was 5,000 pounds to London booksellers—but he arranged as well as he could for the care of his mistress, Sarah Andrews, and his two illegitimate children by her.

Prospects of getting help in the United States now seemed promising. By 1805 the seizure of American vessels by Spain and the suppression of the commercial entrepôt at New Orleans, conceded by the Treaty of San Lorenzo, had embittered relations between the two countries. Also, a dispute had arisen over the boundaries of Louisiana, purchased from France by the United States in 1803. In March, 1804, Secretary of State James Madison had sharply warned the irascible Spanish minister in Washington, Marquis of Casa Yrujo, not to forget the deference due to the government to which he was accredited. Miranda believed that the possibility of war with Spain would create sympathy for his cause.

On September 2, 1805, using an assumed name, F. Martin, Miranda and his secretary, Thomas Molini, embarked at Gravesend on the *Polly* and reached New York on November 9. At once he acquainted his friends, Rufus King and Colonel William Smith, with his designs. Smith, at this time the head of the New York port authority, introduced him to Commodore Thomas Lewis and merchant Samuel Ogden, who both took an active interest in his projects.

To Henry Knox, in Boston, the patriot wrote, "The object of this letter is to inform you that the moment has at last arrived when the great scheme we have had in view for these many years past is to take place." He would send an intimate friend, Colonel William Armstrong, to inform him. Armstrong, who was also to confer with Christopher Gore, was an arms peddler Miranda had met in London.

Miranda himself went to Washington, stopping en route in Philadelphia to see ex-Vice President Aaron Burr, involved in a conspiracy to separate Mexico from Spain. Burr was impressed by the "social talents and colloquial eloquence" of Miranda, but he "refrained from giving him an opportunity to disclose his views about the emancipation of the Spanish Indies." Miranda stigmatized the Mephistophelean politician as a "detestable" and "infamous" man, who betrayed his plans to the Marquis of Casa Yrujo.

In Philadelphia, Dr. Rush gave him a letter of introduction to Secretary of State James Madison, telling of Miranda's role in the French Revolution. "He is still the friend of liberty, and a believer in the practicability of governments that shall have for their objects the happiness of nations, instead of the greatness of individuals. He knows your character and longs to do homage to your principles."

On December 6, 1805, Miranda called on President Jefferson, whom he found conferring with members of his cabinet. When Miranda mentioned the warring nations of Europe, Jefferson said, "We will feed them all while they fight."

"If they pay for it," added one of his secretaries.

The President responded, "To be sure!"

On December 11 and 13, Miranda had conferences with Madison. The Secretary of State said that the government looked favorably on the emancipation of South America, but at this juncture it could not furnish assistance. Miranda responded that the South Americans wanted only such indirect aid as France had given the United States during the American Revolution, and that the authorities should wink at his enterprise.

Madison replied evasively that he did not consider it necessary for the government either to smile upon the affair or view it with anger. Citizens of the United States could do whatever was not absolutely forbidden by the laws, especially in an undertaking which was "honorable and useful."

Miranda considered this a green light and wrote Turnbull and British Minister Nicholas Vansittart (over the years unwavering in his support) that the United States government had given "tacit consent" to his revolutionary enterprise.

At a dinner party that evening, President Jefferson remarked that he had been born too soon to see the splendor of the New World which was steadily advancing toward complete independence. Another green light?

Jonathan Dayton, ex-senator from New Jersey who was present, trotted straight to the Spanish minister, Yrujo, and betrayed Miranda's plans. Yrujo put spies on Miranda's trail and began pressuring the State Department. To get off the hook, Madison said he had warned Miranda that "it would be incumbent on the United States to punish any transactions within their jurisdiction which might, according to the law

of nations, involve an hostility against Spain, and that a stat-
ute of Congress had made express provision for such a case."
If the United States were to undertake hostile measures
against Spain, it would be "not in an underhand and illicit
way, but in a way consistent with the laws of war and becoming our national character." (How times have changed!)

English Minister Anthony Merry reported to Downing
Street that he doubted if the American government had confidence in Miranda. His visit to Washington had "been attended with no material result."

vi

Even so, Miranda capitalized on his conferences with Secretary Madison, assuring Smith and King that his project had
the "tacit approbation and good wishes" of the government
and that there would be no difficulty in the way of American
citizens promoting his plans if the laws were not "openly violated." The government would "wink at the things being done
by individuals."

Merchant Ogden advanced him $20,000 for arming and pro-
visioning a vessel of 187 tons, called the *Leander,* and two
small schooners, the *Bee* and the *Bacchus.* On January 4, 1806,
Miranda drew bills of exchange aggregating 2,000 pounds
upon Turnbull and Vansittart. To the latter, he wrote that
the Washington government was "very well disposed; it gave
me a perfect, tacit consent and left to merchants the option of
doing the rest." Various merchants had "cleverly" equipped
him, and he would leave on January 10, 1806. "I assure you
that the arrangements are more extensive and more solid than
those we had in England. We shall succeed, and before three
months you will know the result. I am forced to draw upon
you and Turnbull for supplies indispensably necessary . . .
[rather than] make my secret known among merchants who
are not personally interested, which might perhaps ruin the
affair! . . . As American merchants are furnishing forty-five

thousand pounds for this purpose, should not those of London advance two thousand for an enterprise which promises them at least an equal benefit?"

Colonel Smith secured the recruits, engaging some directly, others through agents. The precise object of the expedition was concealed; an agent called Fink, a butcher in Bowery Lane, engaged some volunteers to serve in "the President's guard." Regular pay was promised, plus special rewards and advancement. One deluded mortal arranged that a friend should take charge of all the "gold, silver, gold ore, and bullion" which he would bring home. Smith's own son volunteered, and Mrs. Smith wrote Miranda anxiously but expressed the opinion that she did not know of any other person to whom she could with so much confidence entrust her son. In all, about 200 recruits entered the service of a leader whom few of them had ever seen and whose purpose they knew not.

According to the *Leander* quartermaster, arms loaded included 582 muskets, 16 blunderbusses, 15 carbines, 19 ninepounders, 8 six-pounders, 2 brass two-pounders, 2 petards, 440 cutlasses, 297 hangers and sabers, 6500 cartridges, 1586 pounds of ball, 5 tons of lead, and 10,000 musket flints. None of these military supplies was mentioned on the captain's manifest, so that port officials, kept in line by Smith, would not know the purpose of the voyage. Not least of the equipment was a small printing press; war propaganda was, as usual, as important as pikes and sabers. On February 2, 1806, the *Leander* cleared for Jacmel in Santo Domingo, with a fine breeze from the northwest.

Minister Yrujo did not learn of the real object of the *Leander* until a few days later. He dispatched warnings to the governor of Cuba, the viceroy of New Spain, and the captain general of Venezuela, and sent a letter of protest to Secretary Madison. He got the French minister at Washington to protest also. The Spanish minister at Paris denounced to Talleyrand the unneutral conduct of the United States.

Yrujo's protests stimulated the administration to take measures against Miranda's friends. Colonel Smith was removed from office, and he and Ogden were indicted for aiding to equip the *Leander*.

Smith affirmed at the trial that he had promoted the expedition because he believed it was being prepared with the consent of Jefferson and Madison. He and Ogden addressed a memorial to Congress that, though federal officials in New York City had been cognizant of the equipment of the expedition, they had taken no steps to prevent its departure. Public opinion in that city strongly favored the accused men, and eventually they were acquitted. Ogden wrote Miranda a jubilant letter, declaring they had triumphed over their enemies and the oppression of the government.

Jefferson, squirming under criticism in the newspaper *Aurora*, denied that either he or Madison had countenanced Miranda's expedition. After Smith and Ogden were acquitted, Madison declared with some pique that a disclosure would be left to time which would "do full justice to all parties."

The *Newark Centinel* said, "We are among those who wish him [Miranda] success and who would gladly echo his triumphs. Not because we are anxious to see him decorated with the ensigns of royalty or clothed with the majesty of wealth, but because a great empire would be open to the enterprise of our citizens, and an abject and miserable people would become a nation of free men." The *Richmond Enquirer* observed that if the attack proved successful, Spain might "tremble for all her possessions in South America." Its editor hoped a "new confederation of states might start into existence" and that General Miranda might become "the Washington of South America."

vii

Not until the *Leander* had been several days at sea did the commander appear on deck. Youthful volunteer Moses Smith later declared that an "air of authority distinguished him"

Upsala College
Library
East Orange, N.J.

from the other members of the company. "He had on a red gown and slippers," continued Smith, "and his physiognomy showed that he was not of our country. It was whispered about that he was a great general called Miranda, whose name had been celebrated."

The recruits soon realized his real object was to start a rebellion in South America, but they believed that their government had given "implied sanction" to the undertaking, that the British would cooperate, and that once they landed the South Americans would flock to their standard.

Miranda's courteous and conciliatory disposition charmed his men. One recruit felt that their leader intended "to sow the seeds of heroical deeds, of liberty and revolution," and Expeditionary Captain James Biggs wrote home (later he became disillusioned), "He assumed the manner of father and instructor to the young men. He spoke of the prospects of success and of the preparations made for him with great confidence. The glory and advantages of the enterprise were described in glowing colours. At another time he detailed his travels, his sufferings, and escapes in a manner to interest both their admiration and sympathy. He appeared the master of languages, of science, and literature."

He urged the young men to study mathematics and Spanish and expounded to them his ideas on politics.

Biggs described him, "About five feet ten . . . limbs . . . well proportion; his whole frame . . . stout and active. His complexion is dark, florid, and healthy. His eyes are hazel colored, but not of the darkest hue . . . piercing, quick, intelligent . . . more . . . severe than . . . mild. He has good teeth, which he takes care to keep clean. His nose is large and handsome, . . . chest, . . . square and prominent. His hair is gray, and he wears it tied long behind with powder. He has strong gray whiskers growing on the outer edges of his ears as large as most Spaniards have on their cheeks. . . . We may pronounce him a handsome man."

On February 13, 1806, the vessel was hailed by the British

frigate *Cleopatra,* commanded by Captain Wight, who impressed a number of the *Leander's* sailors, claiming they were British.

Miranda visited the frigate with his documents and convinced Wight that his undertaking was "advantageous to the British government" and that the ports of Venezuela would be opened to English vessels. Wight then released the impressed sailors, allowed the *Leander* to proceed, and wrote to the admiral in charge of the British North American squadron, requesting to be permitted to join Miranda's expedition.

General Miranda proceeded to organize the "Colombian Army," appointing officers, whose commissions were run off on the printing press, and having each sign articles of war and take an oath to be faithful to the people of South America. The men were organized into groups of engineers, artillerymen, artificers, light dragoons, riflemen, and infantry. Sergeants drilled recruits, and all were set to studying manuals of war. Carpenters made staves for pikes; "old muskets, pointless bayonets, and rusty swords" were cleaned and repaired.

On March 12, the red-blue-yellow Colombian flag was unfurled from the masthead.

Near Santo Domingo, a bitter dispute arose between Captain Lewis and Colonel Armstrong. "A great deal of indecent warmth was shown on all sides," commented Biggs, "and in the highest degree by the general himself, who appeared, before the storm was over, more fit for bedlam than for the command of an army." Other quarrels about the respective authority of Lewis and Miranda also lowered the general's prestige.

The *Leander* reached Aruba, near Venezuela, April 11. At last, with fewer than 200 poorly armed followers, Miranda was ready to strike a blow at Spanish power.

viii

Warnings from Yrujo had stimulated the captain general of Venezuela, Manuel Guevara Vasconcelos, to direct coast guard commanders to be vigilant. The slow progress of the *Leander* gave the Spaniards time to prepare. When Miranda attempted to disembark near Puerto Cabello during the night of April 27, two small Spanish vessels fired on him.

"The action," said Miranda's secretary, "continued for about forty minutes (without our receiving any injury) when it was deemed prudent to decline the contest, from their decided superiority both in weight of metal and the number of their men. The signal was kept flying for the two schooners to join us. But as the *Bee* and the *Bacchus* . . . were unable to keep up with the *Leander,* they were intercepted." In the words of one filibuster, "the redoubtable Miranda and the almighty Lewis fled," leaving about 60 recruits on board the unarmed schooners.

After a manly defense, the hapless adventurers surrendered two days later. They were carried in triumph to the mainland, thrust into the filthy dungeons of a Puerto Cabello castle, and soon put on trial on the charge of "piracy, rebellion, and murder." Captain General Guevara himself presided over the trial and sentenced ten of them, on July 12, 1806, to be hanged for their "atrocious crimes"; fifteen to serve ten years in Morro Castle in Puerto Rico; sixteen, eight years in a castle near Cartagena. Three young lads were remanded there also, to await the King's pleasure. The heads of the ten condemned to death were to be exposed to the public gaze, and the public hangman was also directed to burn Miranda's portrait in effigy, his proclamation, and his captured banner. Thirty thousand pesos were offered as a royal reward for the traitor's body, dead or alive.

A council of war aboard the fleeing *Leander* decided that the expedition should proceed to Trinidad and solicit aid from its governor. On May 26, 1806, however, the *Leander* was chased and fired upon by the English sloop of war *Lily*. Captain Donald Campbell described the *Leander*'s master as a "perfect pirate, . . . dissatisfied and nearly in a state of mutiny." The ship was boarded and escorted to the island of Grenada.

From Campbell, Miranda learned that William Pitt had died, a victim of gout and the collapse of his last coalition against France. George III had asked Lord Grenville to select a new cabinet.

Miranda's Caribbean cruise piqued the curiosity of the new prime minister. To Lord Auckland, on June 5, 1806, he wrote, "an immense question is opening by this attempt (successful hitherto) of Miranda's on Caracas. The thing was launched by our predecessors, as a matter of connivance only, without any plan for acting in consequence of it. How far shall we now countenance it, or engage in it?"

At Grenada, Miranda was hospitably received by Governor Maitland, who supplied provisions which enabled the *Leander* to sail for Barbados. There Miranda became acquainted with Admiral Lord Cochrane, a tempestuous, arrogant, greedy, and idealistic commander, but the type of man with whom Miranda knew how to deal. On June 9 they signed a pact in which Cochrane promised to support the *Leander* with a naval force and protect her from attack by the Spaniards. He also gave Miranda permission to recruit forces at Barbados and Trinidad. On his side, Miranda promised that English citizens would be assisted in the recovery of their just debts in Spanish America and that the independent Spanish-American nations would concede commercial privileges to England. In a dispatch to Earl Spencer, Cochrane urged that 5,000 English soldiers should be sent at once to aid Miranda to liberate South America. A great market would be opened in the emancipated colonies for English manufacturers.

Miranda also wrote Vansittart, asking him to do everything in his power to induce the new ministry to support his undertaking. He next solicited aid from General Bowyer, commander of the English soldiers in the Leeward Islands, implying that the English government had agreed to aid him with

700 soldiers, arms, munitions, and provisions. General Bowyer declined, nor would the governor of Barbados assist, though he placed no restrictions on recruiting.

ix

Miranda enlisted a score of new men, mostly adventurers and vagabonds. Captain Lewis, thoroughly disliked, was removed, and the *Leander* intrusted to "a very inexperienced young man." They sailed from Barbados for Trinidad, June 20, accompanied now by the *Lily*, the brig *Express*, and the leased merchant schooner *Trimmer*.

At Trinidad, Governor Hislop proved sympathetic and permitted volunteers to be recruited from the insular militia to serve under Colonel de Rouvray and two other English officers; in all, an additional 190 more men joined the expedition.

Writing to Vansittart, Miranda reported that Hislop had given him "a cordial and warm reception, equaled only by that of Admiral Cochrane at Barbados. . . . I was obliged by the pressure of circumstances to draw £688-2-0 Sterling at Barbados, having received at that moment news from the Continent of S.A. that absolutely required the sailing of the Expedition. I hope the government will not refuse the payment of this small sum, in consideration of the magnitude of the object, and the mutual interest of both nations. I shall remain accountable for the payment of the whole."

To Lord Cochrane he wrote, "We learn at this moment that six [French] sail of the line and one frigate are at anchor at Martinique, ready to sail, and in very good order, etc. Under these circumstances H.E. Governor Hislop, Captain Campbell, and myself have agreed to suspend our departure until we hear from you. . . .

". . . Before any force from G.B. can enable us to frustrate their pernicious views, I shall deem it a miracle if the New World by our efforts at this moment is rescued from bearing the disgraceful yoke of France."

Turnbull wrote a letter, not received until much later, asking Miranda to point out a few ports in the Spanish-American provinces to which English ships laden with manufactured goods could proceed in safety, and asked to be appointed "your commercial European agent, as that may enable me to be of service in promoting your views." On June 20, he sent out circular letters in Spanish for distribution in South America. They recited the glorious events that had resulted from the efforts of his old friend, General Miranda, which ensured "an intimate and friendly connection" between England and Spanish America. Turnbull and Son offered the South Americans their services in England or any part of the continent. "You may calculate with certainty that all the products of this province which used to arrive in England via Spain, burdened with imposts of every kind, will have an advantageous market here; the same results will take place with products of English factories that were formerly sent to Spanish America via Spain, because of the saving of the heavy duties. . . . So great would be the economies, these manufactures unloaded in America will not cost one half of their former price."

Informed that the French squadron had sailed for Europe, Miranda decided to make another sortie at once. The colonists "were anxiously awaiting his arrival to free them from the Spanish yoke." He secured additional "English supplies," increased his fighting force to some 300 men, and sailed forth. Admiral Cochrane directed Captain Campbell to take charge of the seven English escort vessels.

x

By coincidence, another bizarre enterprise was shaping up at the other end of the continent. In April, Sir Popham, recently disgraced but vindicated by a parliamentary committee, had been put in command of the English naval forces at the Cape of Good Hope. Aware that his enemies in the cabinet would soon oust him, and knowing of Miranda's plans, he decided, without authorization, to use regular soldiers under General Charles William Beresford at St. Helena to attack Montevideo and Buenos Aires.

He wrote Lord Castlereagh that his project had "not arisen from any sudden impulse, or the immediate desire of gratifying an adventurous spirit," but as the outcome of a plan that he had previously framed at the request of Lord Melville for "a general emancipation in South America, and that the great organ of action in this undertaking" was his good friend, General Miranda.

Early on the morning of June 25, English warships entered the estuary of La Plata River, and two days later scarlet-clad soldiers took possession of Buenos Aires.

Popham wrote Miranda, whom he believed to be still in London, "Here we are in possession of Buenos Aires, the finest country in the world, and from what I see of the disposition of the inhabitants, I have no doubt if ministers would accede to your propositions and send you here, that your plan would take as well from this side as from the other. Try, my friend, to come out. . . . I wish you were here. I like the South Americans prodigiously. God bless you, my dear General."

xi

Rumors about Miranda's expedition had provoked great fears in Venezuela. The viceroy in Bogotá was also apprehensive. General Guevara wrote his government with considerable alarm and took vigorous measures to thwart the patriot-filibuster. Arms were distributed, fortifications strengthened, soldiers stationed at strategic points. The Caracas *cabildo* denounced Miranda as a "conspirator" and "traitor" who had committed heinous crimes, and a thousand Caracas inhabitants contributed to a defense fund "to reduce the traitor to ashes."

All element of surprise had been lost.

Even so, Miranda's expedition reached the bay of Coro during the night of August 1, without being intercepted. A heavy sea prevented any attack until the early dawn of August 3. The vanguard was led by British Colonels de Rouvray and Downie and Lieutenant Beddingfield. They drove the Spanish soldiers from the beach and stormed the battery. Reinforcements landed, took over the little hamlet of Vela de Coro and raised the insurgent banner, then moved on to take over the town of Coro itself.

Miranda took up residence near a city gate, surrounded by his most trusted followers. A horse was kept saddled day and night. He sent out messengers bearing flags of truce, offering protection to inhabitants who returned to their homes.

A proclamation, fastened on the doors of churches and public buildings, stripped all Spanish officials of their powers and placed government in the hands of local courts. Any individuals aiding Spain were to be considered traitors; persons deserting the Spanish service were to be rewarded. All male citizens between the ages of sixteen and fifty-five were summoned to the Colombian colors. The new flag of Independence was ordered displayed in conspicuous places, and all free Colombian citizens were to wear cockades in their hats. The public good "is a supreme law." But no local people swarmed to his aid. Coro remained almost deserted. No supplies or food of any kind were found, so Miranda was obliged to return to Vela de Coro.

On July 13, 1806, Earl Howick, first lord of the admiralty, on receiving Cochrane's report, had already expressed grave doubts about "embarking on this scheme. . . . Can we spare the force?" It meant 3,000 men for Buenos Aires; 5,000 to support Miranda. "Such a force, in addition to what will be required for Sicily," would leave the government "without the power of acting anywhere else," or proper protection at home "if the threat of invasion should be renewed." Two days later, the Grenville cabinet disapproved of Cochrane's decision to aid Miranda with "ships under his command"; he was directed to take no steps "by which His Majesty can be further committed in that enterprise." And so Miranda was left holding an empty bag in the tiny port of Vela de Coro.

Popham was also reprimanded and removed; a new commander appointed. But apparently—since the first moves were auspicious and British prestige was directly involved—the cabinet was impelled to back up the aggression. More than 11,000 troops were landed. But soon the patriots, instead of flocking to the British as liberators, rallied en masse and drove them out.

xii

Juan de Salas, commander of the district of Coro, stationed soldiers to prevent the filibusters from penetrating into the elevated regions where he feared discontented slaves might follow the revolutionary banner. Defense forces were increased by hastily recruited Indians and Negroes and, by August 8, 1806, totaled 1500 men.

Salas cautiously followed Miranda to Vela de Coro and stationed men on the sand hills to await Captain General Guevara who was bringing 4,000 men from Caracas. On August 12 they captured Captain Johnson of the *Leander* and a number of seamen.

A delayed letter to Miranda arrived from Admiral Cochrane (dated at Tatola, July 30). "After the part I have taken to support the success of your plans I hope you are convinced that I have your interest much at heart. . . . You have some warm friends in the present ministry, but I fear also some are not so much so as I could wish.

"Situated as I am now, I cannot openly act, but secretly will give you all the assistance in my power. I will take care that the enemy's ships do not annoy you. . . .

"I must also limit the supplies of provisions but hope before this that you are in the midst of plenty on the main. Should the British Govt. charge what has been already supplied to my private account, I trust that when you have it in your power that the same will be repaid."

The increase in the enemy's forces, losses in the attacking party, lack of assistance from the inhabitants, and lack of water for the squadron led the leaders to decide that the expeditionary force should move to where they could hold a real port against the enemy until the expected English aid could be received. But when?

At 10 P.M., August 13, the General went on board the *Lily* in a violent rain, and by midnight all the forces had embarked. They sailed for Aruba.

On September 22, Captain Dundas of His Majesty's escorting ship *Elephant* warned Miranda bluntly that, if he did not leave Aruba for Trinidad at once, English naval protection would be withdrawn and Cochrane would furnish no more provisions than those needed to carry his followers "to some port of safety."

xiii

The *Leander* reached Grenada on October 21, 1806, and Miranda's followers discarded their revolutionary uniforms. The disbanded men were paid only a part of the wages promised. The owner of the *Trimmer* sued to be paid for the use of his vessel. Miranda had failed; he was bankrupt, harassed on every side for payment of expenses incurred.

He still clung to the hope that the enterprise could be revived and kept on calling for help from England. In November he sent de Rouvray to London to obtain "immediate succours or a categorical answer" from the English ministers. He sent along many pleading letters.

To Earl St. Vincent, he wrote asking him to use his influence in "carrying into execution those benevolent plans that the administration in which your Lordship was so conspicuous a member had formed for the welfare of Great Britain and the happiness of mankind."

To Vansittart, "I pray you to listen to him [de Rouvray] with the same attention that you would give me if I were present; and to introduce him to those ministers of His Majesty whom you judge it proper that he should see at the present moment. Send me a positive response in regard to the future fate of this expedition, in order that I may be able to retain here the persons who are voluntarily devoted to this generous enterprise and who are awaiting with impatience a definitive conclusion. Give me your advice and extricate me from the disagreeable and dangerous position in which I am placed at the present moment."

Vansittart transmitted Miranda's letters to Lord Grenville. He had the impression that the government might decide "to take a very active part in wresting South America out of the hands of the Spaniards," but it wished to have the South Americans show their "disposition to come forward."

As for Miranda, though citizens of the United States had promoted his enterprise, it was more of a British than an American undertaking. English ministers furnished some two thousand pounds to meet the expenses, and when Miranda attacked Coro, more than one half of his forces were Britishers or men under the British flag. Without the supplies obtained from English commanders, the *Leander* could scarcely have kept on, and Miranda could hardly have withdrawn from the Venezuelan coast except for the shield of English vessels.

While Miranda simmered in the Caribbean, the British cabinet hemmed and hawed. On December 19, 1806, Lord Castlereagh took the government severely to task in Parliament for not having been able to make up its mind one way or the other.

xiv

In 1807, the Spanish government published and circularized widely in South America a *Portrait and Biography of the Traitor Miranda*. It stigmatized President Jefferson as a "disloyal friend of Spain" who overlooked Miranda's activities "in order that he might recruit some two hundred men." That "miserable person [Miranda] in order not to lose everything, . . . attacked the Venezuelan coast with a ridiculous force. After the repulse of his first attack, the traitor then undertook to visit the islands of his friends the English, beseeching aid and offering South America as a reward." Spanish Americans everywhere "detest the memory of such a wicked son."

One Venezuelan historian suggests that the dominant Creole aristocrats opposed Miranda because they believed his endeavors were subsidized by English gold. Certainly the sudden appearance of a tiny attacking force did not induce the people of northern South America to rise in arms against the Spaniards and their troops. Yet if Miranda's attempt had been strongly supported by English soldiers, its success might have led to the independence at this juncture of all the Spanish colonies. English merchants, given special privileges, would have developed an extensive and profitable trade. But though England would have liked to have seized much of South America, it was afraid of "revolutionizing."

As it was, Miranda's great expedition was a fiasco. Even after all his waiting, it had been premature. In two more years, Spain was taken over by France, and the whole Spanish empire crumbled rapidly. Two years later he would have walked ashore in glory. But in the year of 1806, he was fifty-six years old. His name, his influence, all his hopes, all his dreams were at stake.

His failure, however, was only a military and strategic one. His name flew across the continents; it stirred innumerable people in the cities, the fields, the valleys, and the mountains. It helped solidify their beliefs and feelings and prepare them for the day Independence would come. The Lautaro Lodge spread rapidly. Its great emissaries were to be Bernardo O'Higgins in Chile; San Martín and Carlos María de Alvear in Argentina; Simón Bolívar in Venezuela; López Aldana and Riva Agüero in Peru.

For the moment, Miranda returned to England, his tail between his legs. But he did not give up. He bent all his efforts to propaganda, starting a magazine, writing proclamations, corresponding with revolutionaries all over the continent. He was ordered by the British government to desist. He apologized, but continued. He did not realize that the hour was close at hand when he himself actually would head up the government of an independent Venezuela.

2

On the Eve

/.V.\ The Spanish and Portuguese colonies in South America were the product of armed conquest. The great Aztec and Inca empires fell before gunpowder and the fabulous horse, aided by native fear and such superstitious myths as the prophesied return of a bearded white god.

After the conquest, Indians were driven under the lash in mines and on plantations, exterminated by bullets and swords and by the white man's alcohol and diseases.

Soon Negro workers had to be imported to mine the gold and silver, the mercury and tin, and to work on the new sugar and cotton plantations, especially in Brazil, Peru, Venezuela, and the Caribbean. In many regions they came to outnumber the whites. In Brazil, the early poet García de Rezende wrote,

> We see so many captives
>   Brought into the kingdom,
> They will become the natives,
>   For if this keeps up,
> They will outnumber us—
>   So it seems to me.

> *Vemos no reyno metter*
>   *Tantos captivos crescer,*

Irem-se os naturaes,
    Que, se assim fôr, serão mais
Elles que nós, a meu ver.

They became the beasts of burden. Old laws in Brazil set forth how sick or maimed slaves and beasts could be disposed of.

After a few decades, the Spaniards did set up the Laws of the Indies—for that age, an enlightened code—intended to ameliorate the lot of the original inhabitants, but distances were great and communications difficult. Mostly, the humane portions of the various codes were ignored while harsher provisions were utilized. Also, at the beginning Spain sent over numbers of enlightened viceroys who did much to lessen local hardships and promote new industries, build roads and bridges, and open up new areas for permanent settlement. The Jesuits, who ruled Paraguay, herded the Guaraní into missions and, though exploiting them, taught them trades.

These missions were among the brighter spots in a continent of cruelty. They were a beneficent feudal system of serfdom in which nomadic Indians were made sedentary and provided with knowledge and more civilized habits. In many ways they were idyllic communities.

The great patriot leader, José de San Martín, was born in such a community—Yapeyú, probably the most important center between the Uruguay and Paraná rivers, where his father was an official administrator of Las Vacas, one of the great confiscated haciendas, and was to become governor. But that was ten years after the Jesuits were expelled in 1768.

How much of the Jesuit way of life still survived when San Martín spent his childhood there is not known; but one of his biographers, Humberto Tejera, feels that the Jesuit system greatly influenced the liberator.

"Life there at the end of the eighteenth century corresponded to a scheme of theocratic absolutism, picturesquely blended with economic communism, all reminiscent of a puritanical idyll. The wealth of cattle and agriculture were its bases. The indigenous Guaraní, magnificent horsemen, navigators of mighty rivers, had been subjugated and converted into skilled gardeners and horticulturists. The Jesuits maintained there a herbarium of four thousand different plants; rose and jasmine gardens; lemon, fig, apple, and pear orchards, in a paradisical climate that made possible the proximity of giant cryptogams, mesquites, and palms. Much *yerba mate* tea was grown, sustaining a large export trade; flotillas of three hundred oarsmen plied the rivers. The Jesuits' ingenuity put floating temples on the balsas, with a superabundance of polychrome images, candles, music, and incense; there, masked Chinese, Moors, Turks, and Persians were conquered by the bellicose saints of the order.

"All had to work, but only a six-hour day. They were organized into guilds of musicians, instrument makers, gold- and silversmiths, blacksmiths and forge workers, painters, scribes. . . . San Martín's childhood in that paradise of perfumed gardens, birds, fish, and tropical butterflies, elaborate choruses, and processions implanted in him an undying pride of having been born in America."

The empire, however, mostly had hardened into a rigid caste system. At the bottom were the Indians and Negroes. Their conduct, their dress, their adornments, their recreations were precisely spelled out by the law. They could not bear arms (except later as members of armed forces); they could not own or ride a horse. Marriage with whites was banned.

Soon enough, since relatively few European women came to the New World during the first centuries, there arose large groups of mestizos, men of Indian-white blood (mamelucos or curibocas in Brazil); mulattoes, men of Negro-white blood; and zambos, Negro-Indians (in Brazil, *cafusos*).

In all the colonies there was a vast nomenclature designating the various degrees of blood in the mixed individuals, even to a sixty-fourth part. But by the time of the Republics, the census in most countries listed everybody not pure-blooded Negro or Indian (*caboclos*, they called them in Brazil) as white.

As a Brazilian once said wryly, "We Brazilians have much more faith in the potency of white blood. In our country, anybody with a drop of white blood is catalogued as white. In your country, anybody with a drop of black blood is put down as Negro."

These new blended racial groups were more or less outlaws from both cultures, the native and the European. They had to live chiefly by their wits, fitting into the interstices of either culture or acting as go-betweens: they became overseers of Indian and Negro serfs, miners, petty traders, muleteers, and, as time went on, soldiers, but not officers—all higher ranks were reserved for the Gachupines, the Saracens, the Goths, as white Spaniards and Portuguese from overseas were called. In general, the mestizos and mulattoes, because they lacked long-standing ties, became as time went on the most mobile elements of colonial society. This was a large factor in their eventual supremacy, quite apart from their greater inherited talents; by the very nature of their birth, they became agile, semilawless, opportunistic, playing great roles in new conquering expeditions, especially in Brazil, where they comprised the majority of the *bandeirantes* who boldly carried Portuguese rule from São Paulo and elsewhere into the hinterland—up the Amazon, into Minas Geraes and Mato Grosso. In spite of the many regulations that tried to keep mestizos from rising in the social scale, the continent was vast, there was much elbow room and many openings for adventurous spirits, and they slipped like quicksilver through the fingers of their rulers.

Thus the mestizos and mulattoes, the Indians and Negroes, were long excluded from even the lowest official ranks of the armed forces and the Church but gradually rose in the militia; and, it is said, a mulatto even became Bishop of Panama. All told, it was a rigid caste Conquest system, but toward the end, ever more rapidly, it began breaking down. The wealthy Creoles—European whites born in the New World—were taking over the reins everywhere, and their rise also brought new opportunities for all the lower orders.

ii

The Creoles themselves differed from colony to colony, for Spain itself had a complicated ethnic pattern. The original population had been Mediterranean stock upon which had been grafted Celtic people, giving rise to the expression "Celtiberian." There was the infusion of Greek, Phoenician, Roman, Moorish and Berber blood from many centuries of occupation. There were the fair, blond Spaniards, products of Visigothic conquest. The Catalán were Provençals, and to this day theater troops play in towns and cities in southern France and eastern Spain. The aggressive, cruder Gallegos and Extremeños of northwest and west often became leading conquistadors. The softer Valencians and Andalusians, with their liquid speech, became clever, insinuating bureaucrats. In the north were the hardy, independent Basques, with their own strange language, their origins surrounded in mystery—perhaps Magyar. Cannot much of the psychology, customs, and history of Chile be the product of the large number of Basques who seemed to favor that land more than other places? Strange Basque names, such as Eyzaguirre, Ezcurra, Yrarrázaval, Zañartú, Zúdañez, echo all down the centuries of Chilean history.

But even whites born of such European parents in the New World—the Creoles—had fewer chances for advancement than European-born Spaniards and Portuguese, though the Portuguese colonizing policy was far more enlightened than that of Spain. Brazil welcomed Jews and other nationalities very early; there was far less social rigidity, greater tolerance and understanding. But for centuries in the Hispanic-American world, the Creoles, with a few exceptions, could hold none of the higher posts in the army, the Church, or the government.

Later, when Spanish strength was seeping away, they came to head the local militias to supplement the dwindling Spanish forces. Nearly everywhere they also came to control the *cabil-*

dos or *ayuntamientos,* the town and city governing bodies, but rarely gained footholds in the powerful regional *audiencias.* Sudden status came with Independence, when the Spaniard in time became an object of contempt. Miranda's secret Lautaro Lodge admitted only "Americans." If denied position and political power, the Creoles inevitably became pre-eminent in the productive life of the colonies. Many had inherited vast estates, originally granted by the Crown to their forebears, and these *repartimientos* included Indians, the serfs they were supposed to catechise. In Chile, scores of such estates extended from the crest of the Andes to the ocean tidewaters. Even to this day, numbers of such imperial patrimonies remain almost intact, some still owned by descendants of the original grantees. In Paraguay even today, a number of such estates contain more than four million acres, and nearly half the land of the country is owned by precisely twenty-five families, who naturally rule the country through obedient military dictators.

Thus an all-powerful feudal land system prevailed and still does. Only near the cities were some small holdings given out to veterans as a reward for their services. The Creoles—though they could not put their hands on the heavy taxes spent or shipped abroad by the Godos, nor on the Royal Fifth, nor on the Church tithes—became the ruling caste. Though import and export duties were excessive and there were heavy-handed exactions, well before the end of the colonial period, and in spite of the many doors closed against them, the wealthy Creoles became the privileged elite, beginning to buy titles and commissions from the Crown, edging into the *cabildos.* That they would eternally submit to the discrimination and humiliations imposed by the mother country and the greedy merchants and bureaucrats was absurd to believe.

In spite of everything, they rose in social and political importance. Ambrosio O'Higgins, a non-Spanish vagabond peddler, rose to be viceroy. More and more sons went off to Spain to buy commissions, as did Pío Tristán y Moscoso (who became field marshal and Peru's last viceroy), Francisco de Miranda, José Miguel Carrera, San Martín, and hundreds more.

Advancement was slow. Often the colonials were harassed by envious plotting; they were the first to be accused if things went wrong, either with army finances and supplies or on the field of battle—as Miranda knew better than any other. But many of them played heroic roles in the Napoleonic wars and, on one side or the other, in the Independence wars.

Other members of the two wealthy Arequipa families, Tristán and Moscoso, became high churchmen—bishops, archbishops, and grandees—not only in Arequipa, but in Spain itself.

And so, by the end of the eighteenth century, when all races and groups, all the submerged cultures, were struggling upwards, the caste system, the ironclad trading monopolies, and the enforced isolation of the colonies began breaking down. Spanish power in the New World, quite apart from the disastrous wars in Europe, was disintegrating.

iii

The process of race mixing was accelerated and continues to this day, resulting in what Mexican educator José Vasconcelos has called "the cosmic race," which he believes will be superior to all other races, for it will have a broader biological heritage and will have access to more varied cultural backgrounds. Thus the nationalities and the racial composition of Latin-American countries at the time of Independence were, and even now are, in a formative stage.

By the time of Independence the differing ethnic and social individualities of the various regions were becoming recognizable. By keeping the colonies isolated from each other and from the world to make for easier supervision, Spain helped create the fierce nationalisms that eventually were to destroy her control and bring about the wars for independence she feared.

The process continues, providing Latin America with a rich, varied, ethnic pattern often widely divergent even between local regions. In *Os Sertões*, published in 1902, in the second

chapter, entitled "Man"—one of the most brilliant essays on
the ethnology of Brazil—the author, Euclydes da Cunha, con-
cludes, "There is no such thing as a Brazilian anthropological
type." He provides a sharp-etched picture of the formation of
definite regional types, due to the varying percentages of the
original stocks and the "mysterious catalytic" force of nature—
cultures, soil, heat, light, rainfall, long continued migrations,
and so on—which have created the different sub-races in that
vast land. Even before the conquest, there were more than
five thousand languages spoken in South America.

iv

The Spaniards sought to control all travel and trade. As
time went on, no one could emigrate to the New World without being able to produce a fine family record, for generations
back, of loyalty and service to the Crown. Travel between the
various colonies was prohibited except by royal consent. Vio-
lations could be punished by death.

Trade between the colonies was also strictly regulated. Many
of the harsh restrictions were to prevent the rise of new industries which might compete with the mother country. Mad
Juana even went so far as to order *all* industry extirpated in
Peru, something that was not and could not be enforced. But
many farming enterprises such as vineyards and wine making,
olive groves and the making of oil, were either forbidden or
their products could not be exported. At one time, even paint-
ing was prohibited, lest it compete with the profitable sale of
works by Spanish artists, what with so many churches always
being built. Paintings by Murillo and Zurbarán, Spanish imi-
tations of Titian, Tintoretto, and Raphael, are strewn over
the continent in churches, monasteries, and museums.

All goods, except a few shipments between the colonies, had
to be transshipped through Callao in Peru and Porto Bello in
Panama—the only two ports where interoceanic commerce was
permitted. In Buenos Aires, cut off from all trade with the

empire except via Lima, Peru, an imported suit of clothes cost 500 steers. In Spain, for a time, the only ports allowed for New World trade and travel were Cádiz or Seville, at great injury to the colonies and to Spain herself.

This simplified controls and made it easier to block free travel and to smell out pernicious books and literature. It was an attempt to keep the New World ignorant of the new ideas and forces that were shaking Europe. There was no doubt, even so, that they would have a similar effect on the overseas colonies. Some years before Independence, one of its leaders, the scholarly Juan Belgrano of Argentina, even had the temerity to petition the ecclesiastical authorities to permit him to translate the works of Montesquieu, Voltaire, and Rousseau. As time went on, anybody of any intellectual stature, even many a Church prelate, was avidly reading the French and English philosophers.

Gradually the close-trade empire system broke down. Smuggling—of goods, books, ideas—became a major industry. It was even encouraged by many New World officials; in Buenos Aires, the warehouses of the smugglers were in plain view across the river. Such illegal traffic broke down the tariff, tax, and price structure; it ruined exclusive trade with the mother country. Brazil became a great smuggling center for New World goods; Spanish merchants often went to Lisbon for merchandise rather than pay higher prices for products from the Spanish colonies.

Toward the end of the eighteenth century, Spain lifted some barriers against American, British, and French shipping. Little by little a breach was being made, through which, presently, a vast torrent would flow.

v

The whole picture was growing clear as events grew cloudier. In spite of the exactions and restrictions of the mother country, the colonies had steadily become wealthier; the population, particularly the lower classes, had been increasing. All colonies were becoming more self-sufficient, beginning to have farm and factory surpluses for export as well as gold and silver and diamonds. Sugar plantations spread all along the northern coastal region of Brazil; sugar had become a leading export from Venezuela, Colombia, Ecuador, and Peru. Argentina was exporting vast quantities of dried meat and hides. Coffee, tobacco, quinine, cocoa, spices, and tropical forest products were in growing demand throughout the world. Chile, though most looms were still household enterprises, became an important textile center, its products superior to those obtainable elsewhere.

Beginning also in the eighteenth century, printing presses were imported. Though at first only ecclesiastical books could be published, much clandestine printing went on. As reprisals weakened, other literature—patriotic poems, books on economics and the natural sciences—was issued; presently, also periodicals. Miranda brought the first free printing press to Venezuela; Joel Poinsett, United States consul and a volunteer in the Independence forces, brought the first free press to Chile.

It could not be said, though, that a new commercial class was arising or that the feudal system was being undermined. Many of the great aristocratic landholders were among those most ardently engaged in studying the seditious literature and accepting its broader humanitarian implications—at least until the French Revolution frightened them.

Toward the end of the eighteenth century, Spain became slightly tolerant of scientific investigation; many scholars went to the colonies from Spain, and the doors were opened to numbers of French, English, and German naturalists.

In the first half century of the Conquest, Spain had welcomed the observations of her great explorers and scholars. But one by one, the classic reports had been buried in the archives. The iron curtain came down. Finally all foreigners were excluded. Spain did not wish outsiders to discover the wealth and beauties of South America, nor did it want news of European affairs, except those in Spain, to reach the New World. It was almost as if America had never even been discovered. But in the eighteenth century, South America was discovered again—a great burst of rediscovery.

Explorer-naturalists opened up that lost world. They climbed the Andes and took observations of the stars; they collected strange plants in the Amazon and Orinoco, struggling, in the face of fever and poison darts and death, through the densest jungles. Toward the middle of the eighteenth century, the French Académie des Sciences, thanks to Newton's theory that the world was flattened at the poles and fattened in the middle by the pull of the moon and sun, tried to measure exactly the length of a degree of latitude in various zones; they sent an expedition to Lapland, and Philip V permitted two such expeditions to South America.

One was led by the great mathematician, Charles-Marie de la Condamine. He crossed Panama and Colombia, climbed the Andes in Ecuador, followed the earlier incredible route of Francisco de Orellana down the Amazon, and went back to France with hardened sap of the rubber tree.

On June 5, 1799, Prussian scientist Alexander von Humboldt, the greatest naturalist of them all, sailed on *El Pizarro* from Coruña, Spain, and on July 15 landed at Cumaná at the mouth of the mighty Orinoco. He and his party headed across the llanos and the rivers and through the jungles in a delirium of excitement. They swung their hammocks in the thatched *hatos* of the natives, ate their *sancocho* of stewed fowl, their cassava cakes, black beans and plantains, drank their pitch-black coffee. They also drank the milk of the famous *palo de vaca,* not knowing it to be the rubber tree. One Negro in the party began vomiting small rubber balls. At Calabozo, Humboldt captured electric eels and received a frightful shock in one leg. He dissected them and was the first to find the Organs of Hunter and the Bundle of Sachs, the eel's dynamo. Perhaps his story of the electric eels aroused more interest in Europe

about Latin America than anything else, for electricity itself
was a mysterious power newly discovered.

Humboldt measured the length of the mighty Orinoco
within two miles; he went on into the most ancient geological
region of the continent, was the first European to discover the
two-way Casiquiare River and, by the stars, calculated the
junction of the Amazon (Rio Negro) and the Orinoco to be
2° 43″, only a few minutes off.

He next explored the mighty Magdalena River and, late in
1801, arrived in Bogotá, not to see the white-towered cathedral
or the massive hill-perched Monserrate monastery, but to pay
homage to one of the great scientists of the epoch, creator of
the Colombian colonial renaissance, José Celestino Mutis, bot-
anist, metallurgist, discoverer of nocturnal variations in baro-
metric accuracy, and a lexicographer versed in native languages who compiled a dictionary for Catherine the Great.
Humboldt looked at his herbarium of 20,000 plants with admiration and delight.

Humboldt did not fail to observe that Antonio Mariño, a
brilliant member of Miranda's freedom movement, was in
prison in Cartagena, with thirty-six-pound shackles on his legs.
He knew that behind "the bolts and bars," as Abel Plenn has
put it, "a new age was being born."

When Humboldt went on to Quito, he took with him one
of Mutis' closest collaborators, young Francisco de Caldas.
Francisco had already discovered the method of determining
altitude by the temperature at which water boils. In Ecuador,
he and Humboldt discovered that temperature decreases 1°
with each latitude north and 1° with each 300 feet of altitude.
Together they climbed 21,000-foot Chimborazo, one of the
loftiest Andean giants. (Caldas was also a revolutionist and
patriot, and in 1816 Spanish General Pablo Morillo put him
before the firing squad, saying, "Spain has no need for
savants.")

In Quito, the Prussian scientist recruited Carlos Montúfar,
young brother of Rosita Montúfar of whom he was so fond.

Both were children of Juan Pió Montúfar, Marqués de Selva Alegre, one of the charter members of Ecuador's only cultural group, the Patriotic Society of Friends of the Country, founded in 1791 and headed by Bishop José Pérez Calama. In collaboration with the secretary of the society, Francisco Espejo, a cholo whose brilliance was attested to by his being head of the National Library, the elder Montúfar had written a revolutionary book, *Escuela de Concordia,* which favored free speech and a free press. It mocked the ecclesiastical educational system and was quickly suppressed as "bloodthirsty and seditious satire." Montúfar was too wealthy and powerful to be touched, but the society was suppressed and in January, 1795, poor Espejo was thrust into a stinking dungeon, from which he was hastily released to die by the end of the year.

The father's spirit burned brightly in Humboldt's companion. Young Carlos went with him all over Latin America and on to London and Paris. He came back to lead armies against the Spaniards in behalf of the second revolutionary junta of Quito, to be exiled, to come back and fight again and finally face a firing squad. His heart was burned in the public plaza.

vi

The whole process of liberation was stimulated by the world industrial revolution, which, though it had not reached much of South America, was creating a new Europe and a greater demand for products. South American trading cities expanded and a strong new merchant class established itself.

In a sense, South America and Mexico helped make possible the European industrial revolution, for the gold and silver sent over from the New World allowed the aristocracy of Spain to buy luxury goods being turned out by France and England. However, in Spain this easy supply of wealth imported from the New World stifled production and enterprise; it was easier to buy needed manufactured products elsewhere than to manufacture them at home.

The early explorations and colonization in the Americas, Africa, and Asia had stimulated not merely the curiosity and greed and enterprise of the European countries; they had promoted more trade and production, a world-wide expansion of commerce, and the use of money instead of barter. A new merchant class was created; in due time, a capitalist class. These new entrepreneurs represented progress and revolution everywhere. Soon they found themselves pitted against the old feudal order, the power of the aristocrats. Well before the Napoleonic era that doomed the old order, the absurdities of sacred feudal rule became sufficiently obvious to bring about the writing of the greatest satire of all time, Cervantes' *Don Quixote*.

Gradually this altered the political pattern of Europe and the Americas. Eventually, as new worlds and countries came into being whose interests no longer coincided with the two arrogantly feuding imperial powers and their selfish systems, an end came to the centuries-old cold war between Spain and England.

The whole world was now ripe for exploitation and trade—if production could be increased. Not only were machines and factories needed, but more political freedom, the breaking up of the closed-guild handicraft system, and the abandonment of feudal land tenure. Strangely enough, because the new machines needed cheap labor, the power and wealth of the feudal lords were temporarily augmented by brutal land enclosures that wiped out ancient communal and small land holdings and forced peasants and handicraft workers to migrate into the cities where they starved or worked for pitiful wages in the factories. This political transformation came about in England by means of two centuries of intermittent civil war.

A similar change did not occur on the continent much before the French Revolution but then was spread ruthlessly across the continent by the Napoleonic conquest. England, therefore, held the lead—a tremendous economic and political advantage over all latecomers. She had an abundance of iron and coal; the solid basis for rapid expansion was available. Industrial upsurge was accelerated at the middle of the eighteenth century by the use of coal instead of charcoal for iron smelting, a revolutionary process that coincided with the birth of Miranda in 1750 in far-off Caracas, and by the time he reached Europe, when he was twenty-one, steam power began replacing water wheels and windmills, bringing about still faster growth in industry and new transportation. In 1785 Cartwright's power loom was introduced. Eli Whitney's cotton gin (1783) demanded a large cheap supply of raw cotton for spinning. Overnight, great textile factories rose in New England, England, and on the continent, and Fulton's steamboat moved on the Delaware one year after Miranda's ill-fated expedition to free Venezuela.

A revolution was also occurring in agriculture—not merely the expansion of commercial crops entering world trade, but a technical revolution: machine-drill seeders, fertilizers, crop rotation. The first steam threshing machine was used in England in 1803, three years before Miranda's expedition.

Mass production was just around the corner—another of Eli Whitney's contributions, introduced in his gun factory in New Haven, Connecticut, and soon taken up by the clock industry.

Thus industry was pulled out of the home and capital accumulation occurred. Division of labor and interchangeable parts transformed the methods and psychology of workers caught in the web of a new, large-scale system that in so many ways stultified their creative instincts.

At first, the old abuses of feudalism—ruthless exploitation from dawn to dark of human beings, particularly of women and small children—were carried over into the new factories. The early manifestations of capitalism were cruel and barbarous. Man really became a slave of the machine, not the contrary, until labor began to revolt, to form unions, to go into politics, to secure protective legislation.

Also, as production increased, new markets had to be found. There was no point in producing goods for people unable to buy them. Yet it was almost ludicrous, the manner in which the new capitalists fought tooth and nail against any ameliorative legislation—against shorter hours, against health safeguards, against improved housing—all elements most necessary for their own profits, expansion, and power. They represented the revolution, yet almost from the outset they were more hostile to political and social change than the feudal elements they were increasingly displacing.

Without ever-expanding markets, domestic and foreign, capitalism must and does slow down; imperialistic wars had to be waged for sources of raw materials and for outlets for goods. Increased wages and shrinking hours that permitted larger employment helped create a wider domestic market. As industrial methods grew more complex, more intelligent workers were needed.

As industrial competition with other countries sharpened and trade became more important, England, France, and Spain all tried to set up closed trade empires backed by imperialist armies—just as Russia, China, the United States, and the new federated Europe are trying to do today. This is a costly and self-destructive pursuit, as history has demonstrated, for the greatest profits are always made by trade with industrialized countries having good standards of living, not with backward countries. Competition hurts certain lines of enterprise, but in the long run all industry prospers, for the wider the market the freer the market and the greater the number of well-paid consumers.

But there was also the need to control raw materials, for this made costs lower for the mother country and increased them for competing countries. All these controls made it impossible for new industry to rise in many parts of the world, and for most of the world the industrial revolution is only beginning to occur, with a repetition of the blood throes of earlier centuries.

Pari passu with these short-sighted national efforts came vast military establishments. The art of war suddenly ceased to be the prerogative of feudal knights in armor, now vulnerable to deadlier weapons. It was based on conscription, in the name of freedom and patriotism, although conscription is the antithesis of freedom. The new armed establishments naturally became based upon industrialization; organized militarism depends upon the constant expansion of the factory system.

Since the new methods demanded an abler working class, education also expanded. Presently, compulsory free education—another contradiction—was imposed nearly everywhere. That education should come to be controlled by the capitalist state was inevitable, to break the feudal and religious monopoly and to instill the right sort of regimentation and patriotic nationalism. History was rewritten and is still rewritten falsely in all the textbooks of the world—not merely in revolutionary countries.

The industrial revolution, therefore, produced the printing press—though power was not applied until 1814—making possible the rapid diffusion of news and knowledge, and also of official and other pernicious propaganda. The development of separatist sentiments in the Spanish colonies dates almost precisely from the introduction of the printing press. Its influence was cumulative, for books long survive to be read by many.

vii

The quickening tempo of human freedom, initiated by the American Revolution, finally reached Europe a generation later. The Revolution went far beyond the previous antifeudal domestic wars of England; it not only smashed feudalism but sought to level all men to equality and absolute freedom.

By then, England, as the industrial leader, had grown afraid of popular freedom and revolt. Abroad, it was soon allied with the very feudal elements it had curbed at home; it sought in every possible way to preserve feudalism on the continent, for that left its own industrial domination without competition and meant better control of colonial markets and sources of supply. (A similar United States-feudal alliance continues to this day in many parts of the world, particularly in South America.)

English efforts to curb the French Revolution, and to crush it, were as fruitless as similar efforts in previous and later eras. It could not be done. Instead it brought about the rise of Napoleon and the military conquest in the name of the revolution of all of Europe. The strange alliances of free England with the most backward feudal monarchies of Europe merely hastened their downfall and the triumph of the French arms. The legions of Napoleon swept through Holland, Belgium, Prussia, Austria, Russia (his first great setback), and the Papal States, and into Spain and Portugal. Napoleon was strong enough to force the abdication of King Gustavus IV of Sweden in favor of a dutiful puppet, Charles XIII, and to set his own brother Joseph on the throne of Spain.

In the end, of course, England blocked the "new democracy" of France, kept Europe divided, and, to enhance her own industrial and imperialist might, put capitalism into a strait jacket for more than a century. The downfall of Europe meant, before long, the downfall of England, also, and the industrial rise of the United States, where for the better part of a century capitalism already had a vast continental empire to exploit and develop before following its own peculiar brand of imperialism.

Napoleon, all in the name of freedom, patriotism, and the Revolution, climbed into the saddle after the sobering period of the Terror, becoming first consul in 1800, consul for life in 1802, and hereditary emperor in 1804. As he concentrated and centralized power in France and abridged political liberties, he continued to expand social and economic freedoms, abolishing the privileged orders, granting "justice," "equal rights," "equal opportunity," and making all careers "open to talent." He created, or his associates did, the enlightened Code Napoléon, which he imposed upon all of Europe by the sword. Thereby he plowed up feudalism the length and breadth of Europe, cracking the hard old pavement and letting the new grass of modern industrialization grow.

Successively Napoleon broke the three coalitions England made on the continent, but he lost the battle of Trafalgar when the combined Spanish-French fleets were wiped out—and thereby lost Spain's empire.

It was in 1808, two years after Miranda's expedition, that French troops put Napoleon's brother on the throne of Spain, where he stayed for five years until driven out with British aid. Those five years were crucial throughout the Empire. All the forces of Independence were coming to a head. The political downfall of Spain meant that within a decade or so its empire would be destroyed.

viii

The French encyclopedists, the physiocrats—Helvétius, Diderot, Rousseau, Voltaire—had had a tremendous influence on New World thinking long before the French Revolution. Spain put up high walls but the sparks flew over, setting conflagrations over millions of square miles. Those ideas even had had a great influence on such enlightened monarchs as Catherine of Russia and Frederick the Great, both of whom invited numerous new thinkers to their courts.

But the French Revolution, the inevitable outgrowth of such radical ideas about human liberation, raised up great fears. Catherine was terrified and ended her friendship with Miranda. In the New World, it split feelings and attitudes and so shook the colonies, already shaken by the American Revolution, that for the moment Independence seemed remoter than ever. When Creoles who had gloried in their enlightenment and denounced the Spanish imperial system came face to face with the possibility that revolution, if it came to the New World, would destroy their feudal privileges, many of them drew back and became reactionaries, frantically determined to uphold the Spanish monarchy and its system at all costs. On the other hand, the ideas of the French Revolution, for the first time, in spite of all the imperial barriers to the dissemination of knowledge, increasingly became the common property of the lower orders—the Negroes, Indians, mestizos, mulattoes, and hoi polloi of the towns and cities.

There is no doubt that England, with a decisive effort, could have quickly overthrown Spanish rule in the Americas, but William Pitt and his successors were fearful that this might spread the French Revolution. (He had the same fears of the new republicanism in his day that Dulles and Rusk have had of communism in our day; he was trying to hold back the whole historical process.)

Napoleon now became—as for the privileged groups in England—the bête noire of the elite in Spanish America. As the tread of his legionnaires crossed Europe, destroying the great estates, fears among the great landholders in the colonies grew stronger. And when King Ferdinand, trying to save himself, gave Spain a liberal constitution and a representative Cortes which included New World delegates, many Creoles (the diehards, at any rate) were suddenly ready to renounce Spain and to work for Independence—if they could contrive it—not to free the people but to preserve the existing system. Then, when the French soldiers took over the mother country, they feared that this meant either permanent subjugation by alien imperialism or the spread of the Code Napoléon and the Revolution to the New World.

All in all, the French seizure of Spain produced a great outburst of independent sentiment in all classes in South America. The jarring controversies among the Creoles were quickly healed. For various reasons, all wished to save themselves from the Napoleonic monster. The popular orders, particularly the mestizos, saw a golden opportunity both for Independence and for a revolutionary system. They were fighting for freedom while the Creoles were fighting to preserve their wealth and power, but for the moment something close to a united front, a combined nationalist movement, won the loyalty of all classes.

The first issue to split this nationalistic front was the question of whether to swear allegiance to the new Napoleonic regime or to ousted Ferdinand VII, a conflict that quickly degenerated into armed strife. In general, however, the local *cabildos* took over administration, at first holding the western countries in trust for the return of a true Spanish sovereign, which meant, almost at once, the kicking out of appointed viceroys and the birth of autonomous governments.

The pressures for outright declarations of Independence became stronger. This too caused new strife and bloodshed. Numbers of premature Independence governments were set up.

In any case, the self-reliance of the colonists increased. In 1806, the year of Miranda's invasion, the colonists of La Plata, with no help from Spain, threw the British out of Buenos Aires and Uruguay, thereby gaining both military experience and self-confidence. Similarly, the frightened efforts in Venezuela to beat off Miranda's 1806 invasion—the raising of local volunteers, equipment, and supplies—also promoted a feeling of independence; it provided similar experience in handling arms and troops and created self-confidence in local abilities. A similar story was to be repeated many times elsewhere, and a new feeling of national pride arose that greatly contributed to eventual Independence.

French usurpation of Spain would never have produced, in itself, the great Independence movement that swept the South American continent, had there not been a score of economic, social, intellectual, scientific, and political trends already at work. The French Revolution and the conquest of Spain were merely the heat that caused the yeast to rise faster; the placing of Joseph on the Spanish throne was merely a fortuitous event which played a decisive role in speeding up the processes of colonial freedom.

Many things were beating on the doors and the barriers of Spanish colonialism. There was the upthrust of all the orders, all the ethnic groups. In spite of Spanish exactions, all the colonies had grown more wealthy. Trade and production, in spite of setbacks from whimsical Crown decrees, had expanded everywhere. A breach had been made in the closed-empire trading system, letting out goods, letting in new goods, and letting in ideas and knowledge. The printing press supplemented the smuggling of proscribed books. Education, while still mostly in Church hands, had been expanded, and more attention was given to teaching Indians, slaves, and mestizos. The age of enlightenment, the work of eager new naturalists and other scientists, and the general acceptance of their efforts (Englishmen, Frenchmen, Dutchmen, and Germans, as well as Spaniards and Portuguese) began rolling back the mists of ecclesiastical and official obscurantism. Little by little, better roads had been built and stage coaches were beginning to supplement or replace horseback and river travel.

Above all, there was growing up a vast local pride, a new nationalism, which caused increasing difficulties and undermined the older forms of dictatorial rule. Bit by bit, Spain had had to make concessions—all too slowly, all too late. Gradualism of this sort is ever the delusion of established power, especially when the relentless Zeitgeist takes giant strides. In essence, the old order fights for the status quo, not progress. But the fruit of Independence was now ripe all over the New World, ready to drop from the gnarled tree of three hundred years of colonialism.

Perhaps, as Argentine Bartolomé Mitre put it, "The colonies were not ready for self-government, but worse would have been their condition governed by laws contrary to nature that condemned them to slow death. . . . The unity of Spain with the kingdoms of the New World under absolutism was incompatible with the representative government and the full equality of all citizens."

As the great Domingo F. Sarmiento put it in his *Facundo*,

"There is no need to consider at length the character, object, and end of the Independence revolution. They were the same throughout America and sprang from the same source, namely the advances in European ideas. South America pursued that course because all other nations were pursuing it." The implacable Zeitgeist!

3

Out of the Pampa Endlessly Rocking

/\/\/\/ On March 9, 1812—a bright autumn day—the British frigate *George Canning* moved up La Plata to Buenos Aires and put ashore Lieutenant Colonel José de San Martín, lately of the Spanish army. Though only twenty-six, he was a veteran of wars in Africa and Portugal and had fought against the French invasion of the Peninsula. By experience and study, he already knew as much or more than any other military leader.

He presented himself almost at once to the junta, a somewhat reactionary Creole triumvirate which had taken over the reign of power in a vast realm of nearly two million square miles. The junta gave him the right to raise and equip a cavalry regiment. And so the Creole San Martín, born in the Uruguayan Jesuit missionary town of Yapeyú, returned from Europe to fight for the freedom not merely of his native land but of all of South America. It was his destiny to liberate half the continent.

By this time the Independence movement was flaring up all over South America except in Peru, the most firmly held and most reactionary of the colonies. But in few places were there the ability, devotion, unity, or resources to support the new-found freedoms, and the immediate results were mostly tragic. Freedom was still precarious.

Following the creating of the 1808 Buenos Aires junta, which merely changed viceroys, revolting Creoles in Chuquisaca, Alto Vera Paz (Bolivia), set up an independent government in May, 1809. La Paz rose up two months later, setting up the Tuitiva junta, "wholly American," which hanged everybody opposed to it. Though Chuquisaca was eventually to become the first capital of an independent Bolivia, both juntas were suffocated by troops rushed in from Peru and Argentina. The leaders were promised amnesty but were sent to the gallows. "The fire I have lit," said one, just before he was strangled, "can never be put out."

In Quito, Humboldt's friend, the elder Montúfar, was jailed in March, 1809, but got out and headed an uprising that set up a "Sovereign" junta. It claimed as its goals "the protection of the true religion; defense of our legitimate monarch (Ferdinand VII) and property." Montúfar became "Supreme Highness," the other members "Excellencies." "It was a revolution of *marquéses*, not of the soil," remarks Alfredo Pareja y Díez Canseco in his *Historia del Ecuador*.

The junta made some show of defense, but its forces were defeated in Pasto, and by October 24 the government was turned back to the Spaniards. In December, in violation of pledges, the latter made arrests, including Montúfar's brother, Pedro. He himself escaped. On August 2, 1810, a mass uprising of the people to liberate the prisoners was drowned in blood, and all the prisoners, many of them chained to the walls, were slaughtered.

Pedro Montúfar had been released three days previously because of grave illness. Another prisoner had previously feigned insanity so well he had been kicked out. Mariano Castillo saved himself by lying among the bloody bodies in the prison, pretending to be dead and not moving even when he received several bayonet jabs.

But the two children of Manuel Quiroga, minister of justice, brought to see him by a Negro slave girl, were hacked to pieces in front of his eyes and the pregnant slave was bayoneted through the belly. Quiroga was then sabered to death.

A month later, ironically, Carlos Montúfar, Humboldt's friend, arrived as the emissary of Ferdinand VII. He set up a new conciliatory junta, but Viceroy Abascal in Lima refused to recognize it, and Spanish troops converged on Quito. The people angrily surged into the streets, an open *cabildo* was called, and the junta was put in charge of Bishop José Cüero y Caicedo. Carlos and his father led various forces to fight the Spaniards. By December, 1811, the Congress of Free Towns assembled, and on the tenth the Bishop appeared before it to demand full independence, which was voted overwhelmingly. A constitution was ready by February 15, 1812.

Viceroy Abascal sent in more troops, from Peru, Panama, Guayaquil, Cuenca, and Guarandá. The patriots worked feverishly: church bells were melted for bullets; powder was made day and night; women gave their jewels. Rural priests organized Indians armed only with bows and arrows. Three thousand volunteers rose up, armed only with knives—"hands flexed, their eyes fixed on destiny."

The patriot forces were driven back, they were penned in Quito, but they were strong; they had cannon on the city's eminence Panecillo, Little Loaf Hill. The women sang in the streets as they carried ammunition and food to the soldiers. Why Carlos Montúfar suddenly ordered abandonment of his positions is not fully clear. On December 8, 1812, the Spaniards, led by Toribio Montes, entered a city from which defenders and citizens had fled en masse. The few patriots captured were shot on the spot.

Only in Argentina and in Chile, where a dictatorship had been set up by the flamboyant Independence leader, José Miguel Carrera (and he, too, was soon to fall before powerful invading Spanish armies), had the first Independence governments managed to survive. The flame had crackled brightly

on all sides in 1810, not merely in Bolivia and Ecuador and
Buenos Aires, but in Caracas (April 19), Bogotá (July 20),
Chile (September 18). All had been isolated outbursts, yet all
had the same doctrines. For the time being, most of the new
governments, though deposing viceroys and governors, ousting
Spaniards, and proclaiming autonomy, gave deposed Ferdinand VII nominal allegiance, but they proceeded to run their
own affairs.

In Buenos Aires, as early as 1808, the Creoles had demanded
self-government and deposed the viceroy, who had failed to
protect them properly against the 1806–7 British invasion
though they had been paying out nearly half the annual revenues of over 4,000,000 pesos—the second largest in South America—for military defense. They proceeded to install a viceroy
of their own choosing, in itself an almost unprecedented act.

But Argentina's real independence—her "First Independence"—came on May 25, 1810. On that cloudy, cold fall day,
a restless multitude, bearing improvised white-and-blue Independence banners, forced the *cabildo* to admit two "ideal and
valiant Creoles" as members. The viceroy was forced to resign
—the fourth in two years—and a three-man junta was set up
to arrange for a Constituent Assembly.

ii

Of all the Spanish colonies, Argentina, since it had had no
known mineral wealth, had been the most neglected, although
it had prospered considerably after it was made a viceroyalty
in 1776 and was enlarged to take in the Banda Oriental (Uruguay and Rio do Sul, now part of Brazil), Paraguay, and half
of Alto Peru (Bolivia), including the rich Potosí silver mines.

From the start, Argentina had lacked a labor supply, a
further barrier to its early development. The indigenous population, mostly primitive Charrúas, Querandíes, and Tehuel-
ches (the Inca empire had not penetrated far into the Pampa),
was small and dispersed, but since little large-scale or other

farming was started, few Negroes were imported. Early Spanish regulations prohibited specifically the growing of grapes, olives, flax, *cañamo* hemp and sassafras, though by the time of Independence great vineyards stretched out from Mendoza and wine making was well advanced.

As Cortés had said in Cuba, the Spaniards had not come to the New World to till the fields, but for gold. The quick peso was the chief aim. The Pampa remained almost depopulated.

But cattle raising and increased need for horses as transportation made the Pampa a source of new wealth. The vast grass empire was soon overrun by great herds and by roving bands of outlaws from all over the continent.

The seizure of native women from the harassed tribes created the mestizo horseman—the Gaucho—the semisavage, raw-meat-eating cowboy of the plains. As described by Ricardo Rojas in his great classic *Martín Fierro*, the Gaucho became "a genuine race that has engraved on its manly breast the seal of our America . . . proud, belligerent, independent." He was a singular mixture of naïveté, astuteness, loyalty, and brutality; at the same time, "a lover of music, a composer of cantos and poetry." San Martín later said, as a partial explanation of his successes, "The backbone of my army was mestizo—and Gaucho."

Foreign trade, wholly in the hands of native-born Spaniards, called Saracens or Godos—no Creole could export or import— was restricted to the one American port of Lima; Argentine goods and imports had to be transported fifteen hundred miles across the Pampa, up to the Andean plateaus of Bolivia, and another fifteen hundred miles to Peru, and put aboard ships to Panama, to be mule-backed across the Isthmus and reshipped in Porto Bello for Seville or Cádiz, Spain. Or else they could be sent an even greater distance by ship on a treacherous voyage around the Horn to Lima. Travelers, if given permission to come or go, had to follow the same difficult routes. No wonder goods coming into Argentina were so costly that only a handful of the wealthy could afford them! Though the Argentines got little enough for their mountains of hides and other wares, by the time the goods reached the markets of Spain their price was staggeringly high. The Gauchos grew bitter, first over the red tape and exactions and secondly because of those robbers, the Porteños—the port people—a distaste that divides Argentina to this day.

The folly of Spain's closed trading empire policy was never more patent than in Argentina, a bumbling, greedy, ignorant bureaucracy cutting off its nose to spite its face. Naturally smuggling became a major industry, in which both Spaniards and Creoles waxed rich. To the warehouses and docks of the smugglers, open for all to see across the river, came the ships of England, France, and Portugal, and some United States vessels. Brazil, too, profited, for it became a depot for goods not merely from Argentina but from all Hispanic America.

In 1777, however, the more enlightened Carlos III opened Buenos Aires to foreign shipping. Since the extended boundaries of the newly established viceroyalty now included such richly productive areas as Santa Cruz and the Potosí silver center, once the largest metropolis in the Spanish-speaking world, Argentina began to prosper and expand.

That strange, wrathful, chauvinist Spanish historian, Mariano Torrente, who in 1829 began publishing his impressive three-volume blow-by-blow *Historia de la Revolución Hispana-Americana*, described the benefits to Argentina under this more liberal policy: the tide of commerce between Buenos Aires and Lima was reversed, and goods from Peru began flooding over the Andes to the Argentine port for all climes. "The population grew rapidly; internal trade extended as far as Cuzco and Arequipa (in Peru); the metallic products of Potosí fecundated the immense Pampa, and the capital was given strength and vitality beyond all calculation."

Thus, paradoxically, remote Argentina came suddenly to have more contacts with the non-Spanish world than any other colony. Its revolution was more cosmopolitan than that of any other region. There was, it is true, only one university, that of Córdoba, founded in 1613, and it would be two centuries before Buenos Aires would have any institution of higher learning, but its writers, before and after the revolution, sought inspiration in French and English literature or turned back to the great Inca traditions, as did Ricardo Rojas, exalting the imperial glories of early Tahuantinsuyu, "Land of the Four Regions."

Thus, other things besides freer trade and geographic expansion widened horizons. For a generation prior to Independence, books were coming in more freely, and in 1806 the first newspaper, *El Telégrafo Mercantil,* was started, soon to be followed by the *Seminario de Agricultura.* The contributors were enlightened men, soon to be found in Independence ranks, such as physicist, scholar, and lover of French literature Manuel Belgrano, leader of hosts, and Gregory Funes, an ecclesiastic but a member of the secret Lautaro Lodge in Europe, later in America. As Sarmiento put it, "Books, events, and impulses from Europe induced South America to take part in the movement imparted to France by North American demands for liberty and to Spain by her own and by French writers."

iii

The first determined demands in Argentina for local political rights came as a result of the expedition of British Commodore Homer Popham, simultaneous with the Miranda raid on Venezuela, when General Beresford came ashore with 1,564 men and took over Buenos Aires. The inhabitants were shocked that the viceroy, Rafael Sobremonte, with far superior troops, large stores of supplies, and strong fortifications, put up no significant defense. The only real effort was made by a Spanish Navy captain, Santiago de Liniers (born in France). He proceeded to raise a volunteer force against the invaders and shortly obliged Beresford to surrender, on terms of safe-conduct to Montevideo, which had also been seized.

Popular feeling was so intense that the *audiencia* had to permit a general junta. It proceeded to arrest the viceroy and strip him and other Spanish officials of office.

Efforts were then made to dislodge the English from the Banda Oriental, or Uruguay, though the British sent in more than 10,000 troops the following year. This, too, was presently accomplished by Liniers, who in turn became viceroy. Soon after, Napoleon seated Joseph Bonaparte on the throne of Spain. At once a conflict arose over recognizing the imposed government or the rival Spanish junta, set up in Cádiz to govern in the name of deposed Ferdinand VII.

In mid-July, 1808, a representative of the junta arrived in Montevideo, to enforce Ferdinand's claim, and also an emissary from Napoleon, demanding recognition of Joseph. Governor Francisco Javier Elío of Uruguay, with elaborate ceremonies and fiestas, on June 21 proclaimed allegiance to Ferdinand, but Viceroy Liniers delayed doing so and tried to remove Elío.

As a result, a new group of civilians and military men took over Buenos Aires, demanded an independent junta, and forced Liniers' resignation. Elío became viceroy until he, in turn, was ousted.

On a dismal, cold, rainy, early fall day, May 25, 1810, the people, infuriated by the trickery of the *cabildo* and the viceroy and led by a secret revolutionary cabal directed by such Independence patriots as Mariano Moreno, Manuel Belgrano, and Bernardino Rivadavia, poured into the plaza early in the morning. The *cabildo* called on the troops to disperse them, but the officers replied they were with the people. Leaders of the *cabildo* then addressed the crowd, asking them what they wanted, whereupon they went back inside and everything was granted. A new triumvirate was set up, the Primera Junta, headed by Cornelio Saavedra.

When the people shouted their answer to the *cabildo* members, legend has it that the sun broke out briefly in glory, and so "the Sun of May"—"the Inca Sun"—was adopted as an emblem. It was stamped on the first coinage put out by the new junta. It was on the adopted shield, along with a Phrygian liberty cap and clasped hands, embraced by laurel leaves. A country-wide election was called to choose a National Constitutional Assembly.

It soon developed into a three-cornered fight in the capital: the Spaniards; the reactionary Creoles, believing in strong centralism; and the radical Creoles, believing in the rights of the people and full Independence. Over and against this was the attitude of the interior, in the end to lead to prolonged civil war that lasted far into the life of the Republic, a regionalism that still operates. The Gauchos and farmers, distrustful of Buenos Aires, were closer to the radical Creoles than to any other group. Injected into this was the struggle—though this played far less part in Argentina than in any other part of Latin America—of the mestizos, Indians and Negroes, slave and free, both against Spanish rule and against Creole rule.

International forces were also involved. The English who, while at war with France and Spain, had schemed for the dismemberment of the empire, now, allied to the independent junta and the Regency, became interested in holding the empire together, though they were quick to seek commercial privileges from independent governments. Resident British merchants threw their influence on the side of the more reactionary Creoles, helped the Spaniards, or sought to mediate differences which would ensure the continued recognition of Ferdinand, not Independence. For a century, the United States followed a similar pro-Spanish policy toward Cuba.

The Spaniards, whether pro-Bonaparte or pro-Ferdinand, sought to limit Creole control, particularly that of the more radical Independence groups. Carlota of Portugal and Brazil actually sought to establish her claim to act as Regent for Spanish restoration and sent Portuguese troops into Uruguay.

iv

The Portuguese court was now seated in Rio de Janeiro instead of Lisbon, for Portugal had become a battleground between British and French armies, victim of the cold war become hot of that day.

More than three hundred years had passed since Brazil's discovery and settlement. Slowly the coastal areas had filled up. Great sugar, cacao, and other plantations had been established with slave labor. Coffee was flourishing in São Paulo and other southern provinces. The gold and diamonds of mountainous Minas Geraes and Goyaz had brought in tides of lusty, brawling people. The bold *bandeirantes*, halfbreeds, mulattoes, semi-outlaws—reckless, cruel, and greedy—had pushed far west to the Paraná River and the highlands of Mato Grosso.

Other groups had followed the Amazon River and the great tributaries—São Francisco, Madeira, Rio Negro—to the very foot of the Andes; some had pushed on into the great northern Amazon plains, larger by far than the whole state of Texas. Negroes, experienced in Africa in handling large herds of as many as 100,000 head, had built up the cattle industry everywhere. They were also skilled metalworkers, as they had been for a thousand years.

By the time of Independence, the population totaled more than 3,000,000, about equal to that of the original thirteen colonies in the north.

In spite of the variety of climates, the manifold aspects of the geographical setting, and the intricate pattern of races—aboriginal, African, European, Oriental—that had produced pagan revivals, Catholic temples, Mohammedan shrines, and Protestant churches that rose white-spired or white-domed out of the green forest, within a century Brazil had a more typical nationalist flavor than any country in Hispanic America.

This was partly due, perhaps, to the readier mixing of the races and to the great open frontier. Ethnic and social barriers in Portuguese Brazil were never so rigid as in Spanish America. Open marriages with Negro and Indian women were the order of the day. As early as 1510, Diego Alvarez married the chieftain's daughter in Bahía and had a large mameluco family. Another famous early mixed family, to become prominent in Creole affairs, was that of João Remalho in São Vicente.

Education was more widespread than in Hispanic America. Most good-sized communities had primary and secondary schools for all, that taught Greek, Latin, Hebrew, mathematics, and theology. Even before the end of the first century of settlement, a definite Brazilian literature—which over the centuries was to become one of the most inspired bodies of writing in the world—was emerging, chiefly books of geography, travel, botany, and patriotic epic poetry, telling of the wonders of the country.

Also self-rule progressed. Even before Portugal set up an over-all colonial administration, local self-government (by Brazilians, not Portuguese) had become well established.

As Pedro Calmón put it in his *Historia Social do Brasil,* "The [town] Câmara of the first century—a Portuguese version of Greek democracy—was the faithful government of the people by the people, . . . respected and strong . . . as it had been in the Peninsula before the monarchical centralization."

Later on the Capitão Mor, the civil and military councils of Crown-appointed governors or captains, brought oppression and brutal abuses, though such excesses did not become pronounced until the eighteenth century, when Portuguese controls were actually slackening. Even so, at all times, control by the mother country remained flimsy—both the freedoms and the abuses were largely Brazilian products—and, as the cities grew in size, the Câmaras stoutly maintained their independence. Real rule in the interior, as Calmón also pointed out, was usually exercised by the heads of powerful Creole or mameluco families.

As was Hispanic America, Brazil was profoundly affected by events in Europe. Queen María, who had ascended the Portuguese throne in 1777, was as mad as a hatter, and government was exercised by her son João, fat, lazy, stupid, and his nymphomaniac wife, Carlota Joaquina, sister of Ferdinand VI of Spain. The slackness of court rule, its corruption and inefficiency, stirred autonomy in Brazil. The Tiradentes—tooth puller—revolt broke out in Minas Geraes as early as 1788. It was suppressed, and the captured were deported permanently to Africa. But the leader, Joaquim José da Silva Xavier, a dentist, paid the supreme penalty.

At dawn, April 21, as described by Frei Raymondo Pennaforte, "the hangman entered his cell to dress him and to beg pardon . . . for having to execute him. . . .

" 'Oh, my friend,' Tiradentes said calmly, 'let me kiss your hands and feet'—then removed his shirt—'The Redeemer was also undressed when He died for Him.' "

He walked out to the gallows courageously, holding a crucifix, to the sound of gay, martial music between lines of troops in gala dress in a procession of cavalry; generals; the viceroy's son; ministers of justice in robes; the trial judge with silver trappings on his horse, the mane braided with pink ribbons; priests; bands of Irmandade da Misericordia monks; and numerous lay organizations singing hymns.

But the revolt indicated that soon Brazil would go its own independent way. An ironic turn of events delayed this process until well after the rest of the continent had been liberated.

In 1807, Napoleon sent Marshal Andoche Junot across Spain to take over Portugal. For once, prodded by the British fleet in the Tagus, Regent João bestirred his plump buttocks. Old mad María and João's wife, Carlota Joaquina, were packed up, and he and the thousand and more members of the royal court piled themselves, their slaves, servants, hangers-on, and all possible portable belongings aboard eight men-of-war and forty merchant ships and sailed off, just as the French soldiers swarmed over the Lisbon hills.

The old worm-eaten, stinking ships wallowed through heavy seas for two months and reached Bahía in January, 1808. By then, even drinking water was gone—for the first time the aristocrats could appreciate some of the horrors of the African slave ships—and they stumbled ashore more dead than alive.

The Bahían people opened their doors and their hearts, fed them lavishly with splendid banquets, showered them with the finest raiment. Carlota was pretty much out of things, because all her hair had been shaved off to get rid of the vermin. Mad María crept about, blubbering, "I'm going to hell." The nobles stalked around, contemptuous and arrogant, arousing little sympathy by their ingratitude. But João had a fat lazy smile for all and made friends.

Two weeks later the whole moth-eaten crew re-embarked and sailed south to Rio.

Rio was more pleasant than Bahía. It was—and is—the most beautiful and one of the largest cities in the Americas, with lovely, contoured bays flanked by jungle mountains, miles of glistening beaches, streets curling about the flanks of the jagged peaks of the Cariocas. Its public buildings were not yet remarkable but several were handsome "palaces." A few impressive private mansions rose above the low unattractive adobe buildings. The *favelas* or slums were larger even than today; the streets were unpaved cesspools of mud and stench, actually not so different from the cities of that day in the United States but certainly far behind glorious Lisbon.

The Cariocas, as the Rio de Janeiro people were called, were even more hospitable and lavish in their entertainment of visiting royalty than those of Bahía. The aristocrats here had more resources. João liked the people, high and low; Carlota, still bald, was petulant and disagreeable. The haughty nobles were not ingratiating. And so, Rio became the capital of the Portuguese empire, what was left of it.

João, with surprising wisdom and energy, set to work eagerly to make Rio a city fit for kings. He cleaned it up, built palaces, and otherwise beautified it. He heeded all grievances, threw Brazil open to the trade of the world, and invited immigration from every quarter. He reformed taxation and the judiciary; established religious freedom; founded a national bank, a medical school, a military academy, a national library and art museum. Brazil, now cut off from the mother country, was economically on its own, which meant that it was not drained by overseas tribute, and under João became one of the most progressive enlightened countries of the times.

World-shaking events occurred shortly. The French overran Spain, and Napoleon imposed his brother, the obese, incompetent Joseph, on the throne; and in Rio Queen Carlota's hair grew back, and she became the female Samson of the court.

As sister of Ferdinand and as the Princess Infanta of Spain, she now schemed to be named the New World regent for the Spanish monarchy, as custodian for all Spain's New World colonies. Brazilian troops were soon marching into the Banda Oriental, eastern Argentina, which in due time was to become the independent country of Uruguay.

v

The revolutionary junta in Buenos Aires faced its worst moments. The reactionary Creoles had gained the upper hand; Paraguay had been lost, first to a Spanish *coup,* then to a popular movement that declared the country sovereign and independent of both Spain and Buenos Aires. Bad Argentine defeats had occurred in the north, and the Uruguayan campaign did not progress.

For the elections for the National Assembly, intense rivalry between Spaniards, royalist Creoles, and Independence Creoles flared into the open. When a Spanish plot to overthrow the junta was discovered, all Spaniards were stripped of their properties in exasperation and banished from Buenos Aires; they were allowed only five hundred pesos and could not come within thirteen leagues of the city.

Numerous uprisings occurred in the interior; each declared independence. And so Argentina was fast becoming a country of many heads. The French philosophic ideas of the cities were scarcely understood in many rural places—the only symbolism that caught the imagination was the simple one of Independence and this, for many, meant independence not merely from Spain but from the rule of Buenos Aires and Córdoba as well. The Gauchos nourished deep grievances against the city Creoles. Thus, if battle was joined between the patriots and royal-

ists, still "a third entity," as Sarmiento called it, was stirred
into consciousness.

"The revolution served to develop this detached, heterogene-
ous party . . . such was the element, full of life and instincts,
that was set in motion by the renowned José Artigas," the
intrepid outlaw who eventually liberated Uruguay. He made
use of these hordes—made them into the blind tool of his will—
to fight European civilization and any regular organization
except his own rule. He opposed both monarchy and republicanism, because both came from the city, and reverenced
authority.

As Sarmiento put it, "The Argentine revolutionary war was
twofold: (1) civilized warfare of the Creoles against Spain;
(2) a war against the cities by country chieftains to shake off
all political subjugation and satisfy their hatred of civilization.
The cities overcame the Spaniards, and were in turn overcome
by the rural districts. The last shot is still to be heard."

Thus to unite all Argentina—in the face of this Gaucho
hatred of the metropolis—was not going to be easy. Besides
that, Spanish forces were advancing on all fronts: Bolivia,
Paraguay, Uruguay, Chile. The Portuguese were marching in.
The new junta hastily raised armies to meet the danger. Belgrano led a big force to Paraguay; Castelli went north to save
Bolivia. Other forces were built up along the Uruguay River
facing the Banda Oriental.

The First Junta soon suffered sharp reverses: the loss of Paraguay, defeats in the north. Stalemated in the east, it was overthrown by the more reactionary Creole oligarchy: Posada,
Pueyrredón, Rivadavia, Passo. It promised to push the war on
all fronts, but, since it had no real support in the interior,
things went from bad to worse.

It was to this governing body that San Martín offered his
services. Granted permission to raise a cavalry regiment, he set
to work at once, recruiting, organizing, and training his grenadiers. His headquarters and barracks were in the old slave
market, El Ribero, which had been left idle by the 1811 eman-

cipation decree. His men had to drill and maneuver for long hours; they had to study military science. Sometimes he routed them out suddenly at night to go into action. Those who did not stand up to his implacable regime were summarily dismissed. "I want only lions in my regiment," he told them.

One commentator remarked that San Martín's grenadiers had three components that made them invincible: the horses of the Pampa, the indomitable skill and courage of the Pampa Gauchos, and San Martín's own superior knowledge and experience of military science, acquired in Africa, on the battlefields of Europe, and from intensive study. Certainly the grenadiers produced "a whole generation of heroes." From the regiment came nineteen revolutionary generals and several hundred officers.

San Martín also set up in Buenos Aires the political and civilian arm of the Independence revolution, the secret Lautaro Lodge which Miranda had started fifteen years ago with the motto, "Union, Strength, Virtue." All members had to be native-born Americans and were pledged "to work with system and to plan for the Independence of America and its happiness, with honor and with just methods."

Over in Chile, Bernardo O'Higgins, member in Cádiz with San Martín, set up another Lodge. In Ecuador, José de Antepara, also a London friend of Miranda, did the same.

Though the Lodge claimed to be nonpolitical and drew in members from all factions if they were dedicated to the Independence cause, it was always involved in behind-the-scenes politics and was the *deus ex machina* of San Martín's whole career. It was primarily an engine of revolution against a common enemy and a defense against internal traitors. One writer characterized it as "the greatest international conspiracy of the age."

San Martín's third major step, shortly after his arrival in Buenos Aires, was to marry María de los Remedios Escalada, a fifteen-year-old girl with enormous black eyes and tiny feet, daughter of a wealthy Creole family. She became the mother of his children and his tireless companion in his later work in building up the Army of the Andes. When she died, he had carved on her marble tomb the words "Wife and Friend."

But his day and night preoccupation was in shaping the grenadier regiment into a perfect mechanism of war, with absolute discipline, absolute loyalty, and unbreakable morale. All officers had to be members of the Lautaro Lodge. To the very end of his long struggle, the grenadiers were the core of all his armies. They fought from Buenos Aires across a thousand miles of Pampa, across a thousand miles of Andes, and along thousands of miles of coasts, from Buenos Aires to Santiago, from Santiago to Peru, and to the snow slopes of Ecuador. They kept on even after San Martín turned the completion of liberation over to Bolívar; at the end, only seven of the original members survived. They rode back together from Ecuador—four thousand miles—to Buenos Aires. By then, fifteen years after the start, all South America had been liberated.

Meanwhile the reactionary junta proposed to set up the Spanish Infanta Carlota or some other member of European royalty on an Argentine throne. No Spanish court, neither Joseph Bonaparte nor the Cádiz junta, would accede to this, which left Belgrano and the other true Independence apostles of popular liberties in a stronger strategic position. When, in 1812, the triumvirate refused to convoke the constituent assembly, it was overthrown by San Martín.

On October 7, 1812, at 11:30 P.M., San Martín led his grenadiers, aided by infantry and artillery under Carlos María de Alvear, a fellow Lautaro member, into Plaza Victoria and surrounded the *cabildo* with drawn sabers.

It was coordinated with civil action. The people were called together by the municipal bell—the Liberty Bell. Some three hundred notables occupied the *cabildo* galleries, among them leading members of the clergy. They presented a proclamation that, under the protection of the armed forces, the triumvirate was relieved of its position and the *cabildo* resumed the authority "given it by the people in 1810 with power to call a truly national assembly."

The assembly met in January, as scheduled, and a new impulse was given to revolutionary defense; Tucumán was reinforced, and a whole new army sent to retake Montevideo.

As Bartolomé Mitre put it, "Thus, in the space of seven months after the arrival of San Martín in Buenos Aires, everything changed. The government was consolidated, its politics defined, the public spirit improved, and the revolution with two armies audaciously displayed the banner of Independence."

vi

By the time the constituent assembly met, Paraguay had separated. All Alto Peru except Cochabamba and Santa Cruz had been overrun by the Spanish armies from Lima. Led by Peruvian Creole Pío Tristán, they moved on into Jujuy, Salta, and Tucumán.

Ignoring the orders of the assembly to retreat to Córdoba, Belgrano, in charge of the northern Argentine army, turned on Tristán in a desperate, savage counterattack and sent his forces reeling back, to Salta and finally to the Bolivian *altiplanicie*. There the Spaniards reorganized, with 4,000 additional Indian conscripts, and began edging back to the Pampa. Northern Argentina was by no means secure.

Uruguay even less. The British tried to pry the Portuguese loose with an armistice. The Spaniards, not the patriots, moved in with a big flotilla and thousands of expeditionaries. Well-seated, they made numerous forays on Argentine coast and river positions. The Buenos Aires government did not have so much as a launch, whereas Spain, aided by the British, dominated the oceans, from the Caribbean to Cape Horn, from Cape Horn to California and beyond.

After San Martín's Buenos Aires *coup* of October, 1812,

which put the uncle of Alvear at the head of the government, Alvear went off to lead the Argentine army against Montevideo. San Martín's grenadiers rode off to protect its flank, control the Paraná River, and keep communications with Paraguay open.

Keeping his grenadiers out of sight and disguised as a countryman in big hat and poncho, San Martín watched Spanish war vessels coming up the Paraná River. They landed in force at San Lorenzo, above Rosario, and marched up a steep barranca with four pieces of field artillery toward the monastery on the llano. San Martín, concealed there, had few guns and no artillery; he drove them back to the shore with sabers and pikes. The survivors hastily re-embarked.

San Martín himself was pinned under his wounded horse and cut on the cheek by a saber and would have been killed except for two soldiers. One ran a Spaniard through with his bayonet and freed San Martín. The other was shot dead, crying out, in the very best tradition, "I die happy; we have whipped the enemy!"

This was the last Spanish effort to control the rivers, and Alvear, coming in at the end of a long siege that had left Montevideo starving, soon took over in triumph. Both he and San Martín returned to Buenos Aires as heroes.

Things were now going better in the north also. Belgrano had moved on into Alto Peru. For a time he swept on to recover all of that part of Bolivia that had been included in the viceroyalty. But by November, he suffered several bad defeats; his army was cut to pieces. He resigned and was presently called to Buenos Aires for trial, as had happened to Miranda in France.

San Martín was asked to take over northern operations. Alvear, instantly jealous, demanded the post. San Martín gracefully agreed. Alvear then became suspicious that his fellow officer wanted to remain behind to control the government, so he insisted that San Martín be sent out after all.

vii

San Martín met Belgrano at Tucumán and rode north with him to Salta, where the townspeople themselves had driven back the Spaniards. Taking over the army, San Martín made no move to push on into Alto Peru. Independence sentiment was strong there, but so were General Pezuela's massed Spanish and Indian forces, all well equipped. San Martín had only 2,000 men, ill-armed, demoralized.

He set up headquarters in Tucumán, drilled his men to exhaustion, and piled up supplies and more supplies. He sent occasional aid to two places still held by patriots in Bolivia, the important centers of Cochabamba and Santa Cruz. Otherwise he spent his time creating a reliable fighting force.

All had to attend classes. "An army that doesn't know mathematics," he told them, "cannot survive."

San Martín pondered the whole problem of South American liberation. To push on into Bolivia was a difficult and dangerous campaign, for it was more easily reinforced from Peru than from Argentina.

Chile, now in chaotic condition and likely to fall again into the hands of the Spaniards at any moment, lay on the long flank of Argentina.

San Martín saw clearly that the grand strategy for the continent must be to win Chile and make it secure. This would place the Independence forces on *Peru's* flank.

His plan included building up a Chilean fleet. "We'll take Peru from the sea. . . . Until Lima is subdued, the war will never be ended."

Peru, then, was the key to everything, the pivot of Spanish power. It cut the continent in half. The seat of the viceroy..lty, Lima, had become one of the shining, beautiful cities of the New World, but the people of Peru, the coast Creoles at least, were—as they mostly are today—bigoted and reactionary, the most fanatically royalist of the continent. They still lived in the conquest era; their very existence depended upon the Spanish rule. There had been little mixture of the races. The highlands were predominantly Quechua and Aimara, sons of the Inca empire. Though exploited in large plantations as slaves or serfs—*yanacones*—many retained their aboriginal communities and their ancestral lands, clinging stubbornly to their own language, culture, and traditions.

The Peruvian Creoles had known the terrors of the Tupac Amarú uprising of less than half a century before. To subdue it had cost years of war and much money and bloodshed, until Tupac was finally yanked into four pieces by horses. Their coast cities, mostly founded as military barracks, were citadels of resistance against the aborigines and the continent. Until those citadels were breached and razed, the war of Independence would not be won.

Once more Alvear wanted to be sent to the north, to win laurels by reconquering Bolivia. San Martín's defensive tactics seemed to smack of inertia.

San Martín graciously offered to resign. He asked merely for the post of governor of Cuyo—a distinct comedown—but there he hoped to build up a force strong enough to cross the Andes and drive the Spaniards out of all South America.

And so, telling no one of his plans, he took up residence in the provincial palace in Mendoza. It was a drab, almost treeless little city, on an arid plain. Its wide streets crossed at right angles and its buildings were single-story adobe, though it had those invariable structures which symbolized the Spanish genius over a continent and a half—the town and provincial "palaces" and a somewhat more impressive cathedral. But these landmarks were dwarfed by the sheer wall of the Andes rising up close at hand on the west, stark and ominous. Only a zigzag trail led up that steep ascent to the two major Andean passes—the highest ones on the continent—Uspallata and Los Patos. (Through Uspallata Pass, Captain General Ambrosio O'Higgins, father of the later patriot, had driven a road of sorts, with stone *tambos* or refuges at convenient intervals.)

Mendoza, even with the two countries on either side in such a disturbed condition, was the gateway of considerable trans-Andean trade. And so San Martín, there in command, supported by his loyal grenadiers, set to work to forge an army that would conquer over "three hundred years of colonialism and four thousand kilometers of zigzag Andean crags."

He was indomitable, scarcely rested, yet he was now a very sick man. Pneumonia, contracted in the northern campaign, had developed into tuberculosis; he had stomach ulcers that caused him frequently to vomit blood; he suffered severely from arthritis. The doctors gave him only a year to live unless he went to another climate and rested. (He was to live to be seventy-two.)

Once, when he was supposed to be sick unto death, he shook his head free from his blood-flecked pillow and appeared like a champion charger among his officers at a banquet, where he lifted his glass in a toast "to the first bullet fired on the other side of the Andes."

He always rose at daybreak, made his own breakfast, brewed his own coffee of which he drank innumerable cups all day, and spent the morning in paper work, receiving visitors, giving orders. He usually made his own lunch, a light repast, and ate it standing up in the kitchen. In hotter weather, he sometimes took a two-hour siesta on a sheepskin-covered cot in the hall. In the afternoon he visited his troops and watched the drills, sometimes taking charge himself.

He watched a slave who had escaped from a Spanish cane plantation and gave him hints. "Learn to saber well, for if you fall prisoner to the Spaniards they'll turn you into sugar." The anecdote went around, and one of the battle cries in later saber charges against the Spaniards became, "Oh, Godo, take this for sugar!"

In the evening San Martín ate a frugal supper and had visitors in. Talk of politics, public offices, and military matters was taboo. Usually he played chess; at ten everybody had to leave, but San Martín often worked on through the night.

He sent engineers through the passes, sometimes as diplomatic emissaries, to spy out the land, locate enemy forces, and make maps. "We cannot make war like Hottentots," San Martín remarked.

One such emissary engineer, Alvarez Condarco, was sent in by Los Patos Pass with instructions to come back by Uspallata. Asked how he would conceal his documents, he replied, "I shall make no sketches; I shall bring back every stone in my head."

San Martín made trips to the Indians of the Andes, the Pehuenches, and held conferences with the Indian caciques, or headmen, to ask for permission to lead his army through the La Plancha Pass. His real motive was to spread the belief among the Spanish officers in Chile that he intended to attack through the southern passes—a ruse that succeeded, for the Spaniards divided their strength.

The story is told well in the *Memoirs* of General Miller, who for years was one of San Martín's aides and later was with Bolívar and Sucre.

"San Martín caused to be sent to the fort of San Carlos, on the River Aguanda, one hundred and twenty goatskins of *aguardiente* or grape brandy, three hundred skins of wine, a great number of bridles, spurs, all the old embroidered or lace dresses that could . . . be collected, . . . hats, handkerchiefs, . . . gloves, beads, dried fruit, . . . an indispensable preliminary to success in any Indian negotiations.

"At eight o'clock in the morning . . . the caciques approached the esplanade in front of the fort with all the pomp of savage life, each at the head of his warriors, their wives and children bringing up the rear. Polygamy being practiced, the wives were very numerous." There were over fifty caciques— Calimilla, Epimán, Goyco, Huanguencul, Jamín, Marilinco, Millalur, Necuañan, Neyancare, Peñalef. "The men wore their hair unconfined and long; their bodies, naked from the waist upwards, were painted with different colors. Following the powwow, favorable for San Martín, two thousand persons, including women and children, seated themselves on the esplanade. As soon as the liquor exercised its influence, all talked together, and shouted, and yelled with deafening din. Quarrels . . . many fought . . . bit and kicked . . . tore out hair by handfuls."

On the fourth day set apart for gifts "each cacique presented the general with a poncho," very well made, with lovely patterns and colors. Of San Martín's gifts, the Indians prized most the hats and embroidered or lace dresses.

After eight days, San Martín left to meet General Pueyrredón in Córdoba. Mendoza merchants then arrived at San Carlos and bartered back most of the gifts in return for more booze. Even so, the Pehuenches said, "Such a splendid palaver was not known in the accounts of tradition."

4

Vales of Paradise

/.V.V.\ Years before San Martín began building up the Army
of the Andes (even before Joseph Bonaparte took over the
Spanish throne), his *compadre* from Cádiz, Bernardo O'Higgins of Chile, was secretly arming and training his workers on
the big 65,000-acre Las Canteras hacienda, with its 3,000 head
of cattle, which he had inherited from his father Ambrosio,
viceroy of Peru, who had died in 1801.

Bernardo made it into the finest ranch in the area. It was in
South Chile, near the Araucanian frontier, actually part of the
famous fertile central Vales of Paradise, in that era the whole
of Chile, which did not reach, except in name, to the southern
icy fiords, though the island of Chiloé, off the Gulf of Relon-
cavi, was settled and well fortified. But the lumber port of
Puerto Montt had not yet been founded and the beautiful lake
and rain country was sparsely settled, except for Araucania,
though Valdivia, where it rained almost every day in the year,
had become a flourishing port. To the north, the country extended little beyond Coquimbo; the whole nitrate desert was
part of Peru and Bolivia and, after Independence, was to remain so for many years. But the Vales were truly a paradise of
fertile valleys where grain and fruit grew magnificently and
where, once Independence had been won, vineyards and wine

making would also flourish, in a climate of eternal spring, superior to that of Southern California but with more rain.

From the corridor of the new "Big House" he constructed at Las Canteras, where he lived with his adored mother, Isabel Riquelme, Bernardo could look over the broad Laja River and far to the east, to where the property ended in the hazy, towering, white Andes. Enormous flocks of white geese honked by; in the fall, when they settled to steal grain, they became so gorged they could not fly, and it was customary to ride them down and kill them with sticks. Occasionally, high overhead, a lone condor flew black against the sky—the mightiest bird on earth, sometimes with a wingspread of fifteen feet, able to reach the very crest of the peaks that rose well over 20,000 feet into the sky. Chile, when it finally reached north to Arica, had 515 mountains higher than the highest mountain in the mainland of the United States. Since the country is so narrow, mountain, valley, and sea are a sacred Chilean trilogy—Nature's triumvirate ruling intimately over the Chilean soul.

Three other forces were at work in Bernardo's being: resentment of his father, who had tucked him away, under the name of Riquelme, as a student in Spain and later in England and then had cut off all funds when he became devoted to Miranda's cause; boundless devotion to his beautiful and clever mother; and a passionate desire for the independence of Chile.

In nearby Concepción, he found his father's former secretary, Juan Martínez de Rozas. Rozas was now married to the daughter of Antonio de Urrutia y Mendiburu, the wealthiest Creole merchant of the river port, but, more important for Bernardo, he was a dedicated disciple of Rousseau and the French enlightenment, as were also his wife and father-in-law. There in the Urrutia mansion, disguised as a social club, or *tertulia*, a select group of spirits gathered to discuss the new ideas, presently to constitute a Lautaro Lodge and to work for emancipation from Spain. Sometimes they rode out to Las Canteras for a country outing, or to the hacienda of neighbor

Pedro Ramón Arriaga, whom Bernardo had converted to his own radical opinions.

In Santiago now was the Argentine Jesuit, Juan Pablo Fretes, head of the convent of the Companía in the main Plaza de Arras, who had been a fellow Lautaro conspirator with young Bernardo in Cádiz.

In 1806—he was then twenty-eight—Bernardo became an official of the Crown, as mayor of nearby Chillán. He had to disguise his true feelings but soon came into conflict with the *intendente,* or military governor of the area, who, on the pretext of putting down sedition and keeping provisions from falling into the hands of any English who might attack, was despoiling the people of the countryside, confiscating their cattle, produce, and goods. He even drove off a considerable herd of cattle which Bernardo had on Quiriquina Island in the river.

It was then that Bernardo began training his men in earnest and laying up arms. He had already won the confidence of the Araucanos, was an honored guest at their tribal and national parleys, and brought back, as foreman of his big ranch and to drill his secret forces, Venanciano, a brave and astute veteran of the Araucanian wars. He also brought in numbers of English and Irish prisoners to work on the hacienda and to aid in training.

In 1808, the captain general of the colony died. The abusive local intendant expected to be named provisional governor by the royal *audiencia,* but Rozas and the Urrutias had enough influence to block this. The vain and somewhat obtuse, if good-natured, General Francisco Antonio García Carrasco got the post, and Rozas became his private secretary. The abusive intendant was removed, and in Santiago Rozas got the Creole *cabildo* enlarged and packed it with his own followers.

From Spain came the tremendous news of the deposing of Ferdinand VII and the seating of Joseph Bonaparte on the throne. All Chile seethed with uneasiness. The governor accepted the change; he had to or resign, but most interior towns declared for Ferdinand. This in itself was a minor revolution, an unwanted exercise of the popular will or at least of the will of the Creoles. It brought on a conflict with the governor that was to have far-reaching consequences.

Some Independence patriots favored going along with the imposition of Bonaparte, for after the naval defeat at Trafalgar he could not enforce his rule effectively; whereas the British, allied with the Spanish junta they had helped set up in Cádiz, would aid promoting Ferdinand's cause, not Independence. Bernardo and his friend Juan Mackenna, Chile's best soldier, a onetime intimate of Bernardo's father and now married into the powerful Larrain clan of big landholders, were of this opinion, but the popular tide was with the advocates of Ferdinand's restoration, so they went along.

Into this precarious situation, while the Santiago *cabildo* was still debating the ticklish matter, came emissaries of Infanta Carlota of Brazil, demanding that she be named regent and caretaker of the Spanish colonies pending Ferdinand's restoration. Then came news of the ousting of the viceroy by the Argentine junta.

Captain General García came down like a ton of bricks, denouncing Carlota, denouncing Ferdinand's partisans, denouncing the actions of the *cabildo*. A wave of arrests followed, particularly in the south. Rozas, also the leading priest of Chillán, Bernardo's neighbor, Arriaga, and scores of others were arrested, taken to Valparaiso, and shipped off to the Inquisition dungeons of Lima to stand trial for sedition. Nightly, Bernardo and Isabel expected the clank of royal soldiers coming to arrest him, but miraculously he was not bothered.

He himself rode off to see General Pedro José Benavente, head of the Frontier corps, to suggest that he be allowed to get together a volunteer corps to defend Chile. He received arms and money and thus was able to drill his forces openly, to unite them with those of Arriaga, and recruit many volunteers who knew his beliefs and purposes. He thus came into command of a large force that would be ready when the inevitable struggle developed.

ii

By this time the Santiago *cabildo,* packed with Rozas' friends, was in an uproar, angrily demanding the release of the prisoners and the discharging of officials responsible for the official persecutions. García dissolved the *cabildo* by armed force.

Its spokesman carried the matter boldly to the royal *audiencia.* "Who," he demanded, "will be safe from such abuses tomorrow? I run the risk today or tomorrow for defending the rights of a religious people, noble and faithful and loving their king, but I will die with glory and satisfaction if my death will liberate my country from shame and infamy."

The *cabildo* gained the ear of various Santiago garrisons, and its armed patrols stalked through the streets day and night. In spite of his palace guard, the governor was helpless and was obliged to back down, Rozas, Arriaga, and other prisoners were brought back from Lima and released; abusive officials were dismissed. Presently the governor turned his office over to the head of the *audiencia,* ninety-year-old Brigadier General Mateo do Toro Zambrano, Count of the Conquest, a grandee who owned the mighty Casa Colorada palace on the main plaza.

The doddering old fellow, scarcely able to cope with the rising tide of Independence, was forced to accept a popular five-man junta—the date, September 18, 1810—to govern the country; whereupon he died.

Rozas was made head of the junta. Before leaving to lead the new government, he visited Las Canteras, inspected Bernardo's well-drilled forces, and knew he had military strength at his back.

"I put my forces at the disposal of the junta. Hasten with

revolutionary measures," Bernardo advised him. "Don't delay."

Rozas, as Bernardo had suggested, sent out a call for the election of a general congress, but otherwise was irresolute, bending to this breeze or that. And he committed what the owner of Las Canteras considered rank treachery. On the contention that Bernardo lacked military experience, he put his brother-in-law, an Urrutia who also lacked experience, in command of Bernardo's forces.

Bernardo concealed his hurt and bitterness but wrote to Mackenna as to how best to improve his own military skill. His friend replied that if Bernardo wished really to know the science of war as it had to be practiced in Chile, he should get more Araucanian veteran officers to instruct him. "First learn how to be a common soldier."

Bernardo sweated it out for long hours every day. He rode to Los Angeles as a representative of Chillán to the local convention that would select the district's delegate to Rozas' new national congress. General Benavente was determined to impose a man of his choice, but at sight of Bernardo, the delegates broke into wild acclaim and chose him unanimously; also fellow-delegate Arriaga, only two years ago under arrest. The convention broke up with joyous shouts; everybody attended a *Te Deum;* and a fiesta with music and fireworks lasted all night.

News came of a royalist counter *coup* against the junta, and the new congress and the two delegates rode off posthaste, reaching Santiago weary and saddle-sore April 5, 1811. They put up with Father Fretes in the Jesuit monastery on the main plaza next door to the Tribunal del Consulado.

Fortunately, Rozas, with a miraculous burst of unwonted energy, had led the forces which, after a bloody battle in the Plaza de Armas, put down the troublemakers. The royalist leader was executed on the spot, and the royal *audiencia* was disbanded for all time.

Nevertheless, the *cabildo* had come into the hands of the Santiago oligarchy of pro-royalists. It opposed Rozas and fought to control the new congress. He finally conceded that Santiago was entitled twelve delegates instead of six. The elections there gave the victory to the oligarchy; all were bitter enemies of Rozas and Independence.

Congress was solemnly opened on July 4 with a military parade, solemn Mass, and a sermon by Father Camilo Henríquez. He made a fiery demand for full Independence.

Henríquez "knew more about the doctrines of Rousseau than those of the Evangels." As priest, newspaperman, and pamphleteer, he had long fought for Independence, had been arrested many times and for long years, and had been deported hither and yon across the continent.

But when the cards were down, the reaction had thirty deputies out of forty-two. The twelve revolutionaries came mostly from the south. They fought for the reduction of the Santiago delegation to the six originally allotted the city; the sessions grew acrimonious, at moments violent. The naming of a new junta was delayed for a full month—and finally was not born of the elected congress at all.

While turbulence was in full swing, the English frigate *Standard,* commanded by Charles Fleming, appeared to take delegates back to the new Cortes or parliament called by the British-created regency in Cádiz, part of British maneuvers to carry on the war against Napoleon. Spain, like a modern Korea or South Vietnam, was the unfortunate battleground for that struggle. New, bitter arguments were stirred up over Joseph versus Ferdinand—or Independence. Fleming also demanded money from Chile, allegedly due in contributions to the Cádiz government.

This shocked even pro-royalist elements, and O'Higgins— who had been kept away most of the time with a frightful attack of arthritis—rose from his bed half sick, in great pain.

"We radicals are in the minority here," he told the congress, "but even so we do not lack the force to prevent the departure of Chile's gold. It is needed here for Chile's own defense against possible invasion."

The bickering grew more bitter when Fleming, conspiring with the worse reactionaries in Valparaiso, arrested the junta's governor there, Juan Mackenna.

Greater uproar than ever resulted; when the majority refused to condemn or oppose the arrest of Mackenna or to oppose the British, the twelve radical deputies rose and left the hall. Now Rozas would have to declare a dictatorship or the whole structure of pseudo-self-government would collapse.

But the danger, it turned out, was not in the threat to Chile's gold, Mackenna's arrest, or the doings of the British troops.

iii

On the *Standard,* Fleming had brought back to Chile Sergeant Major of Hussars José Miguel Carrera, aged twenty-five, fresh from the Napoleonic wars, in which he had been slightly wounded. He came wearing a showy uniform, handsome, arrogant, self-confident. Secretly he was a great admirer of Napoleon, against whom he had fought; secretly he nursed his own selfish, grandiose plans.

Carrera was a member of a wealthy aristocratic clan. His father, Ignacio, a member of the September 18 junta, was now a delegate to the national congress. The younger sons were in charge of local Spanish troops: Juan José, a sergeant major of grenadiers; Luís, only twenty-one, an artillery captain. Their elder sister, Joaquina, a beautiful, relentless girl, was already mixed up in every existing secret political intrigue.

Even before José Miguel came back, the other Carreras had been plotting with the powerful landholding Larrain family to seize the new government. When José Miguel arrived, strutting in his glittering uniform, displaying winning ways to the gullible multitude, the Carreras saw the chance to act. The congressional uproar was their salad dressing.

The blow would be in the name of Chile's Independence.

On September 4, 1811, Juan José led his grenadiers into the Plaza, just as the bells of Fretes' monastery were tolling twelve noon. Luís dragged out four cannon. The doors of the palace of the *audiencia,* where congress was in session, were closed; the deputies held prisoners. Through the gathering crowd, on a prancing charger, rode the glamorous figure of José Miguel, flaunting medals, plumes, and gilded sword. He stalked inside.

He informed congress that eight royalist delegates (seven from Santiago) had been purged. He read off the names of a new junta the delegates would be required to accept.

It was a triumvirate: Juan Mackenna, Rozas, and Rosales, the radicals most feared by the conservatives, though both Rosales and Mackenna were married to women of the powerful Larrain family.

But Rozas fled to Concepción to set up a secessionist junta, which was adhered to by all the revolutionary town juntas of the south.

In Santiago, Joaquín Larrain now schemed to limit the power of the ambitious Carreras and managed to have the new junta appoint members of the Larrain family to all key posts. While riding with José Miguel, he said, a bit maliciously, "All the *presidentes* of administrative bureaus are in *our* house."

After a considerable silence, José Miguel asked, "And who is *presidente* of the bayonets?"

iv

The question was soon answered. On November 15, José Miguel Carrera's bayonets set up a new junta headed by himself, Gaspar Marín from Coquimbo in the north, Rozas from the south. In view of Rozas' rebellious attitude, Carrera asked O'Higgins to substitute.

O'Higgins declined to serve on the grounds of ill health and his firm belief in representative government. But Carrera knew that relations between O'Higgins and Rozas had cooled off. He wished to deepen that division and thus control the south. After urgings from many quarters, O'Higgins finally accepted. It was the chief blunder of his earlier life, and it left a permanent blot on his reputation.

Within a month, Carrera arrested three outstanding members of the Larrain family, including O'Higgins' friend Mackenna, and eight family intimates.

Bernardo tried to get Mackenna released, out of friendship and on the grounds that he was Chile's best military leader, needed for the defense of the fatherland at a time when Spanish invasion was threatened. But Carrera deported him to Mendoza. A few days later, Carrera dissolved congress, and O'Higgins and Marín resigned. In the south, Rozas denounced the usurpation and called up militiamen.

Carrera rallied troops and sent them toward Concepción under Juan José. He himself set up headquarters in Talca and asked O'Higgins to try to mediate the differences with Rozas so Chile's soil would not "be stained by the blood of patriots."

The Concepción junta, after listening to O'Higgins, set forth their minimum demands: that a junta representing north, south, and center be recreated and that a representative senate be established.

Carrera sent warm thanks for their suggestions—and moved troops south.

Realizing that Carrera had merely been playing a cat-and-mouse game with himself as the cat's-paw, and had not bargained in good faith, O'Higgins offered his forces to Rozas, saying they should strike swiftly and hard.

Rozas vacillated, and O'Higgins rode back to Las Canteras disgusted, vowing that he was done with all politics; he would devote himself wholly to the hacienda, and taking the baths at Cato to recover his health.

When Rozas finally moved into the field, Carrera quickly made mincemeat of his forces. He was exiled to Mendoza, where he soon died.

Carrera was a flamboyant soul but profoundly revolutionary.

He ordered that a free elementary school be set up in every place having more than fifty families; created the Instituto Nacional, to this day Chile's leading secondary school; founded the National Library; abolished slavery. He persuaded the United States to send a consular representative—Joel Poinsett—with whom he became intimately associated, even to having him take up residence in the palace. Poinsett brought the first printing press to Chile, and on it the revolutionary monk, Camilo Henríquez, started the country's first newspaper, *Aurora de Chile*.

The Spaniards, using Chiloé as a base, sent a big expedition to retake Chile. Carrera took no precautions, and a powerful Spanish army, magnificently equipped, under General Antonio Pareja occupied San Lorenzo, a port three miles from Concepción.

Bernardo called up all his forces, rode hard to Los Angeles to rally more, then drove hell-bent to help save Concepción, only to learn that it had surrendered. He disbanded his men (except for bands to harass the Spanish advance) with orders to rejoin him in Talca with Carrera. He himself rode there by back-trail short cuts.

He found the dictator with Consul Poinsett at his elbow; they were now bosom pals. Poinsett had become Carrera's adviser on all public matters and his companion in midnight revels. The American had even written a new constitution for Chile. At present, he considered himself a great military strategist and was soon to put the Independence forces into ridiculous and dangerous positions.

O'Higgins proposed an immediate guerrilla attack on the Spanish advance guard, already close by in Linares, just south of the Maule River. Carrera considered it too risky but finally permitted O'Higgins to sally forth, provided he recruited his own men.

That same night, O'Higgins set out with nine hussars, thirteen dragoons, and six militiamen. Penetrating into the Linares outskirts, he learned there were only twenty-four Spanish dragoons, all bivouacked in the plaza. He fell upon them, sending them back as prisoners to Carrera.

He roved the countryside, enlisting many volunteers which he led back to Carrera to enlarge his force. Others were left to carry on hit-and-run attacks on the thin Spanish supply lines.

But the Spaniards moved up to the Maule in force and crossed over by fords improperly protected.

Carrera fled, and O'Higgins and Mackenna (who had been allowed to return to face this dark emergency) held out as long as they could.

The scattered remnants of the patriot army were finally reassembled in San Carlos. Their morale was gone.

Even so, guerrillas were now breaking up the Spanish supply lines everywhere. The patriots, bypassing the main Spanish forces, struck into Concepción and cut them off from the sea. Carrera entered in triumph.

O'Higgins moved up the Laja to gather together his widely dispersed militiamen and grenadiers. After forced marches, he slipped into Los Angeles and took the royalist governor prisoner. The whole garrison came over to him.

By the end of the month, O'Higgins had 1,400 seasoned men. He led them to join Carrera at the siege of Chillán, where the Spaniards had holed up for the winter rainy season.

v

For months, the patriots sat out in the mud and cold while the Spaniards enjoyed warm houses. Carrera showed no initiative. Morale kept deteriorating. O'Higgins broke a Spanish sortie in strength, followed them into the city and, thanks to the Araucanian warrior, Venanciano's, catlike maneuvers, led his men through intricate patios and over roofs. He was ready to take the city when Carrera called him off.

Lifting the siege, the latter retired to Concepción, where he idled.

The Spaniards, growing more confident, made daring sorties

to get meat and supplies and even reached Las Canteras, which they reduced to ruins. Gleefully they carried off Isabel and Bernardo's sister Rosa as prisoners to Chillán.

Pareja was very ill, but powerful Spanish reinforcements arrived under General Gabino Gainza. The Spaniards soon had the run of the countryside.

Carrera had divided his forces. Those of Mackenna were soon in a desperate corner. Bernardo finally convinced Carrera he had to unite the revolutionary elements or they would be cut to bits piecemeal.

In the engagements that followed, José Miguel repeatedly ran away from the battles but always returned to claim the miraculous victories Bernardo produced. It was that way at Roble, an important river ford, where the patriots were attacked from the rear by an overwhelming Spanish force. Carrera fled, but Bernardo rallied his forces with the cry, "Live with honor or die with glory!" He was unhorsed, but he snatched up a gun from a dead soldier and drove the Spaniards in a rout across the river. Even Carrera had to praise him to the junta as "the first soldier, able to heroically unite the glories and triumphs of the Chilean state."

The disaster at Chillán and the record at Roble crystallized public opinion. José Miguel Carrera was incompetent, not even brave.

Arrogantly he blamed his own junta for disasters because it had not sent enough reinforcements and supplies. The junta (which on October 21, 1813, had taken up residence in Talca) ordered him and his two brothers to be relieved of their commands and sent out of the country. Emissaries were sent to O'Higgins to have him take over the supreme command. And so, the invaded country was threatened with civil war.

O'Higgins rode the long road back to Talca—three days and nights of dangerous travel—and met with the junta at 4 A.M. He declined the honor. A divided army, rent by jealousies, he told them, could not stand up against the Spaniards, and much of the army, he made clear, was fanatically loyal to Carrera. But the junta believed that no army led by Carrera would stand up to the enemy.

O'Higgins finally accepted command on condition that Carrera and his brothers be left in charge of their forces. He rode back grimly to Concepción. His task was formidable. The army was disconcerted; wholesale desertions had occurred. The Carrera elements were sullen, even openly derisive; they distrusted O'Higgins.

The junta, exasperated, ordered José Miguel to head the Chilean legation in Buenos Aires. O'Higgins resolutely opposed this.

José Miguel and his brother Luís rode off to Santiago but were captured by royalists at Penco and taken to Chillán.

At the same time, the junta barely escaped a guerrilla attack that seized Talca and menaced the capital. It managed to get together a force of a thousand poorly equipped men, but they were cut to pieces; the Spaniards, ignoring Bernardo's army, raced north.

Bernardo put his troops to forced marches. The conflict became a parallel race of the two armies up the length of the land. Whoever reached the Maule first could control Santiago and would control the country. The patriots had to use narrow muddy trails; the Spaniards had the highway. But Bernardo reached the river a few hours ahead. Santiago was saved—for the moment.

vi

The English—in the shape of James Hillyer and a fleet—arrived and began dealing with the Supreme Director, Francisco de la Lastra, to oblige Chile to obey the demands of the viceroy of Peru. England was still trying to reconsolidate the Spanish Empire. Chile was to go back to the days before September 18, 1810, and submit unconditionally to Ferdinand and absolutism. Ferdinand, it now appeared, might be back on the Spanish throne. The French hold was crumbling before joint Spanish-British attacks.

The viceroy's demands were refused. Hillyer then proposed an armistice until Chilean ideas could be presented to Lima or, if necessary, to the Spanish Cortes.

Armistice negotiations with General Gainza at the Maule were put into O'Higgins' hands. Hillyer journeyed to O'Higgins' headquarters.

Bernardo was not keen on negotiations or any surrender of Chilean Independence, however nominal; he knew the unpopularity of such a course. At once he demanded the complete withdrawal of Spanish forces from Chile. Gainza agreed but said that any such arrangements would have to be approved by the viceroy of Peru. Bernardo brusquely terminated all overtures and resumed the offensive.

Though the Spaniards controlled all south Chile, having taken Concepción—Isabel and Rosa, previously exchanged, were again prisoners—their thin lines to the north were harassed by patriot guerrillas. Approaching winter and rain were further hampering their supply problem.

Gainza sent word he would personally assume responsibility for any decisions.

On the freezing day of May 3, the two army chiefs and their advisers, accompanied by small cavalry contingents, met in a primitive shack on the banks of the Lircay River—neutral territory. In spite of the arguments of his chief adviser, turncoat José Antonio Rodríguez Aldea—a sly little pock-marked man but very brilliant—Gainza quickly realized that O'Higgins was in no mood for quibbling and suddenly dropped all objections. He agreed to everything.

King Ferdinand, Bernardo did concede, would be accepted as sovereign, but only if the existing Chilean government were recognized. The final form of government would be decided by the Cortes, to which Chile would send delegates. But the Spanish army was to retire at once to Concepción and evacuate

Chilean soil within thirty days after ratification of the pact by the Chilean junta. Hostages and prisoners of war were to be exchanged.

Gainza wanted to send the Carreras to Lima. This would have been a great favor to the patriot side, but O'Higgins was adamant; their fate was a Chilean affair, and they had to be freed along with all other prisoners. Lastra, however, asked that they be delivered into the hands of the junta at Valparaiso.

The papers were ready. It was almost dark. While Gainza held a last-minute consultation with Rodríguez Aldea, O'Higgins and his aides paced along the river in the icy wind.

Rodríguez succeeded in getting Gainza to make changes. Legal clauses were inserted that would make the agreements difficult to interpret and enforce.

O'Higgins was furious. "This is not to act in good faith!" he shouted at Gainza. "We shall continue fighting!"

Rodríguez whispered in the Spanish officer's ear, and he replied suavely, "But why should not the two armies wait on either side of the Maule until the two governments reach a decision?"

"We are wasting time. We had everything worked out. Take it or leave it." O'Higgins turned on his heel.

Gainza picked up his pen and signed. Hillyer raced off to Santiago with the documents.

The following day, Gainza pointed out certain defects in the arrangements which made it impossible for him to proceed with evacuation until the points were cleared up. He moved troops to strengthen his position.

O'Higgins sent back word he was marching at once and sent Mackenna to occupy a hill overlooking Talca.

Gainza backed down again and at once started withdrawing across the Maule toward the south. O'Higgins insisted he was not moving fast enough. Gainza said he lacked transport for his supplies. Bernardo supplied oxcarts and wagons.

Gainza established temporary headquarters in Chillán to

prepare for the complete evacuation of Concepción province.

Rodríguez still had cards up his sleeve. Instead of sending the Carreras to Valparaiso he arranged for their escape, well aware that they would create dissension in the patriot ranks.

When José Miguel and Luís reached Talca, Bernardo concealed his dismay and greeted them affably, lodging them in his own house. At once they began scheming to take over command.

Bernardo informed them that henceforth they should not leave the house. "Many officers hate you," he told them smoothly, "and you are in danger."

José Miguel replied arrogantly. "Don't do me favors that merely humiliate me. My friends will want to know why I don't visit them. My enemies are my own risk. Either arrest me or put me to the bayonet."

"I can no longer be sure of your safety here. You will leave Talca at once." O'Higgins sent them off, escorted by two dragoons. A fast courier hurried ahead to inform Lastra. Before the brothers reached Santiago, Lastra's armed men arrested them.

vii

Gainza showed further signs of violating the armistice agreements and gave no indication he intended to leave the country. O'Higgins informed Lastra that he was preparing to resume war.

In the meantime, the Carreristas and the extreme Independence patriots were agitating against the Lircay settlement. Though its temporary advantages had given O'Higgins time to organize and strengthen his army, it was not popular. At the right psychological moment, Carrera eluded his captors and seized the government, declaring himself commander in chief and promising to drive the Spaniards out of Chile at once. Both Juan José and Luís were given higher rank than Bernardo and put in charge of divisions.

O'Higgins arrested Carrera's emissary to Talca. José Miguel then resorted to guile. "My friend—if I can still call you that, for in spite of our differences, my friendship for you has never changed—I don't know whether you or I is the crazy and unnatural Chilean who wishes to drag the fatherland to ruin. Before that happens, we should meet and talk. In our hands rests the salvation or the destruction of a million people who have worked so hard for their liberty. . . . Believe me, my good intentions toward you are not due to weakness. . . ."

But already, to Bernardo's fury, Mackenna had been re-arrested and, along with other friends, sent into exile once more in Mendoza.

O'Higgins received a call for aid from the *cabildo,* which was opposing Carrera's usurpation. He put his army in motion—not for the south to fight the Spaniards, but for Santiago. Leaving the bulk of his forces in two nearby towns, he went ahead with only 400 men, deeming that number sufficient, for there were few troops in the capital. But just after he crossed the Maipú, the alert Carreras ambushed him. The fight lasted all afternoon, then O'Higgins' men were routed by a cavalry charge. Recrossing the Maipú, Bernardo put up at a friendly hacienda and sent word for the rest of his forces to join him.

Two Spanish couriers blowing bugles brought word to him that the viceroy had refused to accept the Lircay agreement, that Chile had to submit unconditionally, that he was sending a new army corps under Colonel Mariano Osorio.

To strike Gainza hard before he could be reinforced was more important than any struggle over control of the government. At once Bernardo dashed off a message to Carrera, suggesting a conference.

Days went by: no reply. He sent another message: the same result. Finally he wrote a note, saying he was coming to Santiago at once.

"I shall meet you tomorrow at eleven in Tango Alley. I will come with ten men as far as the river and proceed with only one aide."

Mostly they agreed to disagree. Further negotiations would be taken up by their subordinates.

But the following evening, September 3, 1814, Bernardo swallowed his pride. With Captain Ramón Freire, one of the ablest officers to come out of the revolutionary struggles, and with Chaplain Casimir Albano, who had been a friend of Isabel and Bernardo since the latter's childhood days, he rode back to the city to put himself unconditionally under Carrera's orders. He asked only one thing: "Send me to the most dangerous point."

The city was tense with the news of Spanish invasion and the possibility of civil war. Now, news that the two leaders had made up their differences brought the populace cheering into the plaza. The two men presented themselves together on the palace balcony. Together they visited the various barracks to prepare for the new war.

Two days later, Bernardo galloped off to the front. The delay had already been costly. Already Osorio, with 5,000 fresh troops and Chiloé veterans, had reoccupied Talca north of the Maule. His forces also included the Royal Talavera Regiment, a corps to which San Martín had once belonged, famous for having covered itself with glory in Africa and throughout the Peninsular campaign.

The patriot army seemed in danger of dissolution. O'Higgins' own secretary defected to the enemy and sent word to his former chief he should do the same: he would be showered with honors and be made the intendant of Concepción.

Osorio reached San Fernando, sixty miles from the capital.

Only the most desperate efforts could hold the Spaniards back. Bernardo discussed defense plans with Carrera. The latter wished to defend the hills near the capital, where the Spaniards could be cut to pieces in narrow defiles. Bernardo pointed out that the Spaniards could easily take other routes. He suggested that forces to hold the fords at the Chacapoal river near Rancagua be sent out at once; if these points were lost, the patriots could then take up a position behind the strong walls of Rancagua, where they could hold out until the main army could hit the Spaniards from the rear.

The bulk of the army was now in the hands of Juan José and Luís Carrera. They bungled the whole operation by failing to reach the fords in time. Juan José, hit by a small Spanish vanguard, fled into Rancagua in wild rout. He sent desperate pleas to Bernardo to save him. Luís retreated north, leaving Bernardo and his own brother in a bad bind.

Bernardo fought to the last ditch to block the Spanish crossing. Wisdom told him to save his men by quickly retreating north and joining Luís, but he could not abandon Juan José in the city. If Luís returned with his division, all would be well.

When he brought his men into Rancagua, Juan José fell into his arms, weeping with relief. "Though I am your superior in rank," he said, "I put *everything* into your hands."

viii

The battle of Rancagua that followed is one of the most bloody, heroic, and important in Chile's history. It decided the fate of the country and determined many of its protagonists for years to come.

O'Higgins deployed his men in the plaza and raced up to the *cabildo* roof. The Talavera Regiment was approaching the city. Never had he seen such fine military precision. And yet, it occurred to him, free-wheeling Chilean cowboys—*huasos*—could break them up.

He hastened down to throw up barricades. On the cathedral towers he raised the flag of Independence and a black banner, which meant war to the death: no quarter, no prisoners.

He sent a courier to urge Luís to hasten to relieve them; another message went to José Miguel in Santiago. "Our supply of munitions is scant, but if Luís has enough, we are saved."

Luís replied he would arrive at daybreak and launch an immediate attack.

All day, fighting was incessant, a rain of steel, repeated assaults against barricades. Time after time, the Spaniards were driven back. The cannon of the two opposing sides belched fire only a block apart. Toward the end of the day, the Spaniards cut off the water supply and set fire to buildings adjacent to the plaza. All night long, the patriots had no rest, having either to man the barricades or fight the fires.

At daybreak, Bernardo climbed up the cathedral tower and peered anxiously across the valley and the hills. There was no sign of Luís' forces.

He rushed from barricade to barricade, encouraging his weary, thirsty men. At ten o'clock, the Spaniards again set fire to buildings and launched a massive assault. Several times they breached the barricades but were killed with bayonets or in hand-to-hand fighting. Finally they drew back.

Juan José pleaded that the patriots surrender. Bernardo brushed him off and raced up to the *cabildo* roof. Not a sign of help.

Another attack was launched. As Bernardo reeled from trench to trench, a shout went up from watchers on the *cabildo* roof.

"Our men are coming!"

With a frenzy induced by fresh hope, Bernardo tore up to the roof. A cloud of dust was approaching—the army of Luís.

The royalists saw it also and began pulling out of the city and heading for the river fords. The Spaniards sent out small mounted guerrilla contingents to try to slow up the patriot advance from the north until they could get all their forces to the south side of the stream.

Bernardo hurled patrols after the main body to hasten their departure. Numbers of cannon were captured.

"They are running away! They are running away!" came in a scream from the *cabildo* roof.

"Who? Who?"

"The whole Third Division."

The defenders groaned and looked at each other with dismay in their haggard faces.

A small band of guerrillas had hit the division's advance guard, which had broken. Panic had spread to the army. Luís had wheeled his horse and fled from the field.

From the *cabildo*, Bernardo, his taut face black with powder, saw Osorio's forces turning about to reenter the city. One company turned around in the middle of the river.

"There is no hope now," he told his officers. "All we can do is die bravely." Juan José, with a pathetic grimace, said they should surrender.

"When I first took up my sword for my country, I swore I would never lay it down until I died or Chile was free," replied Bernardo.

The attacks grew fiercer, but no man faltered. They fired; they met bayonet charges with bayonets; they fought hand to hand with knives and machetes, but they fought, panting for breath, panting for a few minutes more, a few hours more of life. Perhaps, after all, Luís would re-form his troops and return.

Bernardo himself, Juan José constantly at his elbow whining for surrender, had no hope. He was bitter. He believed Luís' flight had been both cowardice and deliberate treachery. The Carreras would prefer to lose Chile, even a brother, rather than have O'Higgins win a victory.

The attacks were unceasing; the flames advanced on the plaza; the heat grew intense. There was no water, not a drop to drink for twenty-four hours.

All their munitions exploded in a roar that shook the city and knocked men off their feet.

O'Higgins took one more look from the *cabildo* roof.

"Saddle up," he ordered. "Everybody mount!"

Two hundred of Freire's grenadiers swung into their saddles. Three hundred others cantered up. These were all the men left of the 1500 defenders.

Freire wanted to put Bernardo inside a hollow square to give him better protection. Bernardo refused indignantly and placed himself at the head.

"Ride!" His arm swept on and up.

They jumped their barricades; they galloped down Merced Street in a storm of fire and death; they hurdled the Spanish barricades and their cannon; they swept on to the edge of town; they leaped a canal; they galloped across the valley and up the slope of Chada Hill. Three hundred of them were left alive.

At the crest in the growing dark, Bernardo paused and looked back across the fields to the smoking towers of Rancagua. He saw the rabble of townspeople seeking safety, several wandering children, a woman carrying her dead husband across a horse.

He rode on, choked and sad, through the night. It was more than just a battle. Chile was lost.

5

Army of the Andes

/•\/•\/•\ Chilean refugees and the shattered remnants of the
Chilean armies toiled through the snow passes to Argentina.
Some had to eat their mules or horses and proceed on foot.
They struggled into the lofty village of Uspallata at the Ar-
gentine side in every state of misery, hunger, and exhaustion.
San Martín rode up with food, clothes, and medicines to help
them; they fell on the food brought to them like a horde of
savages.

Among the first to reach Uspallata were Bernardo O'Higgins
and his men, though he had waited in Santiago until the last
possible moment, to try to persuade Dictator Carrera to make
a last-ditch stand. He brought along Isabel and Rosa.

As Bernardo had led his men on the high rocky trails toward
the frontier, a lone figure had risen at twilight from behind
a big boulder. It was Venanciano, the grizzled Araucanian
warrior. He had taken off his uniform and was now dressed in
the *huaso* cowboy's big hat and bloomers.

"I will go back to Las Canteras," he told Bernardo. "Everything will be ready when you return."

Now the cruel crossing through the snow pass was over.
They were with friends again.

The two leaders embraced each other warmly.

"Take full charge and get these people straightened out," San Martín said. He had been informed about events in Chile, by Mackenna and other persons Carrera had expelled and by couriers from Argentine forces under Colonel Juan Gregorio de Las Heras, who had been sent to Chile to aid the fight against the Spaniards. Now he heard bitter new tales about Carrera and his brothers—the seizure of the government in the hour of greatest danger; the betrayal at Rancagua; lootings, depredations; how he came now with mules loaded with the gold of the treasury.

Bernardo sent Isabel and Rosa on into Mendoza, while he remained in lofty Uspallata to carry out San Martín's instructions.

José Miguel Carrera, his two brothers, and a large force were not long in putting in an appearance. San Martín avoided him, but the dictator presented himself at the governor's quarters. Arrogantly he demanded to know by what right San Martín had put O'Higgins in charge of the fleeing troops.

"To get things straightened out," San Martín told the haughty Chilean, and he added amiably that he would supply Carrera and his men with all necessary food and facilities "and also help you to proceed at once to Buenos Aires," he added.

But to Bernardo, he reconfirmed his orders. "You are in full command." He paused, then added, "Inspect the baggage of the Carreras and their whole entourage." He rode off to Mendoza.

Carrera flew into a rage and readied his forces to fight rather than submit to any baggage examination. He was doubly angered, realizing that San Martín had disregarded his protest over O'Higgins' appointment.

Rather than precipitate a brawl (the forces under Carrera were larger), Bernardo desisted in enforcing the baggage inspection. Turning his duties over to Las Heras, who had just reached Uspallata with a large force of Argentines, he rode with three hundred men to Mendoza.

Carrera, leading the bulk of the Chilean army, hurried after him. He was met by an Argentine official who repeated the order to have his baggage inspected. Carrera said indignantly he would feed everything to the llamas rather than submit to such a humiliation.

But just outside Mendoza still another official, this time backed by soldiers and a letter from San Martín, again insisted on examining Carrera's baggage.

San Martín wrote, "You may rest assured that no one who violates the laws of the state or the authority of this government will be immune from punishment."

With ill grace, Carrera submitted, for he would need quarters and food for his men.

The stolen treasury of Chile was not found in his baggage, as suspected. It was rumored that en route Carrera had been intercepted by Osorio's forces and, to insure his safety in escaping, had made a deal to turn it all over to the Spanish commander.

In Mendoza, José Miguel and his men were assigned to the Caridad barracks. He sent off a furious message to San Martín. "Hardly had I put foot on this territory than . . . . my authority and position were being abused." He reminded San Martín that he was in command of all Chilean troops and officers and would remain so, and that no one had authority to change that in any way. He hoped "the governor would not violate this by acting otherwise."

San Martín replied sharply that Carrera was now subject to the laws and authority of Argentina. "I will permit no one to point out my duties under those laws."

The exchange grew sharper. Carrera continued to deny the right of San Martín to interfere with the management of Chilean forces. "You have no right to make generals out of subordinates." To make O'Higgins, "commander merely of the First Division," a superior was "an insult." He would not permit this being done "even by the greatest potentate on earth."

The other Chileans drew up a memorial reciting the "depredations," "crimes," and "treason" of the Carreras and demanded their arrest and the confiscation of their properties.

Armed with this, San Martín rode over to the barracks and informed José Miguel that he and his two brothers were to leave Mendoza and take up residence in the neighboring San Luís province, "for your personal safety and the tranquillity of the city."

Carrera refused point-blank. He would not accept this added insult to the rights and dignity of his country—not so long as he had arms in hand.

Realizing the arrogant Chilean was in such a state of insane rage that he might be reckless enough to launch his troops in an attack, San Martín left without forcing the issue. But he called Las Heras and his men down from the pass and, further to strengthen his hand, had Bernardo send off Mackenna and another emissary to the central government in Buenos Aires.

Carrera at once commissioned a member of his junta and his brother Luís to set forth on a similar mission.

San Martín barred them from leaving the city. "No member of your junta can leave here," he told the dictator, but after some delay, which gave the emissaries of Bernardo a good head start, he did allow Luís and a colonel to leave.

At dawn, October 30, 1814, San Martín and Las Heras surrounded the Caridad barracks. He gave José Miguel ten minutes to turn over his command to an Argentine officer and then had him and his brother, Juan José, taken under guard to the main San Agustín barracks and held incommunicado.

ii

In November, Bernardo heard that Luís Carrera had assassinated Mackenna. At once, with Isabel and Rosa, he set out for the capital.

In spite of all efforts, Luís was liberated (he claimed it had been a duel) when Carlos María de Alvear, enemy of San Martín and close friend of José Miguel Carrera since the Spanish campaigns, took over the Argentine government. At once Alvear ordered the release also of the two other brothers being held in Mendoza.

Claiming ill health, San Martín resigned as governor of Cuyo. Was this the end of the great plan to recover Chile and free the Americas?

The governor Alvear appointed could not even take over. The people of Mendoza simply refused to recognize his authority, and he departed. It was Alvear who, now without the support of the Lautaro Lodge, had to get out of the Supreme Command. A show of troops led by San Martín's father-in-law, Francisco Antonio Escalada, supported by the entire Buenos Aires *cabildo*, installed Ignacio Alvarez, who closed the palace doors to the Carreras.

But the factional divisions among the Chilean exiles went deep, seeming to make concerted action impossible. The Carreristas, active as ever, said that a small force could cross the Andes in the north and easily seize Coquimbo, and that the Chileans would then throw out the Spaniards.

Bernardo believed that 6,000 men, divided into two columns, center and south, and supported by a sea attack on the coast, would be needed.

The news from the motherland was dark. The cruelties of the Spanish Reconquista surpassed belief—a reign of terror. Official, police, and army brutality ruled the land. Leading Chileans were being tortured and sent to a bleak San Fernando Island prison. No one's person or property was immune. About the only benefit to Chile was that later it inspired one of the country's finest novels, *Durante la Reconquista*, by its greatest writer, Alberto Blest Gana. In it he pictured the pomp, corruption, and cruelty versus the daring exploits of the underground resistance fighters led by heroic Manuel Rodríguez, who was to do much for the restoration of Independence. (Unfortunately, he was an ambitious Carrerista and later was to make serious trouble for the restored Chilean government.)

By mid-1815, news came that an expedition of 10,000 men had been sent from Cádiz to attack Argentina. San Martín then had less chance than ever of getting arms or support. At the somber news, all the exiled Chileans, including Bernardo, offered their services to the Argentine government. However, by September, it was learned that the Spanish forces were destined for Venezuela.

In November, the Argentine army suffered a tremendous defeat at Sipe-Sipe, near the Bolivian frontier, a slaughter so dreadful that scarcely a man was left alive to tell about it.

San Martín, alleging the danger of an imminent Spanish attack from Chile and the strategic location of his forces against any southward advance into Argentina, steadfastly declined to send any of his own forces to the north. The government redoubled its efforts to build up northern defenses.

Bernardo, Ramón Freire, Jesuit Fretes, his nephew (soon to become an Argentine cabinet minister), and Camilo Henríquez, working through the Lautaro Lodge, kept trying to get governmental assistance for the Chilean invasion.

Not until January was the government able to help, and Supreme Director Alvarez instructed Bernardo to return to Mendoza and assist San Martín.

José Miguel Carrera, feeling the coldness of the authorities toward his group, left to try to get help in the United States. There he signed notes as the representative of the Chilean government (which no longer existed) that were to bring disaster to his father and the family for years to come.

Full of renewed enthusiasm, Bernardo rode out of Buenos Aires with Isabel and Rosa and a small contingent of cavalry.

Mendoza had been converted into one vast barracks—more troops, more shops, more arms—even the school children were drilling. San Martín had not been idle a single moment.

He received Bernardo, in the middle of February, with open arms and made him brigadier general in the Army of the Andes, with a personal staff of seven grenadiers. He put him to building a new military city at Plumerillo, three miles out-side Mendoza, work for which Bernardo's previous labors at Las Canteras well suited him. Ground was cleared, drill grounds laid out, trees felled and sawed into lumber, barracks erected.

Presently, San Martín rode off to Córdoba to persuade the new head of state, Juan Martín Pueyrredón, to continue and augment his aid with money and supplies. He left O'Higgins in command at Mendoza.

News came that the new national congress, meeting at Tucumán, had declared the restoration of the Inca Empire and the full independence of Argentina—something never formally done before. O'Higgins got out the army to listen to a special Mass of thanksgiving; he read a ringing proclamation; the blue and white flag of Independence, with its yellow Sun of May, the Inca Sun, was unfurled with an artillery salute and a salvo from the guns of all the soldiers. The church bells rang out.

San Martín succeeded with the Argentine president in get-ting more help than he asked for and redoubled his efforts in Mendoza. He found an obscure innkeeper, who later held high government offices, to be his secretary: "the philosopher," Juan Ignacio Zenteno; he found a genius, a monk quietly kneeling in his cell, to take charge of army supplies: huge, bearded Luís Beltrán, a jack-of-all-trades, who had tried his hand at farming, carpentry, metalwork, and numerous other humble activities. He set up foundries, powder factories, har-ness and blacksmith shops, shops to make shoes and sandals, textile establishments. Llama wool and goat hair, which was dyed blue, was woven into cloth for uniforms. The women of Mendoza—San Martín's wife Remedios, Isabel, Rosa—every-body spun and wove and sewed. Blue and white Chilean flags of Independence were made. Remedios set an example for the other women of the town by pouring all her jewels into the coffers of the Army of the Andes.

Beltrán melted down nearly every church bell in the province, except those in the cathedral, to get iron for cannon, machetes, cutlasses, bayonets, and pikes. He devised special machines to get the heavy artillery over the chasms. Copying the Incan bridge techniques, he made provisional rope-suspension bridges, some of them 175 feet long, with iron anchors to be stuck in stone cracks. The horses and mules of the Pampa had never been shod, for there a plow could be driven twenty miles without so much as striking a pebble. But it was doubtful if the animals could get through the rocky passes, and so Beltrán made 50,000 horseshoes. "If the army needs wings," he remarked, "it will have them; it will fly." He prepared 9,000 rounds, 2,000 cannonballs, 2,000 grapeshot charges, 600 grenades.

The supply problem was prodigious—ammunition, weapons, medicines, food, clothing, shoes, blankets—5,200 men required a great deal even for a march of three weeks or so up to the Andes and through the icy passes, and there was no assurance that food would be immediately available on the other side. Even firewood had to be taken to cook over and to keep the men alive at night. Ten thousand mules and horses were assembled, and for these, too, fodder and grain had to be carried. They had to be provided with shoes, bridles, pack saddles, ropes. Beltrán was the miracle man who rose to every emergency.

Pueyrredón kept his word, though his government was bankrupt. He wrote San Martín in November, 1816, "In addition to the 4,000 blankets Córdoba was to provide, I am sending you now 500 ponchos, . . . all I have been able to get hold of. . . . I have given orders to send you 25,000 pounds of jerked beef. . . . I am enclosing the authorization you requested for the council of that city [Mendoza] and for others in Cuyo. . . . I am sending the clothing you asked for and many shirts. . . . Try asking for . . . blankets, ponchos, or old quilts from the people there and in San Juan. There isn't a family that can't let you have an old blanket. . . . I am sending you 40 saddles. By mail today, I am sending you in a little box, the only two clarinets I was able to find. In January . . . 34,675 pounds of jerked beef will be shipped to you. . . . Here are the 200 swords. . . . Here are 200 campaign tents, and that's all there are. Here's the World, and the Flesh and the Devil. And I don't see how I'm going to get out of the debts I've piled up to pay for all this. Unless I declare myself bankrupt, cancel all my debts, and join up with you so you will have to feed me on the jerked beef I am sending you. Damn it all, don't ask me for another thing unless you want to get word my body was found dangling one morning from one of the crossbeams of Fort Aleza."

But the bulk of the supplies came from Cuyo. "It is amazing," wrote San Martín at the time, "how a region with relatively little population, without public revenues, without commerce or large cities, which lacks lumber and basic materials, has been able to raise by its own resources an army of 3,000 men, stripping itself even of its slaves, its only manpower for agriculture; provide for their pay and maintenance and that of over a thousand emigrees; build up stocks of supplies; manufacture salt, pikes, and powder, ordinance, munitions, cloth; set up barricades and camps; requisition over 3,000 horses, 7,000 mules, innumerable head of cattle; patrol the Andes. America is free. Its enemies cannot stand up against such virtues."

By September, Bernardo had the Plumerillo encampment ready, and the whole army was moved there. Constant contact with the townspeople had tended to weaken discipline. A number of officers, mostly Carreristas, had schemed to rebel and take over. They were discovered, punished, demoted, or thrown out. At the new camp, things were easier to control. Soldiers and officers were put under the strictest regime. Drilling was redoubled, dawn to dark, sometimes all night. Everybody had to attend classes, even the highest officers. A dress parade was held every Saturday.

For rest and amusement, the troops attended Sunday Mass and bullfights in the afternoon or displays of skilled horsemanship, at which Bernardo was adept. They listened to music and engaged in mass singing. The camp Negroes played their own instruments and sang folk songs, which especially delighted the troops.

Finally, everything was ready. Without disclosing the exact time of departure, on January 5, 1817, San Martín led the forces in a final parade into the city. The people had prepared floral arches; they paved the roadway with flowers; they hung flags and brocades and rugs from every balcony. The great cathedral church bells tolled unceasingly in the clear, bright air, echoing back from the Andes.

Solemn Mass was celebrated. With simple words, San Martín told the army they would be leaving any day now, and he placed Chile's blue and white flag of Independence in the hands of the Virgin María del Carmelo, making her the patron saint of the expedition.

"Soldiers, this is the first flag of Independence that has been blessed in the Americas."

A mass loyalty oath to the Independence of Chile and the freeing of all America was taken. The cannon roared out a salute.

A special bullfight was staged. A daring young officer, as toreador, dispatched his bull in fine style, cut off the testicles (a fine food delicacy), and gallantly presented them to Remedios, San Martín's wife.

San Martín had spent as much time and effort on propaganda and psychological warfare as on actual physical preparations. For a long time he had been misinforming the Spaniards about his real plans, as when he had contacted the Pehuenche Indians. He managed to plant other wrong information to fool the enemy. Prominent Chilean refugees were arrested, then deported, so their stories would carry greater credibility. His spies reported to him that the Spaniards actually had sent the bulk of their occupying army to guard the south. The center and north were only lightly garrisoned.

iii

On January 20, 1817, the last mules were loaded—cases of ammunition, guns, pickaxes, shovels; food for a month: jerked beef, flour, hardtack, cheese, onion, garlic, chilis, brandy, wine, toasted corn; grain, hay, and extra horseshoes; the rope suspension bridges, and Beltrán's incredible machines. It required twenty-four hours for all the mules to pass a given point.

The departure took place the following morning. Freire galloped south to make a false feint through the La Plancha pass. Another small contingent went to the northern passes above Coquimbo. The main body would go through the two loftiest snow passes of the whole Andean cordillera: at points, nearly 20,000 feet high. It was late summer, the best time for passing; much of the snow was melted, with little danger as yet of blizzards.

Las Heras, with his faithful 800 and most of the heavy artillery, took the Uspallata Pass, shorter and less difficult. The bulk of the army would go through the longer more difficult Los Patos Pass. Bernardo led off with the Second Division. After an interval he was followed by Argentine General Estanislao Soler, at the head of the First Division. Behind was the General Headquarters, San Martín with a small force. He was suffering dreadfully from arthritis and was coughing blood; the struggle through the passes would not be easy for him and might be dangerous.

Behind came the hospital services, with mules loaded with drugs and cots; the artisans and blacksmiths, in charge of Beltrán. Most of the mules brought up the rear. Franciscan and Dominican monks plodded along, said Mass before each day's march, and gave extreme unction to the dying.

In spite of the careful preparations it was a frightful, unbelievable march. At places they had to traverse slippery, icy ledges a few feet wide over bottomless gorges. More than one soldier slid to his death into the abyss. Feet and hands and ears were frozen. Men reeled to their knees, vomiting with mountain sickness (*soroche*), or dropped in their tracks from weariness. By the time they reached the other side, three weeks later, nearly half the mules and equipment had been lost—sliding to the depths where, if not killed immediately, they screamed until they died. The slightest foot tread or crack of a stick in the thin, brittle, upland air, so lacking in oxygen, could start a slide of millions of tons of rocks, ice, and snow. At one point fifty men were swept away by an avalanche; the march was held up for half a day until a new path could be cut through. And, overhead, the great condors wheeled, waiting for their banquets.

And so for three weeks they struggled on, first zigzagging up the sheer eastern stone walls of the mountains, then wading for miles up the Uspallata River, then filing through the passes.

At last, twenty-one days out of Mendoza, Bernardo could ease in his stirrups and look out over the width of all Chile—the tangled, steep brown foothills, the shimmering green valleys below—and across the lower coastal mountains to the ocean, a vast stretch of blue melting into horizon haze.

The whole march had been laid out according to a fixed schedule, almost to the minute. Though much of the heavy artillery was delayed, right on time, the forces of both Las Heras and Bernardo emerged from the passes. According to a Spanish soldier's diary, 400 men of the Talavera Regiment fled down to Chacabuco, abandoning "artillery, ammunition, baggage, and warlike stores." Bernardo seized San Felipe on February 8. The garrison fled, and he was received with music and flowers by the townspeople. Las Heras took Santa Rosa almost at the same moment, and as they marched on, everywhere the villagers greeted them joyously with flowers and food and help, taking care of the sick.

The two invading forces reunited in Curimón, south of the Aconcagua River and above the Chacabuco Ridge, held by some 600 Spanish troops. Bernardo wished to push on at once, but San Martín, fretting over the delay of the artillery, insisted that the forces needed rest and time to get their gear in shape.

Scouts brought astonishing news. Freire to the south, not expected to make any serious effort, had broken through, eluded the Spaniards, and was racing through south Chile; everything from Cachapoal province to the Maule was already in his hands. Everywhere the people were rising up. Manuel Rodríguez had come out in the open and captured the important town of San Fernando, near the capital. Santiago was in dreadful confusion.

The Spaniards were frantically shifting their forces to the north, not merely to block Freire but to meet the main invasion army.

The strong stone ridge at Chacabuco, a big hacienda center, was the point at which the Spaniards chose to make a concerted stand. News leaked through to the patriots above that already the most seasoned corps, veterans of Chiloé, and the Talaveras, the cream of the Spanish armies in all the world, had arrived in force under Vicente San Bruno, the brutal hangman of the Reconquista. There was little time to lose. Minutes were becoming precious. "We can no longer wait for the heavy guns," San Martín decided.

Battle plans were discussed. Soler was to lead the bulk of the forces along difficult high ground to attack the left flank; Bernardo was to hit the center with 1,400 men but was to avoid any serious engagement until word came from Soler that he was ready; San Martín, suffering dreadfully from the ordeal through the passes, would bring up the rear.

As they separated to prepare their departure, Bernardo caught a baleful gleam in Soler's eyes. The Argentine general was jealous of his Chilean counterpart.

They got underway at 2 A.M., February 12. Bernardo, advancing along a thickly wooded ravine, was spotted at dawn and caught in a crossfire. No signal from Soler. O'Higgins either had to retreat or attack.

He stormed up a stone ridge with drawn bayonets and flashing sabers and, without too great loss, routed the Spanish defenders. Still no word from Soler.

Though it was a somewhat exposed position, he halted until he could get orders from San Martín. The commander in chief told him to keep advancing but to try to avoid any serious involvement until Soler was ready.

O'Higgins had to cross the sharp Nipa Quebrada, a small canyon, under desultory fire. The troops forded the small Margaritas River and toiled up the Halcones hill. Near the crest, 300 Spanish soldiers were entrenched in strong bunkers with artillery that burst into the ranks of the mounted grenadiers bringing up the rear.

It was now 11 A.M., a blistering hot day, made worse by the heat reflected from the stone walls of the *quebrada* where they had taken temporary refuge. In that hot oven, under deadly fire, he could no longer wait for Soler. He ordered a charge, but it was soon halted by another unseen gully and the grenadiers were floundering badly in the rocky terrain. To avoid the deadly fire, he ordered his troops to fan out and then reconcentrate when he gave the order.

Believing that the patriot forces were breaking up, the Spaniards—and they were the seasoned Chiloé veterans—charged down the slopes. Quickly reassembling his force, O'Higgins fell upon them with bayonets and cut them up badly. His men stormed over the bunkers and beyond, only to come face to face with the Talavera Regiment. It charged to aid their reeling comrades.

When it seemed that ground must be given, the grenadiers emerged from a side *quebrada* and hit the Talaveras on the flank. They were routed, but as they quickly reformed on higher ground the contest was far from over.

Soler's men appeared out of nowhere and hit them on the flank.

It was at this point that the Spanish general, Atero, shouted, "We are cut off!" and fled in a gallop that did not end until he reached Santiago.

Leaving his infantry to follow, Bernardo led his grenadiers

galloping along the stone ridge, pounding in pursuit of the fleeing Talaveras. A bearded Spaniard stopped in his headlong flight long enough to touch the fuse to a cannon. The ball whistled close by Bernardo's head.

"His courage was admirable," was the Chilean's only comment.

Their charge took them into the heart of the hacienda village. The entire Spanish army was racing, tumbling down the steep slopes in panic.

A *huaso* came forward, carrying the bloody severed head of a Talavera by the beard, and presented it to O'Higgins. But the donor was no *huaso*. He was Vicente San Bruno, chief of the secret police of the Spanish governor general, Marco del Pont. Bruno, creator of the Spanish terror and torture, hoped to ingratiate himself with the patriots by this gruesome, last-minute treachery. Bernardo had him executed on the spot.

Soler rode up, his face blazing with anger, and shouted at O'Higgins, "By your flouting of orders, your insubordination, you jeopardized the whole battle!"

Bernardo swallowed his anger and said curtly, "This is not the time for recriminations. If you want to do something useful, ride with me after the Spaniards. We can cut them off from Valparaiso and from any escape from the country."

San Martín arrived and congratulated O'Higgins and Soler on the brave victory. He took no sides, but his sympathies were obviously with Bernardo. However, he vetoed the latter's plea to pursue the broken Spanish forces. The patriots were reeling from exhaustion. The Spaniards were bound to re-form, and there might be strong reserves. He could not risk Bernardo's division in such a dangerous adventure.

Messengers arrived with the news that the Spaniards, including the governor general, had evacuated Santiago and were fleeing to the coast. The city was without a government. The people were surging through the streets; mobs were looting and burning the homes of the Spaniards, the royalists, and the grandees.

San Martín immediately sent 200 fast-riding grenadiers to

take over the city and restore order. He set the whole army in motion at once. There was no time and no manpower available to bury the dead; even before the sound of the hoofs of the horses and the tread of the soldiers had died away, the condors swept down. To this day, the curious can come upon the bones of the men who died at Chacabuco. Next to Rancagua, it was the greatest battle of Chile's history and has gone down in the annals of all South America as one of the most decisive battles of the continent.

iv

As the victors rode toward the capital, at their back the snow wall of the Andes they had crossed shimmered twenty thousand feet and more into the sky. They rode into Santiago past six-hundred-foot Santa Lucía Hill that reared up only a mile from the main plaza. They followed the boulevard and gardens along the stone retaining wall of the sometimes turbulent Maipocho River that embraces both sides of the island city and which for centuries had flooded the place until Bernardo's own father, Ambrosio O'Higgins, when governor general, had channeled the brawling currents between massive walls. They crossed over one of the stone bridges built by Ambrosio into a city of flowers, flags, banners, and delirious crowds, straight to the Plaza de Armas, to the *cabildo* and the cathedral and the Church of the Company.

The bells tolled out an incessant din of welcome, and the towers were black with spectators. Nowhere was the red and yellow flag of Spain in evidence. It was amazing how many people had secretly sewed blue and white flags of Independence, ready for this glorious day. They fluttered and billowed everywhere.

The following day, February 15, San Martín ordered a mass assembly of citizens and notables to meet to set up a government. Neither he nor Bernardo attended.

The leading citizens gathered with the *cabildo*. A big crowd milled outside. The session was presided over by Francisco

Ruiz Tagle. He proposed a three-man junta, representing north, south, and center, to choose a supreme director for the country.

But the crowd roared out, "San Martín! . . . San Martín! . . . San Martín!" He was chosen by unanimous acclamation.

Informed of the choice, he firmly declined the post. "I came to free Chile, not to rule it." The head of the new government had to be a Chilean.

Actually, both he and Bernardo had received word from Pueyrredón, even before the march across the Andes had begun, that San Martín was not to accept any post but that O'Higgins was to be given full charge of the new government.

The next day, twice as many people gathered in the plaza. Actually everything was well controlled by the representatives of the five largest landholders in the country. After some talk of trying to get San Martín to change his mind, the crowd began shouting, "O'Higgins! . . . O'Higgins! . . . O'Higgins!" Again the choice was by unanimous acclamation.

The meeting broke up, the crowd headed for the nearby palace of the former Count of the Conquest—the Casa Colorada—where O'Higgins and San Martín were lodged, and carried Bernardo in triumph to the *cabildo* to be sworn in at once.

He had been tested in many posts—as mayor, as deputy to congress, as a member briefly of the ruling junta, as a leader of army hosts. Now all this experience seemed part of a greater plan marked out by fate, by destiny itself. He stood straight and stiff, his hand on his sword, in dress uniform, cerulean blue jacket and tight white breeches. Over his head was the travel-stained flag of the Army of the Andes, the banner of the free Chile, which had preceded their march through the snows and the iron-bound crags—"the banner of brave men and condors."

"In the name of our Lord God and his four Holy Evangels," O'Higgins told those at the ceremony, "I give my word of honor to govern justly and to defend Chile."

Destiny had made him Supreme Director of a free Chile. He had helped create that freedom.

The city gave itself over to days and nights of jubilant revelry. The heroes of Chacabuco were tendered a grand society ball, inaugurated by the singing of the Argentine national anthem (it would be some years before Chile was provided with one). At the great banquet, roast turkeys, with gilded heads, had Independence flags in their beaks. Every sort of entree was served, ending up with the famous almond pastries and *chimbos,* pastry specialties of the nuns of Chile. Many toasts were drunk and speeches delivered, each echoed with salvos from artillery, just outside the mansion, that did considerable damage to the fine china and glassware and the eardrums.

v

There was work to be done. The country was ruined by years of civil war and invasion. Agriculture and industry and enterprise were in a shambles. There were few resources. O'Higgins had to organize and get production going again, to feed and clothe the people, to open the country up to trade to which for centuries it had been closed. The remnants of the Spanish army had to be rounded up and thrown out; they still held Concepción and its ports, Valdivia, and the big, fertile island of Chiloé, and soon brought in more reinforcements from Chiloé Island and Peru.

Freedom also brought conspiracies in this country riven for ten years and more by conflict and bitter, antagonistic doctrines. There were many Spaniards—mostly wealthy—who could not sympathize with Independence. There were many Creoles, ardently pro-Spanish, pro-royalist, also wealthy and powerful. There were Carreristas who hated O'Higgins and would scheme to regain power. The army itself was not without feuds between ambitious leaders. Ill feeling was to spring up between Chileans and Argentines. In the prolonged struggles, the various regions had grown suspicious, the provinces jealous of their prerogatives. The underground fighters, led by

Manuel Rodríguez, nursing his own ambitions, were militant and demanding.

Under the circumstances, only a strong hand could rule. There was no time for the type of representative government O'Higgins favored so strongly. Elections would merely release hidden hatreds and rivalries, set political factionalism in operation, bring more conspiracies and intrigue. The first thing was to make the revolutionary government strong enough to withstand the dangers from within, to solve the pressing economic problems, maintain order, and restore confidence.

(It was inevitable that, as time went on, O'Higgins would grow more dictatorial, would pull away from the Lautaro cabal, as it grew unpopular with Chileans, and surround himself with new advisers. His chances were not good, and in due course the ugly little pock-marked Rodríguez Aldea, the clever turncoat of Lircay days, would win his ear and his confidence, drive away Bernardo's friends and allies, rob the treasury, and, in the end, would ruin him.)

In the meantime, whatever his mistakes, O'Higgins' initial firm policies consolidated the territory of the Republic—except for Chiloé. He built up enterprise and trade; he opened new farm lands, giving them out to peasants. And his strong rule alone made possible the herculean effort of providing money, supplies, and possibilities for the creation of a Chilean navy and to supply San Martín's army to invade Peru, essential if Chile itself was to win peace, if the Independence regimes of the lower half of South America—for that matter of all of South America—were to be free from Spanish aggression.

Among O'Higgins' measures that aroused the loudest outcries were the confiscation of all royalist properties, the abolition of all titles, and the eradication of all emblems of nobility from homes and buildings. For a considerable time, Spaniards were not allowed to leave their homes after dark. Tax reform hit the wealthier classes hard. The judicial system was overhauled.

Measures ending church monopolies infuriated the hierarchy, made up entirely of Spaniards. All over the continent, the Church had excommunicated revolutionary leaders. Except for the lower clergy, the Church had usually backed all the harsh terrorism of Governor Francisco Marco del Pont during the Reconquista. Since church salaries were paid by him, the clergy was a part of the colonial bureaucracy.

On his arrival, O'Higgins had been conciliatory, suggesting that the Bishop follow a moderate policy and not oppose the revolution. But the Bishop, royalist to the marrow and abetted by antirevolutionary elements, became so offensive that, on the night of February 26, mounted soldiers informed him that "the public welfare is above all other considerations" and, on O'Higgins' orders, escorted him and four other ecclesiastics to exile to Mendoza. San Martín took over the episcopal palace in Santiago as headquarters for the army of Peruvian freedom.

The greatest ill feeling was caused by the abolition of church cemeteries and the stopping of all burials in churchyards and churches, a most lucrative source of revenue, for the elite paid large sums for prominent niches inside the temples.

Heretofore, no Protestant, Jew, or "heretic" could be buried in a Catholic cemetery. The bodies of poorer outcasts were left to rot in ditches; people better off had to bury their dead on their own property.

O'Higgins moved the Catholic cemetery off Santa Lucía Hill, which he converted into one of the finest public parks in the western hemisphere.

Another focus of trouble was *guerrillero* Manuel Rodríguez, the "freedom fighter" of the underground, a former secretary of Carrera who was ruthlessly persecuting and killing opponents in San Fernando. When he failed to obey orders of the center to desist, he was arrested and brought to Santiago. O'Higgins offered him exile abroad with a permanent government pension.

Rodríguez admitted he was a restless spirit. "Were I Supreme Director and no revolution occurred within six months,

I couldn't resist making one against myself." He was sent under arrest to Valparaiso, to be deported, but escaped.

It was about this time that José Miguel Carrera arrived in Buenos Aires, with several vessels procured in the United States. He intended to proceed to attack the Spaniards on the coast of Chile. But he hated O'Higgins more than the Spaniards, and Pueyrredón seized the vessels and put all three Carreras under arrest, promising them, since they were now penniless, he would try to get them their regular officer pay from the new Chilean government.

Carrera himself also wrote O'Higgins, protesting against the "abuse," but O'Higgins never replied. To Pueyrredón, O'Higgins wrote, "All the Carreras have ever earned for themselves is to be punished for their crimes." If they set foot on Chilean soil they could expect "no mercy."

vi

Though Concepción was recovered from the Spaniards by April, they still held the strong forts of nearby Talcahuano and controlled the country south to Valdivia. With Chiloé as a base—a sort of Quemoy and Matsu—they launched raids, helped bandits to harass the land, and stirred up the Araucanians against the central government.

The campaign against them seemed to progress too slowly, and O'Higgins went on a tour of inspection to direct operations in person should it seem required.

Word came that four Spanish vessels had put in at Talcahuano with reinforcements, and Bernardo hurried south with a large force to prevent the recapture of Concepción. Las Heras, in command there, under Ramón Freire, was begging for aid.

Before Bernardo could reach the city, he heard heavy artillery firing. The attack was already on.

He raced ahead, but even before he sighted the towers of

Concepción, a message came from Las Heras. "My General and Friend: I offer you a complete victory."

This was followed by a brilliant assault led by Freire on the powerful Arauco fort, held by the Spaniards. But they repelled an attack on Talcahuano, inflicting large losses on the patriots.

Bernardo put the port under siege but could not dent the powerful defenses. By July, the winter rains had become so heavy he had to retire to Concepción.

He did not waste his leisure time. A flaming affair with Rosario Puga, "Diamond Point," the redheaded, green-eyed daughter of one of his colonels (recently she had had a scandalous separation from her husband), kept tongues twittering.

She provided Bernardo with an illegitimate son—Pedro Demetrio O'Higgins—whom he promptly claimed and placed with Petronilla, his other illegitimate child—an Araucanian girl brought up at Las Canteras—in the palace in Santiago to be cared for by Isabel and Rosa.

Not until December 5 were the patriots able to launch another fullfledged attack on Talcahuano. Again they were disastrously defeated.

A tremendous new Spanish invasion force under Mariano Osorio sailed from Lima. It was feared it might land near Valparaiso, and though San Martín's small army for invading Peru was bivouacked near there at Las Tablas, O'Higgins evacuated the south and set up headquarters in Talca, north of the Maule. Fifty thousand refugees, fleeing with cattle, horses, and household goods from inevitable Spanish reoccupation, hampered the troop movements.

The Spaniards followed closely on his heels with 6,000 men and 30 cannon, and O'Higgins gave up Talca without a fight on March 4.

San Martín then brought his forces to San Fernando, where a new headquarters was established. It was a strategic retreat, not a defeat, for the government now had nearly 7,000 men, magnificently trained and armed.

San Martín fell on the Spanish left flank at Cancharayada, and O'Higgins hit them on the other flank with artillery and mounted grenadiers and entered the Talca suburbs. During the night, fighting broke off.

Viewing the battlefield, Osorio lost heart and wanted to retreat back to Talcahuano, but his officers were against the idea. They would be slaughtered trying to recross the Maule. Osorio handed over his command to General José Ordoñez and hid out in a monastery.

Ordoñez quickly shifted the forces and hit San Martín while he too was moving men, throwing them into confusion. A major attack was made.

San Martín hit back with such terrible fire that the Spaniards were sent reeling back. But in a second attack, O'Higgins' horse was shot from under him, and his right arm was shattered. The patriots grew confused and were beaten.

The royalists were then able to surround San Martín. His aide, Juan José Larrain, was killed.

San Martín managed to cut his way out and recross the Lircay River, where he was joined by the remnants of O'Higgins' forces.

It was eleven o'clock of a bright moonlit night as the two defeated leaders rode in silence through the countryside. Half the artillery had been lost and most of the munitions.

O'Higgins, wounded and sick with high fever, had to cross the Lontué River to the Quechueraguas hacienda, arriving there about daybreak, March 20, 1818. Not until then could his wound be treated. The surgeon told him, "If it comes to the worst, you can go to Mendoza and start over again."

"Never. So long as a single Chilean will follow me, I shall fight on here in Chile."

His arm in a sling—as it would be for months—O'Higgins rode on to the rear to San Fernando and there, with San Martín, reviewed the reorganized troops. Losses had been great, but they still had a strong army.

vii

Panic hit the capital, where the rumor spread that both leaders had been killed. People began packing up to flee across the Andes.

Others gathered in the streets and shouted, "Viva el Rey! Long live the King!" A rich royalist had a pair of silver horseshoes made to present to the courageous Osorio when he entered the city.

Just before the defeat, Manuel Rodríguez had finally agreed to take a post in Buenos Aires, but now he turned back, persuaded Colonel Luís de la Cruz, acting director, to call a general popular assembly to meet the crisis, and galloped through the streets rallying the populace.

Near noon on March 23, the plaza and *cabildo* were jammed. A great milling crowd shouted, "Viva Manuel Rodríguez!"

"Don't run away!" he cried out. "We still have a fatherland. Citizens, if necessary we shall die defending it!"

The crowd shouted for Cruz to resign and turn over the government to Rodríguez.

Burly Joaquín Prieto, commander of the Plaza, shouldered forward. "Anyone who seeks to change the established government, I shall put to the sword."

However, Cruz permitted Rodríguez to have a voice in the government.

He worked hard, visited the barracks, handed out arms to the populace, and raised a volunteer regiment, the Hussars of Death.

Minister of War Miguel Zañartú feared that this portended the deposing of O'Higgins. Despite his urgent messages, Bernardo did not come to the capital. Zañartú drove south in a carriage to fetch him.

O'Higgins was in bed with a high fever but, receiving an urgent call on the afternoon of March 22 to meet Zañartú in Rancagua, he mounted his horse and reached the historic city at dawn. Together they drove back at once to the capital, reaching there early March 24.

He ordered Cruz to call a meeting of the *cabildo* that same day. Sick though he was, he formally resumed the Supreme Dictatorship and assured the populace of victory in the forthcoming battle.

San Martín reached the capital the following day. The news of his arrival set the church bells ringing, and great crowds gathered. He addressed them.

"We were defeated—one of war's mishaps—but our army is intact and standing firm. The fatherland exists and will triumph. I pledge my word of honor I shall soon give a day of glory for all South America!"

A council of war was held. Some wanted to abandon Santiago and retreat farther north or to the foothills of Aconcagua. San Martín listened without comment, then called in Luís Beltrán.

"How do we stand in the way of munitions?" he asked.

"To the ceiling! To the ceiling!" answered the monk.

"Why then should we run away?"

"Conscript workers, and I shall soon replace all the cannon lost," Beltrán replied.

In his grenadier uniform, his greatcoat dirty with defeat, his famous, rubber-lined, double-brimmed hat low over his face, San Martín went back to the Maipú, a few miles from the capital, for the last-ditch defense.

O'Higgins could not remain quiet. He rode hither and yon through the city and organized a militia of 1,000 men to resist to the death whatever happened at the front. He was riding down the old Calle del Rey—King Street—when the first cannon shot was heard. Unable to remain aloof, he galloped toward the battle.

He came out on high hills. Below was a vast panorama of the whole engagement. To his joy, he saw that the patriots had hurled back the Spaniards and were pursuing them relentlessly towards Lo Espejo hacienda.

He galloped down toward the banners of the General Staff. Jumping off his horse, he embraced San Martín with his left arm. "Glory for the Savior of Chile!"

"General, Chile will never forget the name of the illustrious invalid hero who presented himself in this condition on the field of battle."

They rode on together toward Lo Espejo to complete the mopping up. The slaughter was so great, it was stopped. The Spaniards lost a fifth of their men. But the patriot regiment of Negroes from Cuyo had lost half its number.

"Maipú," wrote Bartolomé Mitre, "from a scientific standpoint, was the first great battle ever fought in the Americas," not only "a notable model, but a perfect one, in which a parallel attack was converted into a concentrated oblique attack (in the classic tactics of the immortal Greek general, Epaminondas), and for the skillful use of reserves against the weakest flank of the enemy, weak for its formation, though the strongest in the number and quality of the troops."

Only the mounted battalion of Arequipa managed to escape, and it was hotly pursued. Among the prisoners were the highest Spanish officers, but Osorio himself had fled in the middle of the battle, abandoning his carriage and papers.

Among the papers, San Martín found proof of the treachery of scores of Chileans who had offered their services after the defeat of Cancharayada. He went off alone under a tree and there burned the letters one by one. "A time for magnanimity," he remarked.

O'Higgins went back to his bed in the palace, listening to the church bells ringing out the glad tidings of victory.

viii

Meanwhile, the Carreras had escaped from prison; José Miguel to Uruguay; Juan José and Luís to the Chilean frontier, where they organized outlaw bands that preyed on the Argentine countryside. Presently both were caught and held for trial, one for "robbing the mails," the other for "killing a child."

A week or so before the Maipú battle, San Martín had sent his agent, Bernardo Monteagudo, head of the Lautaro Lodge, to Mendoza to see that the two Carrera brothers were shot. But after the victory both San Martín and O'Higgins were in a more generous mood and at the behest of Juan José's beautiful wife and the United States consul, William Worthington (the United States had always favored the Carreras), sent messages, albeit reluctantly, urging the prisoners be treated with magnanimity.

These suggestions, it so happened, arrived two hours *after* the brothers had been shot. "Double-dealing," the Carreristas charged.

Manuel Rodríguez, frequently haranguing the populace, was still parading his Hussars of Death up and down the Santiago streets. All were Carreristas. Bernardo called him to the palace and ordered him to disband his men and deliver the arms to the arsenal.

Rodríguez smilingly agreed, but on the very steps of the palace he told a crowd that the Hussars would continue to enforce proper respect for the people among the rulers of Chile.

On April 16, the reactionaries, angered by the killing of the two "aristocrats"—the Carrera brothers—called the *cabildo* together to demand "democratic" reforms, and immediate junta of three men (to be headed by O'Higgins) and, within fifteen days, a provisional constitution. A national congress was to be elected to convene by August 15. Manuel Rodríguez led a mob to the palace to back up these demands.

Bernardo dressed and received a commission from the protestors. They had hardly opened their mouths when he upbraided them hotly, accusing them of inciting the populace to revolt and anarchy. As they left, they saw Manuel Rodríguez being arrested. He was taken to the San Pablo barracks.

A few days later the head of the *cabildo* was deported; but, with a certain whimsical irony, O'Higgins appointed the other two commissioners who had entered the palace to prepare the fiestas to celebrate the Maipú victory.

On May 23, after prolonged preliminary hearings which seemed to indicate a ramified conspiracy to overthrow the government (though the evidence, as O'Higgins' biographer, Jaime Eyzaguirre, points out, was rather flimsy), Manuel Rodríguez was taken by the Cazadores of the Andes—a daring unit of the Chacabuco battle—to Quillota, near Valparaiso, to stand trial. En route he was shot "trying to escape"—the old Ley de Fuga.

The accounts differ. One was that a body of rebels tried to rescue him; certainly three other men were killed. This was the official version. The other story was that he had been killed in cold blood. It was known that the officer in charge of the Cazadores, Manuel Navarro, a Spaniard favoring the patriot cause, had had two long conferences with Monteagudo concerning the prisoner prior to leaving Santiago. Was this to prepare another bloody purging by the Lautaro Lodge? Eyzaguirre deduces from Monteagudo's statements that he ordered Rodríguez's assassination.

An investigation was ordered. Navarro was arrested and brought to Santiago, where War Minister Monteagudo talked with him. He was sent to Mendoza, "where he enjoyed full military prerogatives." O'Higgins made no public statements, and his enemies accused him of complicity. In the public mind, the culprit was the Lautaro Lodge—and O'Higgins.

ix

Soon after the set-to with the *cabildo*, United States Consul Worthington appeared at the palace again, on May 5. It was evident he was hand in glove with the Carreristas, the reactionaries and the aristocrats who invariably become tearful in behalf of "democracy" when not running things. He offered to act as an intermediary between O'Higgins and the notables—the wealthy *hacendados*—and the hierarchy of the Church. He came, he asserted, as a great friend of "liberty."

"Follow my advice, cure the wounds, and let me help you draw up a constitution, and you will be not merely a man of battle and military chief of Chile, but the father of your country." In this way, he was sure he could convince O'Higgins' worst enemies to keep the peace. The incredible man pulled out from his coattails a copy of the constitution of the U.S.A.!

If there is one single thing that has been conducive to tragic disorder in Latin America for more than a hundred years, it is precisely that the new independent nations adopted unworkable constitutions based on that of the United States. In countries with such different traditions, experience, and social systems, such documents were and still are unworkable. The contradictions have promoted many military take-overs. Even in those rare instances when such absurd constitutions could be enforced, they have not contributed to the welfare of the people—unprepared and uninformed—but have accentuated the rule of the army, the Church, and the large wealthy landholders.

Doubtless O'Higgins was nettled by Worthington's presumptuous meddling (actually the director had already named a commission of seven notables to prepare a draft of a constitution), but he was anxious to obtain recognition by the United States and England, particularly the latter, and displayed no irritation, except when Worthington brought up the question of religious liberty, which had not been violated at all. O'Higgins for the first time in history, in fact, had established the full freedom of all cults. The Chilean shut up his nosy interlocutor by saying he saw no reason to discuss Chile's religious affairs.

On May 8 at 10 A.M., Worthington brought to see him a special United States emissary, Theodore Bland, who it was rumored was prepared to offer recognition. They sat around a table with a red and gold velvet cover, in front of the Spanish flags captured at Maipú.

Mr. Bland announced that the United States was still strictly neutral between Spain and the new countries but was interested in their independence.

The conversation, as reported in Eyzaguirre's *O'Higgins*, went as follows:

"We hope," answered O'Higgins, "that the first free government in the Americas will be the first to recognize Chile's independence."

"We seek no special advantages," Mr. Bland hastened to assure him, "but the United States wishes to see Chile not only independent but provided with those free institutions which will increase her prosperity now that the recent great triumph has thrown out of your territory your last enemy." (Actually the Spaniards still held Valdivia, Concepción, Talcahuano, and Chiloé Island and were helping terrible and cruel marauders such as Vicente Benavides who, with a large force of Araucanians, was pillaging, burning, and killing all through the south.)

"I imagine," said Bland—who apparently had never before been in Chile and knew none of its problems—"that the country will concern itself with adopting a constitution and setting up its own government."

O'Higgins kept his temper. "The present state of the country is such that to call a national congress at this juncture would be dangerous. It is not as yet possible to provide a constitution. However, a method of procedure will shortly be announced for establishing a provisional government."

"I presume you do not refer to dangers from the enemy."

"The enemy would certainly benefit by the controversies and rivalries that would be provoked by a national assembly at this moment. They would certainly foment a spirit of dissension and intrigue. . . . This country has been hurt by premature congresses, and Venezuela and other provinces have been defeated for the same reason. It will be impossible to hold a reunion of this sort until the situation is fully clarified. . . . In revolutionary times, it is dangerous to implant certain institutions by a sudden blow, however desirable and reasonable they may seem, without risking everything. . . . Our people are not like yours. The people have had no familiarity with such congresses, and previously assemblies of this sort lost our cause overnight.

"The Congress of Mexico has ruined the cause of Mexico. Venezuela is already lost; the Argentine congress has endangered the patriot cause in La Plata. We have to live and work wisely and with great prudence."

Bland remained deaf. "Doubtless there are difficulties," he conceded, "but we hope to see implanted a representative system in this country. Perhaps it cannot be done all at once but, by electing a few of the chief officials, the way would be prepared—and if a completely free press is maintained and protected——"

"Now if we could get a few gunboats," interrupted O'Higgins, "we could clean the coast and transport forces to Lima, and the country would then be freed of the colonial yoke. . . . We would see formed on the American continent a great confederation able to maintain civil and political liberty regardless of the particular form of government adopted."

After a moment of silence, he went on.

"The European situation is very cloudy. If a new war comes, Chile should look to its neutral friend, the United States, as its chief support."

But all Bland could do was groove the same rut. "The United States has no selfish interests in the matter but merely hopes to see Chile in full enjoyment of its own independence. . . . My country is free, and liberty has permitted it to prosper as has no other country up to this time. . . . Free institutions are the most adequate for ensuring a flourishing country. . . . We hope the principles of free government are practiced here soon, just as in the United States."

Remarked the official newspaper *El Duende* a few days later, "In the United States, the provinces and the parties could be united in no other way than by a federal constitution of the sort that was adopted. Here it would merely divide that which has been intimately linked. We would commit the greatest absurdity in the world if we take their constitution as our model. Not all good constitutions are good for all peoples."

O'Higgins had not heard the last of the Yankees. Emissary Bland presented himself a few days later on a purely personal matter. He demanded the payment of $4,000 (plus $4,000 interest) owed his son-in-law, John Skinner, Baltimore postmaster, which the latter had loaned to José Miguel Carrera when that leader had visited the United States "as a representative of the Chilean government."

O'Higgins replied bluntly that Carrera had never received any commission from his government or any other Chilean government and had had no right to contract debts in the name of Chile or to equip an armed expedition to Chile. But since Mr. Skinner had apparently put up the money in good faith, the amount would be paid.

Bland left, rubbing his hands delightedly.

The aftermath was not so pleasant. O'Higgins sent the bill to Ignacio Carrera, José Miguel's father, giving him four days to pay half, a month to pay the rest.

Ignacio said it was not even his son's signature, then took the position that, even if it might be, he was in no way responsible for his son's debts.

On Ignacio's declaration, O'Higgins scribbled, "Protest denied. Payment to be made on the third of this month."

When Ignacio still refused to pay, enough of his cattle were seized to cover the obligation.

Bland left the country on July 15, the money in his pocket. Full of gratitude, he wrote his government, "a shaky despotism here . . . fearing even the mention of the people." But though so glad to get the money gouged out of Ignacio, Bland

—as was Worthington—was particularly wroth at O'Higgins' treatment of the Carrera family.

They were to suffer still more at O'Higgins' hands. José Miguel was now head of a large force in northern Uruguay, and it was reported he intended rushing across Argentina to invade Chile. Secret correspondence, via United States businessmen, between him and the members of his family and to leading notables was intercepted. When the code was deciphered, it was found that he had arranged a plot to assassinate "the barbarous assassins" and "bastard adventurers at the head of the government." O'Higgins was to be confined on Las Canteras; San Martín and Monteagudo were to be killed.

The whole Carrera tribe, old Ignacio and the women, were arrested. O'Higgins did nothing until a hand-picked senate, in accordance with a provisional constitution adopted by "popular" vote, assembled in October. He then laid the documents before that body.

Court proceedings were instituted against all the Carreras, several notables, and a number of high ecclesiastics. All were bankrupted by the costs of defense, and the subsequent fines and property seizures swept away every piece of property, every stick of furniture. The women were sent to Mendoza to serve long sentences under guard in convents. Old Ignacio died in prison.

x

By this time Chile had a navy of five gunboats.

It had been started with the brigantine *Aquilla*, which blundered into Valparaiso soon after Chacabuco, because the patriots had left the Spanish flag flying for exactly that reason. It was rebaptized the *Pueyrredón*.

A few months later the *Wynhaven*, with 44 guns, belonging to the British East Indies Company, came into Valparaiso and was bought by a loan from the Valparaiso merchants for 130,-

000 pesos and a draft of 50,000 pesos on the Argentine government. It was renamed the *Lautaro*.

Soon after, a U.S. corvette of 20 cannon was purchased and renamed *Chacabuco*. Another United States ship with 16 cannon was renamed *Araucano*. Presently the *Cumberland*, with 64 guns and a 500-man crew, was bought in London and renamed *San Martin*.

One of the first duties of the *Pueyrredón* was to bring back the prisoners Marco del Pont had sent to Juan Fernández Island. Among them was the artillery colonel Manuel Blanco Encalada, twenty-eight years old, who had fought at Rancagua and crossed the Andes, and who soon distinguished himself at Cancharayada and Maipú. He was named admiral of the navy.

O'Higgins journeyed to Valparaiso to see four of the navy vessels depart to try to intercept a flotilla of eleven Spanish transports being sent under the escort of three armed vessels around the Horn to Peru.

As the Chilean vessels slipped over the horizon, he remarked, "With four little ships, Spain discovered the New World and won a great empire. With those four ships, we shall take it away from her."

By the time the engagement was over, Chile had sixteen ships in her navy. O'Higgins contracted for the services of a famous British sea dog, none other than Lord Thomas Cochrane. He was somewhat under a cloud, having been dismissed from the Royal Navy for peculation, but though he was arrogant, tactless, and greedy, his abilities were unquestionable. He was a disciplinarian of the old school who did not hesitate to use the cat-o'-nine-tails.

O'Higgins met Cochrane on his arrival at Valparaiso (December, 1818) with great military and official pomp, and the Englishman and Mrs. Cochrane—Catherine, a beautiful and charming lady who delighted the Chileans—were taken to the capital for a round of festivities: a banquet in the palace, a showing of Shakespeare's *Othello*.

Consul Worthington met him at the first ball and described him as thin and very tall, sandy-haired, freckled face, not attractive physically, very blunt and tactless in his remarks, disliking pomp. The consul informed Washington that Cochrane's arrival in Chile, "boded no benefit whatever for North Americans." The admiral seemed "to believe that our government envies Hispanic prosperity, fearing it would result in the weakening of the United States. With these ideas he awakens feelings contrary to our cause."

His appointment did not sit well with the actual commandant of the the navy, Blanco Encalada, who had just won new laurels by his sea victory over the great Spanish flotilla.

The nose of the Lautaro Lodge was also out of joint, for it had been grooming a very capable Chilean mariner, Captain Martín Guise, to head the navy.

Cochrane was very condescending toward both Blanco Encalada and Guise but was careful not to offend the Lautaro Lodge or San Martín, whose army presently would invade Peru. But Cochrane was not the type to listen to anybody but himself, and all too soon bitter differences developed. Quite some time later, he discovered his secretary, José Antonio Alvarez Junto, whom he was sure was a spy for the Lautaro Lodge and San Martín, with "his hands in my correspondence" and kicked him out of his job, off the vessel, out of the navy. Alvarez had powerful friends, and the affair took on scandalous proportions.

Cochrane continued to have troubles or to make trouble. O'Higgins had constant headaches with him. Though the budget was being drained of every penny and the country was groaning under taxes to get the San Martín expedition prepared, at the blackest financial moment Cochrane demanded all his pay at once and an increase in his salary. O'Higgins dug up the money.

Later Cochrane raided up the Pacific coast, captured many prizes of war of all nationalities, then demanded fifty per cent of the proceeds. Later he upped this to one hundred per cent.

O'Higgins gave in. Cochrane asked for permission to buy a confiscated royalist hacienda in the south, where he wished to retire, because he wanted to live in Chile as a loyal Chilean the rest of his life. Clearly he expected the property as a gift. O'Higgins gave it to him.

This aroused such a scandal that even Cochrane winced. He ordered the property sold and with a grand gesture contributed the proceeds to the government. But all the rest of his life—which he did not spend in Chile—he complained of Chilean "ingratitude."

Besides hating San Martín—though both men showed a certain restraint—on the eve of the Peruvian invasion Cochrane quarreled with Captain Guise, took his ship away, and put him in the brig, ordering him court-martialed. The government refused to permit this, and the British admiral resigned in a huff.

Guise challenged Cochrane to a duel, which the British lord ignored.

Curiously enough, almost the entire navy backed Cochrane. So did the Lautaro Lodge, which took the stand that his authority at this juncture had to be maintained at all costs.

It required all O'Higgins' powers of persuasion to smooth down Cochrane's feathers, to bring him back, and at the same time get him to restore Guise to his command and postpone all charges until *after* the invasion.

It was during the blockade of Callao, after Chilean forces were invading Peru, that Cochrane and Guise patched up their differences. The Spanish fleet refused to venture forth from the protection of the big guns of the powerful Callao forts. Cochrane, determined to inflict damage on the vessels, which included the flagship *Esmeralda,* the finest vessel of the Spanish Main, arranged for a dangerous raid and called for volunteers. Every man in the navy stepped forward.

In the dark of night he set out with a little fleet of small launches. Guise was in charge of one. Cochrane sang out,

"Remember our duel? The one who gets on the bridge of the *Esmeralda* before the other will be the winner."

They were discovered. The forts shelled them. But they raced on and climbed aboard the flagship to fight a hand-to-hand battle with the crew, nearly all of whom were killed.

In the midst of the fighting, Cochrane heard a voice from the bridge. "Here I am, my lord!"

"All charges dismissed!" roared back Cochrane.

xi

In preparing for the Peruvian invasion, San Martín was plagued with delay after delay and was desperate for lack of money. The Argentine government had repeatedly promised help, but none had ever been sent. He raced off to Buenos Aires.

There he received a promise of 500,000 pesos at once, but he was held up in Mendoza all winter because of snow in the passes. Presently, Pueyrredón informed him he would not be able to send the money, not any at all. San Martín then seized 200,000 pesos being sent to Buenos Aires by Chilean merchants and gave them orders on the Argentine treasury.

Pueyrredón honored the drafts, but only with tremendous difficulties. He wrote San Martín, "If any more drafts show up here, we will go bankrupt and sink."

But San Martín had cash for the treasury of the Army of the Andes. Returning to Chile, he informed the senate of the promised 500,000 Argentine pesos and got it to put up an equal amount. The senators grumbled, for Chile had already put out a million pesos on the fleet. They grumbled still more when he came back to ask for nearly 300,000 more for the navy. This, too, they reluctantly granted.

It soon became evident the bankrupt Argentine government could send nothing. It was plagued by revolts and was close to anarchy. Not only that, it was terrorized by the report of a new, powerful Spanish expedition of 20,000 men setting out from Cádiz to attack Buenos Aires. Pueyrredón sent word to Chile to send back the Army of the Andes at once and to put off the invasion of Peru until a more propitious moment.

The Chilean senate was upset and sent word that such a step would ruin everybody and not help Argentina. The Peruvian viceroy would be free, if the expedition were abandoned, to concentrate all his forces in Bolivia; Argentina would then be caught in a major squeeze—an attack on the port and an attack from the north. The expedition from Chile simply had to go forward, if not with 6,000 men, as planned, then with 3,000—enough to raise revolution throughout the country. That, and that alone, would save Argentina.

But Pueyrredón again ordered San Martín and his forces home, and so he led a token force back over the Andes to Mendoza. There he fretted with frustration. A month passed into a long year.

His health was at the breaking point. Using this as an excuse, he resigned from the army, saying he was going to take the baths at Caquenes. He sent Remedios, his wife, to Buenos Aires—the last time he was to see her alive—and again crossed the Andes.

Bernardo met him with a great military parade and made him a general in the Chilean army. He was reinstalled in the episcopal palace and toiled day and night pushing invasion plans.

Cochrane, after attacking Callao several times, had rampaged up and down the Pacific coast, striking terror to all ships. Determined to put an end to the Spanish holdout in Talcahuano, he arranged with General Freire for a combined sea and land attack.

Bernardo vetoed the plan as too risky. But Cochrane went ahead. Sneaking men ashore in small boats before dawn, he made daring assaults against the supposedly impregnable forts. The surprise was complete; the attack a complete success.

All Chile rang with jubilant applause. O'Higgins had to

hold back any censure for insubordination and, instead, sent the admiral warm congratulations.

Cochrane now suggested he take aboard the 2,000 troops Freire had had on hand and sail for Peru at once. Cochrane wanted San Martín out of the picture.

It seemed a good way to cut through all difficulties and delays. But O'Higgins could not bypass San Martín, nor was he ready to risk another adventurous sortie. The fate of the continent, as well as Chile, hinged on the outcome of the Peruvian expedition. Every care had to be taken to ensure its success.

Actually, San Martín's preparations were almost completed. Consul Worthington, aware that an attack was imminent, called on O'Higgins, to find out what kind of government would be set up in Peru. (There were rumors that San Martín was now inclined toward monarchy; the English and the Brazilians were urging this solution everywhere.)

For reply, O'Higgins read him the proclamation to the Peruvians which had already been prepared. "We do not come to rule you, but to free you. The Peruvian people will set up their own government in accordance with their own wishes."

It did not satisfy Worthington. "But suppose the people choose for monarchy?"

O'Higgins thought the proclamation was clear enough.

"You know," persisted Worthington, "the monarchical form of government is in disrepute even where it is practiced."

Worthington left the palace unsatisfied, still suspicious, both of San Martín's intentions and the reliability of the Peruvian people.

On August 17, 1820, O'Higgins journeyed to Valparaiso for the departure of the expedition—this time with Isabel and Rosa. The Senate had provided San Martín with detailed and lengthy instructions regarding almost everything. Bernardo, telling nobody, tore them up. He made it clear to San Martín and to Cochrane that the expedition was wholly under the Argentine's command—both the fleet and the army. In fact, in private he told San Martín bluntly, "If Cochrane gets out of line, you have the authority to kick him out entirely and make Guise admiral in his place."

August 18 and 19 were utilized to put the last of the supplies and troops aboard. On Sunday, August 20—O'Higgins' birthday—he reviewed the fleet from a launch with San Martín and Cochrane.

The whole port was gay with banners—the customs house and the government buildings, high Artillery Hill with its ancient Spanish fort, all the houses climbing up the hillsides. It was midwinter, but Valparaiso, as it is all the year around, was gay with scarlet bougainvillea vines, roses, and geraniums.

In a formal ceremony, Bernardo handed San Martín a commission as field marshal and captain general of the Chilean army.

"What flag are you flying under?" an aide asked San Martín.

"The Chilean flag, of course," he replied.

No expedition had gone forth better prepared. It had drained Chile's life blood, but the men had food for six months, uniforms for three years, munitions for five.

Bernardo stood with Isabel and Rosa on the high hill, watching the sails fill like white birds, as the twenty-one ships headed out to the open roads and vanished one by one. Before the last were out of sight, he pointed out to sea.

"On those tablets of wood depend the destinies of America!"

6

Freeing the Empire of the Incas

◢◣◥◤ Peru—Spain's largest, richest South American colony, embracing Bolivia and Ecuador and, at an early period, also Chile and Argentina—had gone through the terrible Tupac-Amarú post-Incan uprising, late in the previous century, which had strained resources, had cost widespread bloodshed and misery, and had thoroughly frightened the Creoles, not merely on the big slave estates in the Andes but also on the coast.

For this and other reasons, the unrest in the continent that followed Miranda's incursion in 1806, the commotions of 1808–1810, did not manifest itself in Peru, except in outlying Ecuador and Bolivia, or Alto Peru, and the uprisings there were put down implacably—at least, ashes dampened the fires.

Even so, Peru was a divided country. The dry rainless coast, with its occasional fertile valleys, was a world apart from the imperial realm of the Andes and even further removed from the vast Amazon jungles beyond. The coast, though it had a large population of Indians and Negroes, mostly serfs (*yanacones*) or slaves, was a focus of military and political absolutism and trade, ruled by Spanish bureaucrats and soldiers—and by Creoles. Lima, the city of viceregal pomp, was delightful both for its magnificence and its dreamlike climate, but it was not rooted in the country as a whole; rather it was a unique manifestation of conquest luxury and power.

Lima is located in the always-springlike valley of the tiny trickle known as the Rimac River. It never rains; "thunder and lightning occurred once a century." It looks out over the sea, guarded by the mighty Callao forts, whose sheer stone walls, rising from the water's edge, "more powerful than Gibraltar," are to this day still used as the chief citadels of military rule. For several centuries it was the only lawful trading post for all South America and grew fat on commerce and monopoly.

An English traveler, Naval Captain Basil Hall, described it soon after Independence. (The words are re-translated from the Spanish.) "Seen from the waterfront of Callao or closer at hand, no city presents a more splendid appearance, owing to its numerous cupolas and towers, which rise up from its elevated location and give it a strange Moorish aspect. . . . For a mile along the entrance avenue, one passes between a double row of beautiful trees, with public promenades along both sides and with elegantly decorated stone benches." Hall also described the coming and going of carriages and prancing riders. "At the end of this grandiose approach a handsome triumphal arch . . . [is] surmounted by the Spanish Crown."

Lima became a thoroughly corrupt city. The imported clergy, like the imported bureaucrats, were also thoroughly corrupt. Lima had been the seat of the terrible Inquisition, the G.P.U. of the times, which tried, imprisoned, or burned "heretics" and others from all over the continent.

Lima's great patron saint, the most pious and charitable Santa Rosa, a hysterical girl who disfigured her beautiful face and body for the glory of God, ruled the emotions of all devout *Limeños* and still does.

But in imperial Lima, the arts and sciences were further advanced than elsewhere. There was published the first South American newspaper, *El Merucrio Peruano,* and Peru's San Marcos University was the oldest (along with that of Mexico) in the New World, almost as renowned as Salamanca in Spain. Since Lima was the center of South American empire, where wealth and arms were most concentrated, its resistance to new ideas cost the South American revolution ten extra years of bloodshed. The die-hards truly die hard.

The long brilliant rule, 1810 to 1817, of aged viceroy General José Fernando Abascal y Souza, had brought the colony, in spite of the seesaw of European wars, to the peak of power. Abascal had successfully put down all revolts and had sent armies through Bolivia into Argentina, Chile, and Ecuador. In 1817 he had been succeeded by General Joaquín de la Pezuela, who, though less resolute, previously had recovered Bolivia and had whipped the Argentine revolutionary armies.

San Martín saw clearly that, until Lima was won, there could be no peace on the continent. Belatedly, in 1820, his army was now on the way.

ii

San Martín had not neglected to prepare the ground for invasion. His march over the Andes in 1817 had announced for all with ears to hear that Spanish rule in the continent was doomed. Peruvian intellectuals, who had secretly operated in a Lautaro Lodge for some years, now felt hope stir. A few had sent messages to him, and he had hastened to send a secret emissary to arrange for continued contact.

Also he sent, among others, three young Peruvian officers. One turned traitor and caused the arrest of several underground leaders, but other emissaries were able, as Mariano Torrente put it, "to pervert the public spirit and stir up the provinces." One, he noted, a certain Pecit y Paredes, even plotted to assassinate the viceroy, either on his promenades or by having him poisoned by a member of his household.

San Martín's agents succeeded in spreading the Lautaro Lodge among the viceroy's own troops. By 1817, the Spanish general in Alto Peru, José de la Serna, realizing how shaky the morale in his army had become, tried to remedy it by mixing Peruvian volunteers and conscripts with Spanish regiments, hitherto kept entirely separate. This merely hastened disintegration.

Early in 1820, the authorities uncovered a plot in Tupizo (Bolivia), led by Colonel Agustín Gamarra (later president and dictator of Peru) and other officers. They were too popular to be punished, so the government merely removed some of them discreetly and bought the others off with promotions and rewards.

And so the "political horizon little by little was darkened by clouds . . . the menace of the coming tempest." The clouds darkened still more on the eve of the invasion when news came that troops in Andalucía, Spain, destined for the pacification of America, had revolted, tired of the long, bloody, futile business. Presently a "constitutional revolution" shook Spain itself.

Soon, the appearance of the Chilean fleet off Callao and the pronouncements of San Martín, O'Higgins, and Cochrane that Peru would be invaded, encouraged the Peruvian underground. In a few short years, prostrate Chile came to control the whole Pacific coast and indeed, next to England and Spain, became the most important sea power in the world.

Even so, in 1820 the viceroy still had 23,000 armed men, though spread over a vast area. San Martín's expedition had only 4,430 men and 12 pieces of artillery, but the men were well armed, imbued with fervent crusading zeal, and carried equipment for 15,000 men.

Seventeen transports were escorted by 8 warships, with an aggregate of 247 cannon and 1,600 marines, 600 of whom were foreigners, mostly English. Army funds on hand, in cash or letters of credit, totaled 180,392 pesos. The flotilla was led by Cochrane, in the flagship *O'Higgins*. San Martín and his staff were on the *San Martín*, also a powerful war vessel.

After fifteen days at sea, the forces were put ashore at Pisco,

150 miles south of Lima—much to Cochrane's disgust, for he wanted to land close to the capital and attack at once. But San Martín wished to avoid military encounters in the hope that the mere presence of the liberating army and the propaganda he issued would provoke revolt. He wanted the Peruvians themselves to be the ones to free their land.

By August 13, the entire expedition was ashore. The Ica garrison of 500 men had fled before 50 men of the cavalry of Las Heras, who had landed first, six miles south of the port. At once San Martín threw out scouting parties across the fertile Chincha Valley.

The printed proclamation—that which O'Higgins had showed Worthington—was given out. "Remember that our great duty is to consolidate America and that we do not come to conquer but to liberate the peoples. The Peruvians are our brothers." To his troops he also issued regulations (setting forth severe punishments) against looting or mistreating inhabitants.

"The time for oppression and force has passed," he announced. "I come to put an end to that [Spanish] epoch of sorrow and humiliation."

All slaves who took up arms were declared free, and 600 from nearby haciendas joined up.

iii

Viceroy Pezuela reinforced his forces blocking the road to Lima, proposed an armistice, and offered to negotiate. This suited San Martín perfectly.

The emissaries met at Miraflores, six miles from the capital. The royal delegates demanded evacuation of Peru and recognition of Ferdinand VII. San Martín's spokesman countered with a demand that the patriots be allowed to occupy the Argentine portions of Bolivia and that the Spanish garrisons in Quito and Chiloé Island also observe the truce.

Toward the end of the prolonged talks, the viceroy attended in person. The patriots then added the proviso that he must also declare Peru independent.

Talks broke down October 1; the temporary armistice ended October 5. San Martín had gained nearly two months.

At once he sent a strong mounted division to raid through the Andes, under Colonel Arenales, an experienced guerrilla fighter. He was an austere disciplinarian who always saddled, groomed and even shod, his own horses, mended his own uniforms, and carried his own food, usually parched corn and jerked meat.

Arenales fell on the viceregal advance units guarding Lima and crushed them. Two royalist militia companies and their officers deserted and joined him. He captured a 100-mule supply train, then swung up into the mountains.

San Martín re-embarked his army and sailed north. They sighted San Lorenzo Island, close to Callao, on October 29. War vessels were left to blockade the port, while he landed his forces twenty miles north at Ancón. At once he sent 200 men to take Chanclay and scout for horses, cattle, and food. They raked in much booty and retired at the approach of a strong royalist contingent from the Azanpuquío base near Lima. The Spaniards were smashed in a narrow defile.

The good news came that Guayaquil in Ecuador had revolted—the so-called Revolution of October 9. This was serious for the Spaniards, for they had made their main supply center for the whole Pacific coast there, and vast quantities of arms and supplies were lost. The new Guayaquil junta was headed by the notable poet, José Joaquín Olmedo, who swore "to maintain independence, be faithful to the patria; to defend it, to promote everything concerning prosperity, and fulfill his duties legally." He was a remarkable political leader who believed in civil liberties and human rights and had the courage and the iron hand to kick out the military leader of the revolt when he committed abuses. At all times he kept the military well in hand.

This was the time—November 5—when Cochrane seized the Spanish flagship *Esmeralda* from under the powerful guns of the Callao forts, and 120 Spaniards died on the decks. The vessel was renamed the *Valdivia*. Cochrane called on San Martín to attack Lima at once.

Instead, San Martín moved his forces further north to Huaura, ninety miles from Lima, an open port but with deep water, and settled there in a healthy, fertile valley to follow a policy of watchful waiting for the next six months.

It was a strategic location that prevented the viceroy from trying to recover Guayaquil by land and from sending troops to northern Peru.

The Spaniards sent out the Numancia Battalion, mostly Venezuelans, to harass San Martín. He was delighted. His agents, among them the beautiful Manuela Sáenz Thorne—later to play such an important part in Bolívar's life—had already subverted the officers, one of whom was her half-brother, José María Sáenz. Now, on December 3, they deserted en masse to the patriot army. Ceremoniously San Martín made them custodians of the army flag.

From then on, the royalists suffered desertions. On December 8, thirty-eight officers and cadets escaped from Lima and joined him.

Everywhere, the Spaniards were kept busy, particularly in Alto Peru, chiefly by plots of insurrection among their own forces. One sought to assassinate General Antonio Pedro Olañeta. Executions were frequent.

"When the chief edifice begins to fall apart," wrote historian Torrente, "there are never enough props to shore it up."

By the end of the month, San Martín had thrown all enemy forces out of the entire Huaylas Department, almost without a fight, and 70,000 inhabitants swore allegiance to Peruvian independence.

His chief of staff, Las Heras, was maneuvering through the north, and soon all provinces there were in open revolt, driving out the royalist garrisons. Cochrane, with only a small landing force, seized Arica and Tacna. In the port of Trujillo, the Spanish general, actually a Peruvian Creole, Marqués de Torre Tagle, said to be a Lautaro Lodge member, called an open *cabildo* meeting and recommended turning the plaza over to the patriots. The royalists, led by the Bishop as spokesman, hotly objected. Bernardo Torre Tagle put him and sixteen other protestors in jail and raised the Peruvian Independence flag—red and white with a dawning sun over the Andes, shining upon a tranquil sea. At once, he forced northern Piura into line on the side of Independence.

With all the north, the country's chief granary, with more than 300,000 people, secured at his back, San Martín now had a rich source of new recruits, food, and supplies. Thus, with only a few insignificant skirmishes he had won a major part of the northern coast and lower highlands and had brought about uprisings in both Ecuador and Bolivia.

As Humberto Tejera put it in his *San Martín:* "The campaign of San Martín against the viceroyalty of Peru was . . . more than an aggressive military campaign . . . a policy of patient waiting to instigate the disintegration of his enemies by themselves alone; a sowing of revolutionary spirit in the country which, having had the greatest colonial splendor and silver opulence, was considered to have the greatest addiction to Bourbon absolutism."

Lima was now cut off from the sea. San Martín proposed to cut it off from the land. In due time it would fall like a rotten fruit from the tree. This task was largely entrusted to Arenales.

iv

After his surprise attack that had wiped out the viceroy's forces south of Lima, Arenales swung swiftly into the mountains and, by forced marches of forty kilometers a day, fell on Huamanga, a rich farming town and important communications center, then Tarma, one of the paradises of the Sierra. By November 21, he controlled the whole important Jauja

Valley, a region rapturously described three hundred years earlier by Conquistador Pedro Pizarro, brother of Francisco, in all its abundance, beauty, and fine climate. And though, since Incan days, the area under cultivation had declined, it was still one of the gems on the crown of Peru.

Arenales set up a local autonomous Peruvian government and armed volunteers, mostly Indian, then advanced on Cerro de Pasco, an important mining center. The Indian city of Huancayo, the major highland city in central Peru, was soon taken.

Meanwhile the Spaniards descended from Arequipa and Cuzco, the ancient Inca capital, and, joined by a strong force from Lima, retook Huamanga, putting 10,000 Indian recruits to flight or to the sword without mercy, and moved on to Huancayo. The place was looted and burned. They then returned to Lima.

The patriot forces soon recovered Huancayo and organized a new force of 5,000 Indian troops.

With the bulk of his forces, Arenales, after a triumphant march of a thousand kilometers through the Sierra, the very heart of Peru, rejoined San Martín on the coast. He had set revolt aflame throughout the Andes and had cut or endangered all Spanish supply lines.

By 1821, Viceroy Pezuela realized that Peru could not be successfully defended. The royalist extremists—frightened by the liberal turn in Spain, disgusted with what they considered the viceroy's military bungling, and fearing he planned surrender—decided to oust him. On January 29, 1821, General José de la Serna, head of the army, reviewed the troops at Azanpuquío with two other officers and gave the viceroy, hero of so many battles in Bolivia, four hours to resign.

He retired to the Magdalena hacienda and soon after took his family to Europe on an English vessel, which they boarded by a miraculous zigzag through the blockading Cochrane ships.

Assuming power by this military *coup* was in itself a breaking of tradition and Spanish authority. La Serna invited San

Martín to send representatives to a conference "to end the struggle between Spaniards and Americans."

The meeting was held at the Torre-Blanca hacienda near Retes, not far from Lima and now the chief patriot encampment. At once the San Martín spokesman rejected any discussion about recognizing Spanish authority. The only basis on which they would confer was "full recognition of Peruvian independence."

The Spaniards then offered to surrender Lima if they would be given free passage to the Sierra. This ruse was rejected.

La Serna was hit by calamities. Food was almost lacking. Yellow fever swept the city and much of his army. Arenales had resumed his forays, leaving the fever-stricken coast with 2,800 men, most hardly more than skeletons, to cut off assistance from the Sierra. He recaptured Pisco, Tarma, and Huancayo. News of more conspiracies and insurrections, as in Huarochiri, Yauyos, and Jauja, came from the interior.

La Serna, as had his predecessor, realized that, as Torrente put it, "the spirit of innovation had made such rapid progress" that everything seemed to rest on quicksand, that Lima could not be saved. But there still seemed some hope in the interior. Royalist General José Canterac was operating brilliantly and recovering lost ground.

If Lima was a prostrate city, the patriots were also on the cross. The epidemic spread to Retes and Huaura. San Martín himself was stricken, and at one time only a thousand men were able to stand duty. The rest were wobbly on their feet. Except for the movements in the Sierra, the whole situation stagnated.

v

On March 25, 1821, a Spanish frigate flying a white flag came into the harbor at Huaura and put ashore Spanish emissary, Manuel Abreu, an old-time friend of San Martín, for four days. Abreu then went on to Lima, where he suggested to La Serna he hold *private* talks with the patriot leader.

The overtures were rejected, San Martín saying he would accept only propositions openly made. News came through of a truly bloody insurrection in Cuzco; General Pío Tristán, wealthy Creole there who had ruled the plaza after his defeats in Argentina and Bolivia, put the revolt down by luck, courage, and astuteness.

San Martín moved his forces boldly back to Ancón. Lima and Callao were now isolated by sea and land. Starvation grew worse. Again Cochrane insisted on an immediate attack. But San Martín sat down once more to await developments and any proposals.

Delegates from the viceroy arrived May 4, 1821. Again they were told that only full Independence was acceptable. La Serna then proposed a sixteen-month armistice, hoping perhaps to get help from Spain, already drained to the point of ruin by the long struggle.

Very well, then hand over the Callao forts as a guarantee. If, at the end of the period, the armistice had not been violated, they would be handed back intact. To San Martín's surprise, La Serna meekly agreed, provided he could first remove twelve pieces of heavy artillery.

A temporary twenty-day truce was arranged, during which La Serna and San Martín discussed all points. San Martín's forces were still in a bad way also, and he was ready to concede much. As he wrote O'Higgins, his men were exhausted; 1,200 were sick. He needed more help. This plea, while talks were going on, could possibly be considered dishonest. But La Serna was certainly not honest. He sent secret word to the Sierra troops to redouble their efforts to seize strategic positions before an armistice was declared.

San Martín agreed to the full independence of Peru under a regency until a satisfactory Spanish prince could arrive to take over the throne. This was worse than the Lircay compromise. It carried San Martín out of the mainstream of the revolution and left a stain on his name. There was no popular support for monarchy anywhere; all revolutionary sentiment was for a republic. This San Martín had always supported; it was a basic doctrine of the Lautaro Lodge.

The two leaders, meeting in Punchaucay on July 2, then discussed the details of the march of the patriot troops into Lima and the celebration, by both forces, of a declaration of Independence.

San Martín's reputation was partly saved by the fact that La Serna's officers refused to accept the pact and insisted that no steps be taken without consultation with the Spanish government.

La Serna then asked for an armistice, dividing the territory of Peru, until this could be done. San Martín refused such a delay. Though all bets were off, neither side was inclined to break the *de facto* armistice. San Martín pushed his propaganda inside and outside the city.

Soon the Lima *cabildo* openly demanded peace. The military men, furious, threatened the *cabildo* members. But instead of moving in for the kill, San Martín quietly pulled his forces back to Huaura. He was still playing a cat-and-mouse game.

La Serna knew his position was hopeless. He ordered his mountain forces to seize Huanacavelica, the lofty mercury town, at all costs, and on July 4 delegated his authority to Marqués Montemira, a Creole. He left for Jauja, recently recaptured, and for Huancavelica, with 2,000 men, mostly convalescents. They suffered dreadfully from mountain sickness, bleeding at mouth, ears, and nose, and many perished.

Lima was left defenseless, with merely 1,000 sick soldiers, though 2,000 men were holed up in the Callao forts on short rations.

Panic hit the city. The priests and aristocrats had described San Martín as "a devil with horns" who would put everybody to the sword. The Spanish notables fled to the forts. The churches, monasteries, and convents filled up with refugees, bringing their valuables and household goods, cluttering up the space before the altars so badly that holy services could hardly be celebrated and, after a few days, creating a terrible stench.

A citizens' committee called on San Martín for protection.

His first move was to pull off all guerrillas, whom the *Limeños* particularly feared, and throw a ring of regular soldiers about the city and send in food. "The people are not the ones who make war," he told the shuddering *Limeños*.

Finally, the authorities made a formal request that his soldiers occupy the city. On July 9 a division marched in and was acclaimed by the populace. But one of Peru's worst earthquakes hit the city right after, raising dark forebodings, sending the people scampering to the churches with candles and screams.

With only one aide, San Martín slipped in after dark on July 10, quite incognito. But at the viceregal palace he was recognized by two priests, who showered adulation upon him. Before he could slip away, a crowd of women surrounded him. Many fell on their knees, calling him their "savior" and trying to embrace his knees.

Shouts went up, "*Viva* our general!"

"No! No!" San Martín called back. "*Viva* the Independence of Peru!"

He was swept off to the *cabildo*, which had been hastily convened. They made proposals for running the city. He listened without comment and, after a few more female embraces, managed to get back to the camp he had established at Mirones, halfway between Lima and Callao.

The next day he ordered all Spanish emblems torn down from buildings and substituted them with the words, "Lima Independent."

Four Chilean flags, captured by the Spaniards in the Rancagua battle, were sent back to O'Higgins, and all Santiago turned out for solemn ceremonies and prolonged festivities.

San Martín made little effort to pursue the Spaniards fleeing to the interior, where the Spanish forces were melting away. He did send out a proclamation that, if the Peruvians would help, all Peru would be free within forty days. Actually he ordered Arenales to come to the city to help in the reduction of Callao.

Arenales, who had been training 4,000 new recruits during the armistice negotiations, was dismayed. Many of his men were *Serranos,* who simply would not follow him to Lima. He sent word to San Martín, "To concentrate all our strength in Lima will be as disastrous for us as it was for the Spanish." Sadly he set his men in motion. They arrived in Lima on the day official Independence celebrations were being staged.

But though Peruvian Independence was now a fact, something that could never be taken away, San Martín's lethargy at this juncture was to cost the new republic four more years of war that might have been unnecessary.

vi

On August 3, at the behest of Peruvian patriots and the Lautaro Lodge, San Martín reluctantly accepted the post as head of the government, with the title of Protector, but "only until the war is over."

A bit apologetically, he wrote O'Higgins he would hold that high office no longer than one year at most. "My one desire is to retire to private life and live quietly and peacefully."

His first edict, drawn up by his new secretary of war, none other than Monteagudo, head of the Lautaro Lodge, was directed against the Spaniards. Those who swore to uphold Independence would be respected, but most—including the bishop and other heads of the church in the interior—were deported and their properties confiscated. For the moment such seizures were the chief source of revenue for the bankrupt regime.

A month after his accession to power, the old enemy of both

O'Higgins and himself—José Miguel Carrera—heading a marauding force on the frontiers, was captured and executed in Mendoza on September 4, 1821, as a "bandit" and his head nailed over the *cabildo* doorway.

Shortly after this, Spanish forces, led by Cantarac, swept down from the Sierra, crossed the desert and almost died of thirst, but drove into Callao under the guns of the forts.

On the eve of this attack, Cochrane had chosen that ticklish moment to demand 200,000 pesos back pay and another 200,000 for his officers and men. The meager Peruvian treasury did not have that much. But when the Spaniards threatened to recapture Lima, San Martín for safety took all they had, 285,000 pesos, and put it aboard the *Lautaro* in Ancón. Hearing of this, Cochrane seized it, took it aboard the flagship, and distributed it all pro-rata to himself, his officers, and men.

None of San Martín's protests availed to get back one penny. He ordered Cochrane to resign. Cochrane said he was no longer under the orders of a foreign dictator; his loyalty and his ships belonged to Chile. He declined to take any orders whatever, he sent a number of vessels to Chile, and with the rest ranged up the coast as far as Acapulco, Mexico, chasing stray Spanish vessels.

San Martín wrote O'Higgins, "It is impossible for me to enumerate all the crimes of that noble pirate." O'Higgins urged caution and conciliation, halfway took Cochrane's side, and suggested they were both to blame; they had permitted the Lautaro Lodge too much power. By then O'Higgins was a four-square dictator himself and had surrounded himself with far worse advisers, among them a number of ex-royalists.

But by September 21, after Canterac's forces had been driven back to the Sierra, more by failure to find food than actual fighting, Callao surrendered in late September. The garrisons were allowed to march out. Officers and civil officials were obliged to agree to leave the country within three months. And so the best fortified Spanish stronghold in the Americas was at last in patriot hands.

San Martín carried on many constructive enterprises. He organized a strictly Peruvian legion—infantry, cavalry, and artillery—looking to the time when his Argentine and Chilean forces could be sent home. He abolished serfdom and slavery, all forced labor, and corporal punishment in schools. He founded a national library and various schools. Freedom of the press was guaranteed. But more and more he was submerged in Lima's effete, corrupt intrigues among prelates, military men, and aristocrats, and he also embarked on a sweet love affair with the beautiful Rosita Campuzano, a Guayaquil beauty.

A little over four months after he took his exalted position, San Martín called a congress to meet December 27, 1821, to adopt a "suitable" constitution and organize a definite form of government. Simultaneously he handed over the authority jointly to Torre Tagle and Bernardo de Monteagudo and shut himself up in the Quinta Magdalena, as the viceroy had done, "to observe without participating in government."

Basil Hall interviewed him there. "An extraordinarily cultured man, free of all affectation, extremely cordial and charming. The benevolence of his character is evident from the first moment. In short, I have never seen a more irresistible person."

It was perhaps in the Quinta that San Martín wrote his impressions. "The struggle in Peru has no ordinary characteristics. This is a war not of conquest and glory but wholly of ideas. It is a struggle of new liberal principles against prejudices, intolerances, and tyrannies . . .

"I do not aspire to military fame," he remarked, perhaps preparing for complete withdrawal, "nor do I have the ambition to be the conqueror of Peru. I merely wish to liberate the country from oppression."

But there were still 19,000 Spanish troops above the city, led by veterans of years of war, and San Martín was less inclined than ever to confront the ardors of a new prolonged campaign.

By 1822, Bolívar, by then successful in all Greater Colombia and Ecuador, sent Joaquín Mosquera to Lima to negotiate a treaty of "Union" with Peru as a preliminary to a similar arrangement with Chile and Argentina. This was signed by Monteagudo on July 16. He called it "the first step in international arbitration throughout the world."

Bolívar also wished Peru to cede Ecuador to the Grand Columbian Confederation. San Martín intrigued against this and went north on a small vessel, the *Macedonia,* reaching Guayaquil July 26.

Bolívar had reached there some weeks earlier. The two great liberators "embraced under the Arch of Triumph of Ecuador and the New World, in the region of volcanoes and evergreen palms."

The result of this meeting was to be more fateful for the future of South America than a dozen battles.

7

The Making of a Liberator

⚠️ The moment of truth—what William James would call a religious experience—came to young Simón Bolívar, the Venezuelan aristocrat, on the Aventine Hill in Rome when he rhapsodized nostalgically to his former tutor, Simón Rodríguez, about the "empresses and courtesans, the martyrs and apostles, criminals and heroes" of the Eternal City. They "accomplished almost nothing for humanity." Flinging out his arms, he announced his dedication to a lifelong crusade. "On my life and honor, I swear not to rest until I have liberated America from her tyrants."

For Rodríguez, a political exile who had taken the name Robinson, the youth was none other than Rousseau's Émile, in flesh and blood. This pledge above the city of the Caesars must have seemed a personal reward, for, as a tutor in Caracas, he had taught Simón—from the age of nine to fifteen—mathematics and Latin, to be sure, but, above all, Rousseau's teachings, which in those years (the boy had been born in 1783) were proscribed by Church and state.

"Of the lessons he gave me," Bolívar once declared at the height of his career, "not a comma has vanished. They have

162

always been present in my mind. I followed them as trustworthy guides."

Bolívar came from a Basque family that had lived in Venezuela more than two hundred years, since the founding of Caracas in 1567, and had become one of the wealthiest in the colony. The first Bolívar had been a public scribe, preparing Indian petitions to the *procurador,* and had spent a spell in jail for failing to pay his taxes. Simón's own father had become a marqués, a title available to Creoles who had the thousands of ducats necessary to purchase it from the Crown.

As tutor, Rodríguez opened young Simón's eyes to the realities of race and class distinctions in the empire, the harsh burdens and restrictions laid upon Indians and Negroes, mulattoes and mestizos, even on white Creoles. It was almost a crime not to have been born a Spaniard.

The lessons were cut short when Rodríguez was arrested for complicity in the premature Nariño revolt in neighboring New Granada (Colombia) and, though he was freed for lack of evidence, anybody on the government's suspect list sooner or later would be imprisoned. He fled to Europe without farewells. For a year thereafter, Bolívar was tutored by the exiled Chilean, Andrés Bello, who was to become one of the greatest writers and thinkers of the continent.

Soon after, Simón was sent to Madrid to live with his mother's brother, one of the wealthiest men in Spain.

Madrid at this time was the center of the world, Europe's most powerful, luxurious, and gay city, ruled over by the corrupt court of stupid Charles IV and his adulterous queen, María Luisa. Young Bolívar had access to the highest court and society circles.

He fell violently in love with delicate, beautiful María Teresa del Toro, daughter of another Venezuelan marqués. Because of their youth, permission to marry immediately was withheld, and María Teresa was whisked off to a country estate.

Simón became a close friend of a courtier known as Mallo, one of Queen María Luisa's paramours, in competition with Prime Minister Manuel de Godoy (who did so much to wreck the Spanish Empire). Perhaps because of his friendship with Mallo, Simón was surrounded by a mounted police guard one afternoon while riding outside the Toledo Gate and accused of wearing lace cuffs and diamond cuff links, forbidden to mere overseas colonials.

Bolívar, small, slim, agile, was as fine a horseman as any Venezuelan *llanero*, a breed unsurpassed in all the world. Drawing his sword, he galloped off.

Mallo had enough influence to prevent his being punished, but Simón was ordered to leave Spain. The humiliation branded his innermost being with hatred of Spanish rule.

In Paris he felt the currents of new freedom and lively cultural activities. Fascinated by Napoleon, already crowned with so many victories for France, Bolívar saw in the Code Napoléon the embodiment not only of the French Revolution and the new equality of man but a true guide for New World freedom.

Presently he was allowed to marry María Teresa, and they sailed back to Venezuela. A prolonged, idyllic honeymoon was spent on a family estate in the forests of Aragua, but nine months later she died from fever. Only Simón's older brother prevented him from committing suicide. He swore never to marry again.

To forget, he decided to tour Italy and Greece with his former tutor, Rodríguez, a long-planned expedition. It was 1804. He was just twenty-one.

Hardly had he reached Madrid than his hatred of Spain was refueled. On the pretext of famine, all colonials were suddenly ordered to leave Madrid. Fuming, Bolívar went on to Paris, an embittered emigree. The trip to the southern lands had to be postponed.

Paris was returning to its old ways. Society was resuming

its former splendor, though sharply divided between the old guard and the upstart Bonapartists. Simón gave himself over to the gay life of a wealthy young blade about town. The finest dressed dandy in Paris, he kept superb horses, pranced down the boulevards, went on hunting parties, threw Lucullan feasts attended by the leading personages of the country, was adored for his dancing, practiced fencing, and gambled heavily. His money gathered about him a swarm of fawning gentlemen-panhandlers, but he also enjoyed the company of leading thinkers, artists, and writers and managed to read more of Rousseau, Voltaire, Montesquieu, and the Encyclopedists.

He haunted the salon of beautiful young Fanny de Villars, married to the Duke de Villars, an aged, wealthy field marshal. Soon she became Simón's mistress. He called her "Teresa" after his first love, his dead wife. Perhaps she knew why. It was a happy relationship, so far as the feverish Bolívar could ever be happy, for he found in her both the physical and intellectual inspiration he needed. In her salon he met the redoubtable René de Chateaubriand, possibly also Madame Récamier and Madame de Staël. Another important personage was General Eugène de Beauharnais, stepson of Napoleon.

"What do you think of my charming young friend?" Fanny asked the general.

Beauharnais peered at the small, slender, olive-skinned Bolívar and said, "He's quite a sparrow, a *moineau.*"

Bolívar took it to mean "monkey" (in Spanish, *mono*) and bridled. He would have slapped the general, precipitating a duel, had not Fanny managed to calm them down.

Whether Fanny's child, born about this time, was Bolívar's nobody knew. If so, it was to be his only offspring, unless there are others off the cuff.

Napoleon was crowned in Notre Dame. Bolívar considered it, for all his continued admiration of the glory surrounding the Corsican, a gross betrayal of the revolution and refused to attend as a guest in the Spanish ambassador's box. Another admirer of Napoleon who admired freedom more was Beethoven, who erased his dedication to the *Eroica*.

From his windows Bolívar watched the bands, the marching troops, the shouting crowds, and felt sickened, yet found the spectacle inspiring.

To his friend, Mariano Tristán, a wealthy exiled Peruvian, he remarked that tyranny had risen from the foundations of freedom, yet it was a sweet thing for a hero to have the applause of the multitude, even if the people did not know whether they were cheering a tyrant or a guardian of their liberties.

Tristán y Moscoso came from the wealthiest, most powerful Creole clan of Peru. His relatives were grandees, bishops, and archbishops in Arequipa and in Spain. But he, too, smarted from the imperial tyranny. Refused Crown permission, as a colonel of the Spanish army, to marry a commoner, the lovely plebeian French girl Thérèse, he had thrown up his commission and career and was now living with her—as wife or perhaps mistress—in a Paris villa. Simón was attracted by beautiful Thérèse, whose name evoked his most poignant memory.

(Mariano and Thérèse were to be the great grandparents of the French painter, Paul Gauguin, and their daughter Flora was to start the first labor unions and the feminist movement in France. Mariano was to die, forgotten, leaving Thérèse and his children in utter poverty, but his brother Pío, was to go on to glory, to lead great royal armies across the Andes and to become field marshal and Peru's last viceroy. Years later, Bolívar, then the triumphant liberator of Peru, would meet with him in Arequipa and strike a deal by which Pío was made a general of the republic. Later he became president.)

All his life, Napoleon had a peculiar fascination for Bolívar, and later he imitated some of his methods. Years afterward, in the struggle in Venezuela, he told his faithful Irish aide, Daniel Florencio O'Leary, that he both hated and admired Napoleon. "After he made himself emperor . . . and I saw him break down the pillars on which liberty had been set up . . . even his glory seemed to me to be infernal, the flames of a volcano rising destructively over a world in chains."

Simón became nervous and restless. Fanny describes him as pacing up and down the garden like a caged creature, tearing at twigs and flowers, snatching fruits from the boughs, biting into them and tossing them away, until she had to protest at his destructiveness. In the house he yanked at the curtains, tore books to pieces. "He could not sit still for ten minutes without ruining something." He had "a mania of movement."

He plunged into everything with excess. One night he lost every cent at the gaming tables and was obliged to borrow from Fanny. She made him promise he would never gamble again. He kept that promise for twenty years, then was shocked, one night, when he thoughtlessly engaged in a game with his fellow officers, that he had broken it.

But for now he was still engrossed with Fanny, writing her long, passionate letters, though he saw her every day, pouring out his ideas, his dreams, his frustrations. He gave up all his wastrel companions.

"What a desert my life is!" he wrote her. "As soon as I have what I want, I hate it." Dame Fortune had ruined him "by laying a bag of gold" in his path. Otherwise he would have "made glory" his cult . . . "as a man of learning or as a friend of freedom." He was only twenty-three.

One night at a great banquet to which he had invited, along with Fanny, leading senators, generals, and churchmen of France, the stupidity of the conversation made him bite his lips, and when a churchman adulated Napoleon, he flared up and denounced that hero as "a traitor to liberty, of aiming at tyranny, of destroying the rights of the people." He upbraided the generals and clerics who abetted him, those who "had put religion under the shadow of bayonets." He shouted down all protests, and the guests left hurriedly.

Greatly alarmed, Fanny's brother-in-law urged him to leave France immediately. Bolívar refused. "I want to know whether a stranger in a strange land can express his opinion of its government, or whether he is thrown out for doing so."

Nothing happened, but presently, hearing that Rodríguez was in Vienna, he rushed to see him. His tutor, now Robinson, was puttering around with chemistry experiments for an Austrian nobleman. Robinson saw at once that Bolívar was spiritually and physically ill. He murmured, "Enjoy yourself. It is the only way at your age for you to recover."

For the youth, burning for action, seeking some lodestar by which to guide his life, everything Rodríguez now said seemed empty sophistry, his grandiose theories divorced from all reality.

In despair he wrote Fanny, "The doctors do not give me long to live."

Soon he was back in Paris. Fanny held his hand again. But this was a real turning point in his life. The pivot was a great man, Alexander von Humboldt, who, with his companion, Aimé Jacques Alexandre Bonpland, was back in Paris from years of exploration in the New World. Humboldt had visited with Bolívar's relatives in Venezuela; he had penetrated the great jungles, had crossed the llanos, had followed the great Orinoco to its sources, and had discovered the junction of the Orinoco and Amazon rivers. Through his eyes, Bolívar looked at his country with a fresh understanding, saw the grandeur and greatness of it; a new pride was born, a new love for his native soil and the Venezuelan people. He talked with Humboldt nearly every day.

Yes, Humboldt told him, the New World countries could become great beyond all dreams, but only if freed from the Spanish yoke. "What a splendid enterprise! The people are ready. But where is the man strong enough to carry it through?"

ii

The words made a profound impression. In his petulant mood, Bolívar had tossed aside all Robinson's fine platitudes about human freedom and liberation. Now he wanted to listen again, to exchange ideas free of interruptions. And so he revived their old plan of touring the southlands.

They set out through northern Italy with knapsacks on their backs, sleeping in farm wagons, on haystacks, in country inns, meeting and talking with the poor people. Over their bread and cheese and wine, under the olive trees beside the ripening grapes, they read Tacitus aloud; they talked their souls out. A mongrel dog took up with them. Bolívar was heartbroken when it left them. Robinson laughed at his tenderheartedness.

They looked up the shrines where Rousseau had lived in Italy. Bolívar's path crossed Napoleon's again. He saw the Corsican crowned with the iron crown of Lombardy in the Milan Cathedral, a great military display. Bolívar, whose thoughts were running to personal achievement and glory, was impressed, and he made no critical remarks. "I fixed my eyes on him and the crowd saw only him. How simply he stood, surrounded by his glittering staff: Everybody near him was covered with gold and lace; he wore only epaulettes, a hat and a suit without ornament. I was delighted."

He got in with the Manzoni crowd in Milan and various top salons in Florence and Rome, where he met or re-met Lamartine, Madame de Staël, Danish sculptor Bertel Thorvaldsen, Chateaubriand, and Lord Byron. Strangely enough, the American made no impression on Lord Byron, though years later he was to name one of his vessels for the liberation of Greece *Bolívar*.

The Spanish Ambassador took him to see the Pope. Bolívar refused to kiss the Pope's slipper.

The Ambassador was shocked and apologetic. The Pope smiled. "Let the young Indian do as he pleases."

Outside, Bolívar exploded, "The Pope seems to hold the Cross in little esteem for he wears it on his foot; even the proudest kings set it on their heads."

All Rome chuckled over the interchange.

The city excited him. He was in a constant fever, rushing

to look at ancient palaces, broken columns, the works of Hadrian and Trajan, the tombs, the inscriptions. He read, in these mementos of past grandeur, the story of "the long struggles between tyrants and the people." On a sweltering August day, he and Robinson climbed up the Aventine. There, overlooking the seven hills of the Eternal City, his whole being crystallized into an unshakable determination to free the Americas, much as had St. Francis been given his holy mission in a storm-riven night of lightning on a mountain in Tuscany; as Miranda, a few years before this in New York, had also seen the vision of a free America. "On my life and honor," Bolívar told his companion, his eyes on the great city, "I swear not to rest until I have liberated America from her tyrants."

A year later, he set out, so to speak, for the wars. He simply had to get back to America, to Venezuela. Fanny gave him her miniature to wear around his neck as a talisman, sending him off like a knight of old on his great mission.

Just before he boarded ship, he wrote her, "I am seeking a new way of life. . . . Most likely I shall build a hut for myself in the forests. . . . I shall tear off as many twigs as I like there without offending anybody. . . . But the great conqueror (Napoleon) has just begun his invasion of Spain, and I should like to be a witness of how America regards the great event."

He had a premonition that the sun of liberty was about to rise over the New World. What kind of a Venezuela was he going back to?

iii

In 1499, on his second voyage, Columbus discovered Maracaibo, a swamp village on piles, to be renamed little Venice (Venezuela), later to become one of the great oil-producing districts of the world—with no great improvement in the lot of the inhabitants.

Many early explorers had come to Venezuela, looking for El Dorado, including Sir Walter Raleigh, who went on into the Guiana highlands, and, finally, von Humboldt, looking for the truer gold of knowledge.

In his long-enslaved land, Bolívar arrived. A few weeks in the United States during his voyage had reinforced his ideas about freedom. But the fate of Miranda's expedition, which occurred shortly before his arrival, could scarcely provide consolation or hope for the young patriot's own expectations. The Venezuelan people had not stirred to Miranda's cry: the Indians, the slaves, the ordinary people had remained indifferent. Even the Creoles, some of whom had secretly espoused new French ideas, had rallied against the heretical agent of British and Yankee gold in spite of their years of grumbling. They had poured out their money and jewels to repel him and burned his picture in the public plaza.

Bolívar got a prodigal son's welcome in Caracas. He was feted everywhere as a seasoned man of the world—the civilized world. He cut a figure. His income was not less than 20,000 pesos a year, and he was sought by lovely Creole heiresses. But his own secret feeling, those first few months in this dirty provincial city of twisted hill alleys, was homesickness for the splendors and culture of Paris.

Torrente later described the Caracas of that day and its people. "The capital of the provinces of Venezuela has been the chief forge of the American insurrection. Its invigorating climate has produced the most politically minded and audacious men, the most enterprising and energetic, the most vicious and scheming, and those most outstanding for their precociousness and intellectual talents. The vitality of those natives competes with their voluptuousness, the vigor of their expression with their clarity of ideas, the stimulus of glory with the ambition to rule, and their sagacity with their maliciousness."

As early as 1711, the mulatto Andre Sato tried to become king of Venezuela. In 1748, a wealthy cacao grower tried to overthrow the trade monopoly of the Quipuzcoa Company, an uprising in which Miranda's father had been involved. In 1797, a conspiracy of elements favoring the French Revolution was discovered. A prolonged two-year trial resulted, but a new, sterner captain general speeded matters up, hung some of them, deported others, and released those least culpable.

Bolívar did not divulge his real purpose in returning. His one gesture was to get up at a banquet table of notables, mostly representatives of the king, to toast for the Independence of the Americas. The shock was as terrible as that he had produced in Paris. Governor General Manuel María Casas, who was present, banished him to his country estates for a few days.

It was no hardship, for he spent most of his time there anyway and besides had already gotten together a congenial group of Creole intellectuals around the groaning banquet board. They batted about new dangerous ideas; the events of the world were discussed. Among those attending were Andrés Bello, the great Chilean scholar and Simón's former tutor. Bello, a stern classicist, recited Corneille and Tacitus to the gathering; fiery José Félix Ribas, the journalist, an uncle-in-law, who until his death was Bolívar's closest aide, quoted Voltaire. In attendance were General Montillo and Marqués del Toro (who had been a father-in-law). The governor sent his son out to tell Bolívar, "Too many visitors."

The news of Joseph Bonaparte's 1808 usurpation of the Spanish throne with the help of French bayonets reached Venezuela in July by English newspapers from nearby Trinidad. Bello translated them for the governor general: Venezuela was no longer subject to Ferdinand VII but to Napoleon's puppet brother. Governor Casas concealed the news from the people for a few days, but two French officers rode up from La Guayra, the port, to inform him of his new obligations.

When the *audiencia* met with other notables to swear allegiance, he collapsed. People swarmed into the plaza about

the palace. "Down with the tyrant Napoleon! Long live Ferdinand!" They rushed to say Mass for the deposed king. They
poured out their jewels and money to aid the Spanish cause,
and they demanded a self-governing junta. If Venezuela was
to be saved for the Crown, only the Creoles could save it.

The Negroes, the Indians, the mestizos and mulattoes, the
intrepid, hard-riding *vaqueros* of the llanos scarcely knew
or cared about these world-shaking events. (Not until 1808,
when a newspaper, the *Gaceta de Caracas,* was first published
—it so happened, on the printing press that Miranda had
brought with him on his ill-fated 1806 expedition—did news
reach the interior easily.)

The Creoles grew more demanding. One group, insisting on
an independent junta but with allegiance to Ferdinand, was
badly mistreated by the governor. Most were exiled or jailed.
The Bolívar brothers escaped, for they had resolutely refused
to sign such a namby-pamby petition. They wanted full independence without strings. The between-worlds people were
the ones hurt.

The Bolívars and the radicals gained additional immunity
in 1809, when the Cádiz junta sent over a new captain general, Vicente Amparán, and militia head Colonel Fernando
del Toro. Both had been friends of Simón in Europe; besides,
del Toro was a relative of his dead wife. Their views were
liberal. Bolívar was made a militia lieutenant of the White
Battalion of Aragua.

But official tolerance for Bolívar mostly vanished when, in
March, 1810, once more he toasted the Independence of Venezuela. He was not molested, but his friends and fellow thinkers
were rounded up and jailed.

Bolívar and his friends began promoting a real conspiracy
and collecting arms on his estate. They planned to assassinate
or seize the governor and force him to set up an independent
junta.

News came April 13, 1810, that the French had taken Cádiz,
that the junta had been disbanded and a regency set up. It

stirred everybody. Clearly now, some argued, Venezuela belonged neither to France nor Spain.

Five days later, the Bolívar conspiracy, led by the Chilean
priest José de Madariaga (Bolívar was outside the city), went
into action. They obliged the mayor to call a session of the
Caracas *cabildo* the following day, Holy Thursday, one of the
most sacred religious holidays. The governor was called in.
He was instructed to hand over his authority to a junta.

"We will consider it after Mass," he said piously, knowing
there would be a guard of honor in the Church.

He also called out troops.

One of the conspirators slipped into the church, put a knife
at the governor's ribs, and forced him out through the guards
and back to the *cabildo*. By now, a vast crowd had gathered
in the plaza to listen to fiery Independence speeches. They
edged the governor back inside.

He was deposed, arrested then and there, and, with other
Spanish offenders, taken to La Guayra and put upon a ship
for Spain.

A twenty-three-man junta was named, "that glorious day of
April 19!" It held for full national autonomy but avoided the
word "republic" and still swore allegiance to Ferdinand.

The following night, Bolívar and his brother Juan rode
into town with Bello and presented themselves to the junta.
Juan was sent as a diplomatic agent to the United States.
Simón was made a colonel forthwith and appointed a diplomatic emissary to London. He took with him Bello and a
young poet, Luís López Méndez.

iv

Bolívar had been warned that Miranda must be viewed as
having rebelled against the king, but if he could in any way
promote the success of the mission in London he should not
be "slighted." The emissary was expected, rather, to cooperate
with the Spanish ambassador in London, for the English, sup-

porting the deposed Spanish monarch and the newly formed
regency and striving now to hold the Spanish Empire together
in his name, had become antagonistic to Miranda. He still
had some entree to high officials, but they were intercepting
his correspondence, warning him to desist from propaganda,
and even threatening him with deportation—a complicated
policy of duplicity with which Downing Street was familiar.

The Spanish ambassador was not at all friendly to Bolívar;
indeed, he protested against the impropriety of the British
foreign officer receiving a diplomatic emissary from a colony.

It was not surprising, therefore, that Miranda and Bolívar
became inseparable. This, too, became known to the Spanish
ambassador; his government had had spies dogging Miranda
for a quarter of a century.

"You know," Bolívar told him, half facetiously, "I'm supposed to be on the Spanish diplomatic staff, and the Spaniards
have a thirty-thousand-dollar reward on your head."

"Not enough to pay my debts," retorted Miranda, but he
added, "That cursed Spanish junta and now the regency, and
this country—vacillating and disgusting."

Actually one of Bolívar's chief reasons for coming to England—he later told his friend and aide, O'Leary—was to induce
Miranda, whom the young Venezuelan considered "a great
military genius," to return with him "to aid the cause of
America."

In London, his good opinion of Miranda was reinforced.
He listened attentively to Miranda's ideas and those of the
secret Lodge who surrounded him. He was impressed by
Miranda's great vision, his continent wide projects, his strange
dream of recreating the Inca empire. "He took the impression-
able Bolívar to the top of a high mountain and showed him
the promised land."

The British officials received Bolívar properly if not enthu-
siastically. He got no recognition, no money, no trade treaty,
no military aid, though an overage gunboat was put at the
disposal of the Caracas authorities.

Apparently neglecting his duties, actually to gain sentiment for his cause in a most agreeable way, Bolívar played around in British high society, which was his true métier. His slender figure, romantic animated olive features, fine horsemanship, and his impeccable ballroom manners made him a favorite and also a source of news; his doings were faithfully recorded in the British press, but he won nothing more from the government and prepared to leave with Miranda.

The British government refused to let Miranda go. Bolívar left Bello and López behind in Miranda's quarters to help push the matter and sailed on September 19 on the British brig *Sapphire*—the only way to get through the French-Spanish blockade.

Miranda planned to follow two weeks later. The Spanish ambassador moved heaven and earth to prevent this, but Turnbull and half a dozen leading merchants of the country brought such pressure to bear that the Venezuelan was allowed to embark with his secretary, Thomas Molini, on the sloop of war *Avon* on October 10.

v

Bolívar's report to the junta in Caracas was received coldly. It had wanted tangible aid from England, but all he was bringing back was Miranda, whose very name filled many ruling Creoles with the fear that this hoof and horns revolutionist would break apart their little world of wealth and power.

Not that the regime did not need a competent leader. Just prior to Bolívar's return, the patriot force of 4,000 men, armed mostly with old-fashioned pikes, had been badly routed at Coro. The troops had been in charge of Marqués del Toro, who had ridden through the llanos to meet the enemy "with a comic-opera bodyguard" and a "whole mule train laden with his big wardrobe trunks." Bolívar's own brother, who had returned from the United States, was killed. Presently a serious counterrevolutionary plot was discovered among the troops in the capital. Could Miranda save the day?

Making the best of the inevitable, the junta prepared to greet the returning hero with a proclamation of welcome. At the same time they rebuffed Bolívar, and he retired to his country estate, bitter and rebellious, to brood darkly.

He saw plenty of trouble ahead. The talk of the convention favored the adoption of a constitution that would copy that of the United States, and this Bolívar saw clearly would be inapplicable to Venezuelan realities—a real disaster. But he put aside his pet and was waiting at the landing for the *Avon* and Miranda.

That hero came riding into port on December 11, arrayed in his old 1793 French general's uniform with appliquéd gold leaves, a curved saber, spurs on his high boots. His hair, white now, was powdered, and he wore a single gold earring. A few hours later, he entered Caracas on a white charger. He was given an enthusiastic reception, but far from what he expected; there was marked coolness on the part of some officials. What most upset him were the troops, a small, defeated, ragged band, mostly barefoot, lacking all order and discipline.

Curiously, the junta ordered all documents relating to Miranda's past revolutionary activities against the Crown destroyed and made him head of the army with the rank of lieutenant general.

Miranda was in a savage mood when he went to a banquet tendered him by Bolívar and chaffed his host for being a colonel without knowledge or experience.

Bolívar replied stiffly he would be quite willing to serve in the ranks.

Miranda set to work at once to get recruits and to drill them. He was a relentless dawn-to-dark taskmaster, often eating his breakfast on the maneuvering grounds. Finally he ordered a dress parade. Off to one side, an officer in uniform was performing horsemanship stunts. Cheers went up. Mi-

randa, choleric over such lack of discipline, ordered the horseman brought into his presence. It was Bolívar. Miranda
dressed him down harshly and demoted him. Bolívar was too
angry to reply.

But they stood together on the issue of Independence, and
both came into conflict with the new national congress, which
convened March 2, 1811, to which both had been elected deputies along with some forty others. It convened in the old cap-
tain-general's palace, with a military parade, a *Te Deum* by
the archbishop, and sumptuous ceremonies. It still swore allegiance to King Ferdinand.

Bolívar and Miranda soon began using the Patriotic Society,
ostensibly a club organized to promote industry and commerce
but actually a revolutionary group, to promote their own Independence ideas.

In a fervent public speech to the organization, Miranda
denounced congressional shilly-shallying. Why were they still
inquiring what Spain wanted? Why did they not inquire what
the Venezuelan people wanted? "Let Spain keep her slaves
and sell them to Bonaparte. . . . We mean to be free. . . .
Let us fearlessly lay the foundations of South American Independence. . . ."

As in Greece, reported the writer Miguel Luís Amunátegui
in his life of Bello, Miranda's "eloquence was not inferior to
that of the great Pericles . . . and moved the multitude . . .
as a tempest heaves the billows of the main."

Two more speeches by Miranda, and great demonstrations,
inspired the congress to adopt the Act of Venezuelan Independence on July 5, 1811.

With Independence, the upsurge of Venezuela was amazing.
Immigrants rushed in from all the world. Industry and agriculture revived. Roads were repaired, bridges built, new broad
promenades were laid out in Caracas; the city was cleaned up
and beautified. The arts and sciences were vigorously promoted. Schools and special academies were open throughout
the country. New newspapers were started. Books were printed.

As one English eyewitness reported, within less than a year the revolution "had assumed a grand, brilliant, and imposing aspect. People everywhere discussed their rights with the same familiarity they used to discuss about God and the king." The new youths eagerly imbibed education and "gave hopeful promise of forming the future pillars of the state."

vi

What broke the patriot cause was the terrible earthquake of Holy Thursday, 1812, which wrecked much of Caracas, killed ten thousand people (a fourth of the population), and filled the remainder with superstitious fears that sent them shrieking hysterically to the few churches left standing.

Bolívar and a few friends worked day and night, helping extricate the wounded, getting relief funds and food, cleaning up the debris. The disaster had occurred on the anniversary of Independence, and the clergy were out in force, shouting to the multitude, "Sodom and Gomorrah! On your knees, sinners, you have insulted the majesty of our virtuous king! God's arm has fallen on your heads in punishment."

Yet much of the death toll was due to there having been so many people crowded in the churches on this holy day!

Bolívar, in a torn, dirty shirt, his sweaty face grimy, came upon a monk in the great market shouting against the government and frightening the people. He chased him off, using restraint not to run him through with his sword. Jumping on a broken column, he cried out to the hysterical mob, "Nature has joined forces with tyranny! Forward! We shall force even nature to obey us!" To the pious, such words were blasphemy.

The whole country became a religious revivalist encampment. Great hordes of people gave themselves over to singing, wailing pilgrimages and to mass orgies of hysterical religious indecencies. With this came a wave of reaction against the revolution, a blind, ignorant, overwhelming tide.

The few towns still held by the Spaniards had not been hit

by the quake—a further sign of God's intentions. Led by the Spanish naval captain from Coro, Domingo Monteverde, the royalists pushed rapidly through the stricken towns. Valencia fell.

The situation was desperate, and Miranda was made general in chief with absolute power to take any necessary steps. All national funds were placed at his disposal to use as he saw fit. The constitution and laws were rescinded, and the only law he was obliged to consult "was the supreme law of the salvation of the fatherland."

Whipping together what forces were available, some 3,000 men (Bolívar rounded up 1,000 more), Miranda set forth on May 1, 1812, to occupy Valencia again. He assigned Bolívar, who had regained his commission, to hold Puerto Cabello and Fort Felipe, which served as a prison for several hundred Spanish officers and was also the chief arsenal, with all reserves of guns and munitions. Miranda considered it the very key to his strategy, able to outflank any enemy advancing on the capital.

But Bolívar, deprived of action at the moving front, took it as a deliberate slap in the face and went with bad grace, displaying "resentment and offended dignity."

He put a trusted officer in charge of the San Felipe citadel and took up lodgings in the city hall, where he spent his time with books and music and pretty girls he picked up on the plaza.

Miranda won a small victory over the Spaniards, but when he was within twelve miles of Valencia his scouting force of 500 men deserted to the royalists, and he retired to Maracay, west of Lake Valencia. Here he imposed the most Draconian regulations, drilling his troops unmercifully. Cardplaying and drinking were banned; theft was punishable by death.

On May 17, his powers were enlarged to allow him to make appointments of all military and civilian officials in the country, giving him control over foreign relations. The great powers invested in him, he told the country, would be used solely to promote "the liberty and independence of my native land." He promised never to lay *down* the sword or abandon his position until he had "avenged the injuries of our enemies." Thereupon he would "again become a simple citizen."

He rounded up Spaniards and thrust the archbishop, Colley Pratt, still fulminating about God's wrath as shown by the earthquake, into Guayra prison. At the same time he offered freedom to all slaves who enlisted and a grant of land after three campaigns.

He carried on an extensive correspondence with friends and governments throughout the world. He was still bemused by the idea that a free Venezuela could not survive without foreign aid and he failed to show any military initiative.

Though now clearly superior in men and weapons, having 5,000 troops and much artillery, when he learned that Monteverde, who had few weapons and no artillery, was preparing to advance on Maracay, Miranda withdrew to Victoria, a key strong point for the defense of the capital.

Monteverde seized San Mateo and launched an attack. He was beaten back with great loss of men and matériel; his forces began to melt away. Still Miranda did not act.

Disaster struck in Puerto Cabello. On the hot afternoon of June 30, gunfire sounded from the fort. Bolívar hurried toward it. His officers, he realized, even before getting there, had turned traitors and had freed the prisoners. Both were cutting down those who opposed them.

Bolívar raced back to town and rallied a few town troops, but all the guns and ammunition were in the citadel. He hurried 200 mounted men to try to recover it. Only seven came back.

On July 5, Miranda received an urgent message dated July 1 from Bolívar. "General: An officer unworthy of the name of Venezuelan has taken the fort of San Felipe with the help of the prisoners and is bombarding the town like a loco. If your

Excellency does not attack at once, the place is lost. I will hold it with all my strength till you come."

Miranda folded the note and said to his aide, "Struck to the heart."

Bolívar's next message, half incoherent, came from Caracas. "I have done my duty. If a single man had remained capable of standing by me in a fight . . . I would have fought. It is not my fault they all abandoned me. I wish I had not saved my own life but had buried it in the ruins of a city which would then have stood as the last symbol of glory and freedom. . . . Since I have lost the last and best fort in the country, how could I help losing my own mind too?"

In Puerto Cabello, the Spaniards obtained 40,000 pounds of powder, lead in abundance, and 3,000 muskets and now menaced Miranda's flank.

Stories about the Puerto Cabello debacle differed greatly. Some believed it was a deliberate plot—perhaps like that of Carrera later at Rancagua, Chile—to destroy Miranda so Bolívar himself could gain greater glory. In any case, Bolívar had shown criminal negligence.

Whatever the truth, the blow broke Miranda's spirit, and it spread panic everywhere. Three fourths of the country was back in Spanish hands, and the forces pushing in from all sides soon threatened the capital. Miranda's forces began deserting in great numbers. Negro slave uprisings occurred all over the country. The Creoles, dreadfully alarmed, demanded that Miranda make peace with Monteverde.

He called a joint meeting of his officers, cabinet, and notables. The most insistent on surrender was Marqués Francisco de Casa León y Iturbe, Miranda's finance minister. He was sent to discuss surrender terms. The unpleasant feature of the arrangement was the marqués' promise he would see that Miranda received enough to be able to live abroad. Two days later the marqués went over to the royalist side, for which he was well rewarded.

It was agreed that the patriot troops would surrender their

arms and that the royalists would respect lives and property of all under arms and all government officials. The pact was ratified July 25.

vii

Miranda's surrender seemed a mystery to everybody. The United States emissary, Alexander Scott, called it "a shameful and treacherous capitulation." Whether Miranda was an "agent of the British government," or whether he had merely "a base and cowardly heart," the North American St. Peter could not decide. In any case, he concluded, Miranda was "a brutal and capricious tyrant . . . destitute of courage, honor, and abilities." Later he wrote about "sequestration, imprisonment, and cruelty almost unexampled."

Unknown to his associates, Miranda made arrangements to slip out of the country. He sent a trusted aide to Caracas to send all his papers, books, and silver plate to La Guayra and had the commandant there hold a vessel for him. He also sent the 22,000 pesos via the English merchant with whom he had dealings, George Robertson (10,000 before the signing of the armistice, 12,000 afterwards). His baggage, including several trunks with silver plate (and effects belonging to Bolívar), were all sent in Robertson's name.

Whatever the truth in the ugly allegations, Miranda believed it folly to risk a decisive engagement at this time. He was discouraged by the treachery at Puerto Cabello, by treachery in his own camp, and by desertions from the ranks. The Creoles were plotting against him. The tide of reaction seemed to grow, while the spirit for Independence among the people seemed to be ebbing away.

His fellow revolutionist, emissary to Washington Pedro Gaul, later stated that during the surrender negotiations Miranda told him, "Let us look toward New Granada where I count upon Nariño, who is my friend. With the resources we can . . . obtain there and with the officers and munitions

we can take from Venezuela, we shall again regain Caracas.
. . . It is necessary to allow Venezuela to recover from the
earthquake and the royalist depredations."

As he pointed out to the country, the republic, thanks to
perfidy, fanaticism, and fraud, now held little more than
Caracas and its port. His diplomatic efforts had failed; there
was no hope of foreign aid.

On July 26, he slipped out of Victoria to Caracas. An officer
tried to kill him. Miranda shut himself up in his house alone.
A few days later, July 30, he left for La Guayra to leave the
country.

The port was already a madhouse: officers, civilians, women,
children, horses milling about, racing up and down the beach
trying to get aboard any craft. It had become every man for
himself.

He did not see Bolívar who was there also; in fact, for three
weeks, since his surrender of Puerto Cabello, he had been
racing back and forth between Caracas and the port, evidently
trying to get out of the country.

By chance, the *Sapphire*, on which Bolívar had returned
two years before, was in the harbor. Securing permission to
leave on it, Miranda had his money and baggage sent aboard,
also Bolívar's trunks. That afternoon the commandant of La
Guayra, Manuel María de las Casas, beholden to Miranda for
everything, demanded 4,000 of the 22,000 pesos. Miranda said
there were so many people to be taken care of, he could hand
over only 800.

The wind died down, he could not sail until ten the next
morning, and he put up at the commandant's house.

While he was sleeping, two rooms away, eight officers, including the commandant, Bolívar, and the civilian governor
Miguel Peña, plotted to seize him. Bolívar—according to one
of those present—insisted that Miranda should be killed as a
traitor and had to be restrained then and later, when they
sneaked into his room. Years later Bolívar's aide, Daniel
O'Leary, said that his superior had "invariably" told him "he

had wished to shoot Miranda as a traitor but was withheld by others."

While Bolívar's aide, Colonel Carlos Soublette (whose sister Isabel later allegedly became Bolívar's mistress), held the lamp over the bed, the hero of Puerto Cabello yanked the covers off the sleeping Miranda and bitterly upbraided his chief. Undoubtedly he was eaten by his own shameful failure, and so now found it shameful that Miranda should run away. Bolívar wrapped himself in sentiments of glory, freedom, and honor and turned on all the verbal spigots of hate against the fallen hero.

Miranda was taken to the San Carlos prison to be turned over to Monteverde. The prison warden then ran up the Spanish flag. In this utterly disgraceful manner, the Reconquista came to Venezuela, as presently it was to come to Chile.

Robertson's firm in Curacao kept the cash, alleging it was for payment of debts incurred by "the dictator."

The silver plate was seized by the Curaçao authorities, but several trunks were found empty on arrival.

Miranda's papers were sent to London, where they were appropriated as personal property by Lord Bathurst of the British War Office. From time to time the Bathurst family permitted scholars to examine them.

Miranda ended up in the military prison at Cádiz where, in 1816, he died in the hospital. Asked by a fellow prisoner if his chains were not heavy, he replied, "Not so heavy as the ones they put on me that night in La Guayra."

Several of Bolívar's associates in the betrayal of Miranda escaped. Others were imprisoned. Bolívar hid out in Caracas in the home of Marqués de Casa León, until safe-conduct could be arranged. He wrote from his hide-out to a mistress (name unknown), sending her money. "In haste. I am not able to see you again. Honor and fatherland call me."

Bolívar, thanks to Marqués de Casa León's intervention, was personally handed a passport by Monteverde in the palace, on August 26, in gratitude for his services in delivering Miranda into Spanish hands. Bolívar said, somewhat lamely, that he did it "for his country" because Miranda was a "traitor."

Bolívar was to return four times with armed expeditions and great proclamations, was finally to win control, was to free half the continent, and was to win the glory he coveted so strongly. In the end, he was to suffer a disgrace as bitter as that of Miranda.

8

The Battle for Gran Colombia

/\/\/\ Monteverde, tearing up the armistice provisions and
two proclamations he had issued, instituted a reign of terror
with frightful reprisals for everyone connected with the Independence movement. The victims were herded into prisons
and murdered, without regard for age or sex. Mass shootings
followed. The shouts of liberty were displaced by the groans
of slavery. In December he rounded up some fifteen hundred
patriots who had participated in "the criminal" act of setting
up the 1810 junta.

"Monteverde is a ravening wolf," said one, and eyewitness
José F. Heredia wrote, "A group of despicable mulattoes, who
had taken part in the rebellion . . . were made *prendedores.*"
They brought "shame upon the good Spaniards before whose
eyes countless horrors were being perpetrated in the name of
the most generous nation and the greatest king in the world."

By then Bolívar was safely on his way, but the 12,000 pesos
he took with him were confiscated when he landed in Curaçao.
So were his properties in Venezuela. Utterly penniless, he was
forced to eat the bread of charity. He was thirty years old.

Gradually, as he rode like a madman up and down the rocky
shore of the island, new dreams took hold of him.

He wrote out a magniloquent, half-idiotic and contradictory

manifesto. It began with a flashy prologue. "I am a son of unhappy Caracas . . . I have come here following the flag of Independence which waves so gloriously over this country." (Curaçao was a British possession!)

He denounced Miranda as despotic and arbitrary and "obsessed by ambition and violent passions, . . . unwilling to sacrifice his own feelings to the liberty of his country. . . .

"Instead of leaders, we had philosophers; instead of soldiers, sophists; instead of laws, philanthropy; instead of tactics, dialectics."

There had been too much "humanitarian leniency . . . the hallmark of too tolerant governments. . . . It was not the Spanish soldiery who thrust us back," Bolívar set forth, "but our own party squabbling." The strife of politics cannot be tolerated during such grave a crisis, he concluded. "We must inspire terror" and "not concern ourselves about laws and constitutions until freedom and well-being have been restored." This was exactly the situation under Miranda.

Three months later, Bolívar sold the gold medal on which he had had his portrait painted during society revels in London and used the money to take passage to Cartagena.

The foothold of liberty then was small. All the south of New Granada, namely Ecuador (which really belonged to Peru), had fallen to the Reconquista when patriot General Arredonda's forces had run away in one of the Andean snow passes, believing the creaking of ice in the morning sun to be the artillery of the advancing royalists.

New Granada was now in confusion, with three Independence governments wrangling with each other: Cartagena, Bogotá (Sante Fé), and Tunja, all menaced by royalists and Spaniards. Cartagena had declared itself "independent of every nation on earth." How long it would remain so was doubtful.

When Bolívar reached there it was already full of hundreds of Venezuelan refugees, who strained the meager resources. The young man charmed President Torices, who had his strange manifesto—to which had been added what seemed a mad scheme of recovering Venezuela—printed and distributed and gave him a commission as colonel in the New Granadan army under Commandant Pedro Labatut, a Frenchman. Since the latter had a force in the field under Colonel Castillo, and he himself was preparing to attack Santa Marta, he denied Bolívar permission to leave on an expedition of his own.

The Venezuelan disobeyed the command and got together a motley force of 200 Indians, mestizos, and Negroes in the adjacent bamboo-hut village of Barranca on the Magdalena River. Yet he had said in his manifesto, "Only trained armies can cope with the myriad setbacks of a campaign."

"I sought out the handsomest mulattoes," Bolívar wrote later. "I wanted them to cut a figure. Most of them owned nothing but their courage."

On Christmas day, 1812—one writer says December 22—he set out up the river at night in *bongos,* tree-hollowed boats propelled by long bamboo poles, and his naked river men surprised the Spaniards in Tenerifa, where the patriots won a few arms and where 300 more men enlisted, plus "twenty young men of good family."

They moved on up the river. They took Mompós; they took El Banco, Tamclamcque, and Puerto Real, and by January 8 they swarmed into Ocaña, a considerable town. Bolívar's fame spread all over the land; on the tongues of rumor, he already had a big army.

Commandant Labatut ordered him back to Cartagena to face a court-martial for insubordination. Bolívar went over his head to President Torices, who gave him permission to march on. He also called on Bogotá for backing.

He headed east—500 strong, now—across twelve miles of arid plain seamed by huge ravines, then through jungles, and with mules, guns, and supplies started up the Andes, finally reaching the high cold pass. Here he could look down on Venezuela. Below him was the last city of Colombia, Cúcuta, named after the local Indians (later to become an important oil center) on the large Táchira River. It was guarded by a strong Spanish force, to which were added four units who retreated as he advanced.

Bolívar swirled down on them February 28, in a surprise attack. After four hours of savage fighting the Spaniards abandoned their artillery and supplies and fled across the savanna. Standing on a hill above the cemetery, Bolívar read another flamboyant manifesto to his men and the curious townspeople.

Soon Castillo's forces moved up and ordered Bolívar and his men to accept his command. While they quibbled, Bolívar sent fast messengers to Cartagena, Tunja, and Bogotá, asking for support. The executives of all three places—Nariño was head of the Tunja government—backed him, but Castillo had the ear of the Bogotá congress. "Don't sacrifice the armed forces of the country to the extravagant ambitions of a madman," Castillo wrote them. Bolívar was a foreigner, who wanted to use needed resources of men and arms for "a crazy expedition into Venezuela." The Congress squabbled.

President Torices of Cartagena cut through the Gordian knot by making Bolívar a New Granadan citizen and a general of the army.

The new general moved across the river to Táchira, where he paid his soldiers and proclaimed, "Your liberating arms have reached Venezuela. The Spanish legions will vanish . . . as night yields to day. All America wants its liberty and salvation at your hands."

Meanwhile, in his rear, the Spaniards advanced with a powerful force on Cartagena, and the president frantically ordered Bolívar to bring back his troops.

He was in no mood to obey. "Forward!" was his cry. When one of his officers, the New Granadan Francisco de Paula Santander, a Creole of Cúcuta, refused to proceed, Bolívar told him bluntly, "Unless you march at once, one of two things will happen—either you will shoot me or, what is far more likely, I will shoot you."

Santander marched and in due time became one of the leaders of the revolution and later on two times president of

Colombia. (He remained closely associated with Bolívar for fifteen years—in admiring friendship, rivalry, hostility—in the end betrayed him.)

Bolívar led his force down the mountains and hills through small villages and towns which acclaimed him madly and provided him with recruits and arms. His force began now to look like an army—an army following a strange Don Quixote who knew nothing whatever about the science of war. But that has been true of a large share of the successful military leaders of history.

ii

From the beginning, Monteverde had been plagued by conspiracies, assassinations, uprisings, guerrilla warfare, "banditry." He lost all of eastern Cumaná province to Santiago Mariño, who invaded from nearby British islands. Other revolts were led by the touchy mulatto Manuel Carlos Piar, and by José Francisco Bermúdez and his brother. Juan Bautista Arismendi took over Margarita Island.

Ferocious atrocities were committed by both sides. Brutality bred brutality. The Spaniards did not hesitate to cut off ears, noses, tongues, penises; sometimes everybody in whole villages was mutilated. One Spanish general kept a trunkful of ears which he handed out to his men to wear on their hats. Pregnant women were slit up the belly. Men with flayed feet were lashed to walk over glass. Prisoners were branded with numbers. After the battle of Gameza in New Granada, Spanish general Barreiro had his prisoners tied back to back so as to be able to run a lance through them two at a time.

The insurgent leaders, many of them unlettered men, according to the Spaniard Torrente, were mostly "ferocious anthropophagi"—cannibals. In one large band, officer rank was determined by the number of human heads—fifty decapitations won a captaincy.

Castillo, for the moment serving with Bolívar, almost went

back to Colombia when the leaders of one band, led by Ricardo
Briceño, sent him the bloody heads of two Spaniards and a
letter, written in blood, offering up to fifty pesos a head. However, Briceño, rushing forward without orders, was captured
and executed along with all his officers and most of his 250
men. It evoked a bloodthirsty reprisal proclamation from
Bolívar.

One Spanish general, deserting to Bolívar's side, said, "I
intend to kill every Spaniard, then I shall kill myself so there
won't be a cursed Spaniard left in the world."

Soon Mariño's forces began advancing toward Caracas.
Much of the rest of the north was seized by an Italian adventurer named Bianchi. Other outlaw bands moved up from
the Orinoco. Monteverde had to draw back toward the capital,
finally ducked into Puerto Cabello. The forces in the capital
began melting away. In one day the last 1,300 were reduced
to 200 men.

Bolívar became concerned lest the city fall before his men
could "share the glory," but told the Cartagena authorities,
"We are marching like lightning." The alarmed Caracas authorities saw no hope and asked for assurances of generous
treatment from Bolívar if they surrendered. Once more turncoat Marqués de Casa León y Iturbe sallied forth to arrange
terms.

He found Bolívar most receptive. "My beloved friend!"
Bolívar told him, "I would sooner be at peace with you than
with the whole Spanish nation, for I love you more than peace.
. . . I owe you everything you can ask." The leader then proclaimed, "I shall prove that the chivalrous Americans know
how to pardon those they have conquered and to show the
greatest moderation toward an enemy who has outraged the
rights of man and trampled his sacred duty underfoot."

This was in August. Eight months after Bolívar had set forth
with a handful of ragamuffins, he had conquered the great
empire of Venezuela. And he was still the chivalrous gentleman! "The gentleman," they called him, whatever he did,
until he died.

He rode into Caracas under triumphal floral arches and wept. Twelve girls pulled him from his horse and put him in a Roman chariot which he drove the rest of the way to the plaza. It is not recorded that he bared his chest in a Roman toga. But he was Caesar now, though more appropriate would have been the armor of Don Quixote. Byron had not yet written his *Don Juan*.

While in Caracas, Monteverde had been able to pry out only 5,000 pesos for his final campaign. Bolívar slapped on a forced levy of 120,000 pesos. Liberty, it was quickly evident, did not come cheaply.

iii

Monteverde, in Puerto Cabello, refused to recognize the surrender and repulsed all attacks. A prolonged siege was instituted.

In Cumaná, Mariño, who had already proclaimed his own independence with the title of Dictator and Generalísimo of the East, rejected a decoration from Bolívar's new "Order of Liberty." The country and also the revolutionary forces were still badly divided.

The vast number of war prisoners was a serious problem. Seven times Bolívar tried to get Monteverde to arrange a prisoner exchange. Military Governor Arismendi in La Guayra found them difficult to manage. Bolívar sent him word. "You have too few men and too many prisoners. I therefore command you to kill all prisoners now in the fortress and in the hospitals."

Eight hundred and seventy were slaughtered—many were prominent Spaniards—one of the worst massacres in the history of the Americas.

Subsequently Bolívar tried to justify the black deed by saying it was to prevent a repetition of the Puerto Cabello disaster. He was not going to "sacrifice" his country and his "honor" a second time. "People who call me cruel misunderstand me."

In Caracas a toast was made at a banquet by Bolívar's faithful aide and uncle-in-law, General José Félix Ribas, that each guest kill a prisoner. Thirty-five heads were displayed in the plaza in front of the cathedral.

Bolívar's biggest headache came to be not Monteverde, bottled up in Puerto Cabello, but a cattle dealer on the Orinoco, Tomás Boves, who rallied the hard-riding *llaneros*. Those free-wheeling outlaws of the plains spent their lives in the saddle, "lived on beef, wild honey, and milk," and adored fighting more passionately than love. Boves was a leader they could understand: squat, massive, low-browed, with a vulture face and deep gray eyes. Vindictive, cruel, he liked to kill. His best record, he boasted, was to have murdered more than 300 in one day. His lieutenant, General Tomás Morales, a ferocious Canary Islander—and no people were more savage—loved arson and murder. Any village he captured went up in flames.

Boves was beaten back a number of times but gathered fresh recruits and slogged ahead till he had 3,000 men and threatened the capital. Bolívar led the defense in lovely Aragua Valley—where he had spent his nine-month honeymoon of delight—and won.

It was a Pyrrhic victory, for it was summer fever time, and his men deserted in droves. The next battle—for San Carlos—was lost. Boves then advanced on Valencia, swearing he would kill Bolívar by strangling him with his own hands. The place surrendered after getting the promise of respect for lives and property. Boves held a reconciliation ball, then slaughtered all the finely dressed guests; all but the musicians. "I love music," he commented.

Bolívar's forces were smashed again, and he flew to Caracas, where he issued a proclamation that everybody—men, women, and children—had to emigrate, under pain of death. The city's incredible confusion and terror as the outlaw *llaneros* approached was described by Major George Finter. "The ringing of bells; the fugitives who escaped the slaughter of the preceding day, covered with dust, galloping through the streets, soldiers running from house to house, with drawn swords to see that the order was obeyed. The old and young, the lame and the blind, men and women, were running up and down in confusion."

Many took refuge in the churches and convents; mothers with clinging children implored those with mules to carry them, but danger destroyed all pity.

"The whole cavalcade moved forward, some on mules, their wives and daughters behind them; others galloping forward to save themselves." Some 30,000 swarmed out of the city in wild disorder, most without clothing or food, heading for Barcelona on the northeast coast. They made the march of Bolívar's troops slow and difficult.

"These ill-fated immigrants had to traverse a desert country of more than three hundred miles, over steep, rugged mountains and unfordable rivers, without any shelter from the inclemency of the weather . . . no place they could derive subsistence, except from the precarious food supplied by the trees of the forests or the wild animals. . . . Their shoes and dresses were . . . torn to pieces . . . feet streaming with blood." Women abandoned or killed their children. Those who fell behind were killed by the pursuing *llaneros* or eaten by jaguars. It was supposed that upwards of six thousand souls perished in this migration.

The disaster brought Mariño and Bolívar together in a last-minute, uneasy alliance.

A council of war was held. It was decided to send most of the forces to the coast islands. Uncle-in-law Ribas was at this council, wearing his usual red Phrygian liberty cap. His head and the cap were presently to be exhibited in an iron cage on the road to La Guayra.

Bandit Bianchi was also at the meeting. He raided the church treasury and made off with all the gold. When caught, he claimed that it was money owed him. He was allowed to keep a third of it.

The country was lost once more, and Mariño, Bianchi,

Bolívar, and others abandoned their men and the refugees
and traveled together on a small sailing vessel to Cartagena.

By this time Napoleon's regime in Spain had crumpled.
Ferdinand was back on the throne, but a mere British puppet.
The British were now helping him get back his New World
empire, and the sky darkened for the cause of Independence.

iv

Despite defeat, Bolívar's prestige was still great, and he was
put in charge of all the Cartagena forces. He managed also
to unite under his command the troops of Bogotá, where he
soon marched.

But Castillo was once more inciting the people and the press
against him. He flung at him, time and again, the shooting of
the La Guayra prisoners and issued a pamphlet, accusing him
of sacrificing thousands of Granadans solely to save his own
property in Venezuela, that he had since fled into exile with
the notorious bandit Bianchi. Bolívar turned the cheek by
proposing that Castillo be made a brigadier general.

By then the Spaniards were approaching Cartagena in force.
When they finally besieged the city, the defenders held out
bravely for 106 days. But it was not Bolívar who shared that
glorious defense. Well before that he had resigned his command, fled to Curaçao, then on to Jamaica.

For the moment he was broken in body and mind. One
observer described him. "This man is in the flower of his
youth but seems to have nothing left but his eyes. The flame
has burned the oil to the last drop."

A wealthy Jamaican, Maxwell Hyslop, believing in his cause,
gave him a house to live in. Gradually his living room and
veranda were filled up with maps and books. News of the
troubled world he had left came only at rare intervals.

Reading avidly, thinking, brooding, gradually he fitted the
Venezuelan struggle into the frame of history and world affairs
—and above all into the frame of South America and the New

World. In spite of British support of Ferdinand and the Spanish Empire, he saw imperial England as the inevitable and deadly rival of Spain, especially now that the threat of Napoleon was no more. The English lust for trade, dominion, and power demanded either the conquest or the freeing of Latin America.

Just as Miranda had done, he now proposed to the British—in what must ever be considered moral blindness—that they seize Panama and Nicaragua as recompense for aiding the Independence movements with money and arms. "Both the balance of world power and England's interests demand the salvation of America—orphaned by British policy, French ambition, and Spanish stupidity." Great Britain, if she would now act boldly, could have almost the "sole enjoyment" of the wealth of America. How can Europe, he asked a bit querulously, "permit the old snake to void its poison on the most beautiful part of the world"?

Belatedly he was arriving at many of Miranda's long-held views about foreign aid, views mostly futile and mistaken, but this has been the delusion of liberators and so-called statesmen of Latin America from that day to this. Face to face with the heartbreaking obstacles and suffering that any struggle for true independence inevitably entails, few even to this day have learned that their countries can be "saved" only by their own people, not by any outside government, however powerful.

Here, meditating in exile, Bolívar looked over the home scene ruefully—and his impressions are still applicable. "Our peoples have been kept in a state of childhood for three hundred years. . . . They have been forbidden to cultivate European crops, to manufacture goods, have been forced to do nothing but grow coffee, sugar, indigo, cotton, to keep herds on the savannas, and to mine the earth for gold—for the masters of the country."

The solution, he believed for the moment, lay not in creating one or two large countries but perhaps seventeen different ones. Big countries felt themselves obliged to expand their frontiers, even if they had less need. In modern parlance, all became imperialistic. Like Rome and Spain, however, he averred, they were bound to perish sooner or later. "Permanence is the essence of small republics." They should, however, be closely allied in congeries of states. The Caribbean countries should pivot on Panama; Venezuela and Colombia should be one country or closely federated; Brazil, an empire in itself, should remain a kingdom, otherwise such a vast area could not be governed. Peru, the most corrupt and difficult to liberate, should be broken up, but the independent republics should then be federated.

At first glance, the idea of a single South American nation was grandiose, and even seemed feasible since all had "the same race, the same language, the same customs. . . . Actually it is impossible, for their situations, interests, and characteristics are too diverse." And yet . . . and yet . . . "How splendid it would be if the Isthmus of Panama could be to us what the Isthmus of Corinth was to the Greeks! May heaven grant that we hold a great congress there one day to negotiate war and peace with the other three continents. Panama between the great oceans could become the center of trade; its canals could speed up communications between the continents. It may yet be that the capital of the world will be founded there."

Ten years later he would celebrate that congress, but the canal he dreamed of was never to be built by the New World nations as a communal effort and a symbol of peace, but as an instrument of the trade and power politics of a single non-Latin nation.

v

Bolívar's enemies did not forget him, even in his quiet retirement. One night an assassin, sent by the Caracas Spaniards, plunged a knife into his hammock—and killed a friend. Bolívar himself was elsewhere, enjoying himself in the hammock of his beautiful mistress.

The bread of charity grated on his proud nature, and he fretted for action. His dreams began crystallizing into definite plans. He sailed off to Haiti, the first Latin-American republic, to ask President Alexandre Pétion for help.

The black president must have been somewhat suspicious of this elegant white Creole dandy but did help him, on one condition: that Bolívar immediately abolish slavery.

The liberator was also aided by a wealthy exiled Venezuelan merchant and shipowner, young Manuel Brión, who had fanatical faith both in Bolívar and New World Independence.

They set forth on a brigantine and six small, ancient, high-pooped vessels not so different from those ships with which Columbus had originally discovered America.

The refugees who accompanied Bolívar that fateful day in 1816 were soon engaged in a petty pecking-order controversy, quarreling over rank and command, particularly Soublette, Mariño, and the touchy Jamaican mulatto, José Antonio Piar, a squabble still not resolved even after they landed on Margarita Island off the northeast coast.

Governor Arismendi at once handed over authority to Bolívar in a church ceremony. Bolívar seized up a gold-headed cane and proclaimed himself Supreme Ruler of Venezuela.

"Venezuelans! The third period of the Republic is dawning." His first edict was the liberation of all slaves. "Now and henceforth there is only one class of Venezuelan men. All are citizens!"

As soon as the small force got on the mainland, it split up. Piar and Mariño refused to serve under Bolívar and marched off with small groups in different directions.

Bolívar rallied 600 poorly armed men and headed for the capital. Into the teeth of the powerful enemy in his path he flung the ringing words, "An army with arms and every kind of ammunitions is on the march under my orders to set you free. I will destroy the tyrants and restore your rights, your country, and peace." His first official act would be to call a national congress.

He was defeated by General Morales, Boves' terrible Canary Island hangman. Once more Bolívar—this denouncer of Miranda—deserted his troops and fled.

The populace began shouting, "Down with Bolívar!" and he and Soublette (also a betrayer of Miranda) barely managed to row out to a brig, *India Libre,* lying in the harbor. Soublette, when an old man, said his memories of the event were clouded but tried to exculpate Bolívar, saying it was all complicated "by a passionate love affair, and we know that Anthony, in the very teeth of anger, wasted irrevocable moments with Cleopatra."

Bolívar was pronounced "dead' by the Spaniards. Other Venezuelans carried on the struggle in remote corners, and Piar (as did Santander) seized the opportunity to declare himself the true leader of Independence.

vi

Upstream along the Orinoco and Apure Rivers, far in the interior, General José Antonio Páez, a rough-riding *llanero,* not dissimilar to Boves but an Independence fighter, was striking hard. He won important victories at Mata de la Miel and Yagual. But in the northeast, royalist general Aldana seized Barcelona and shot 1,400 armed patriots and private citizens.

In Haiti, Pétion received Bolívar with marked coldness. It was mostly Brión who, during the next five months, helped him buy arms.

Once more, on New Year's Day, 1817, Bolívar landed on the coast, at Barcelona. That same month San Martín and O'Higgins started their heroic march over the Andes.

With 300 well-armed men, Bolívar set up a provisional government. His proclamation was ready, of course. He demanded a congress to which he could submit his resignation. "The fatherland is orphaned so long as the government remains in the hands of a soldier. . . . We shall soon liberate all Venezuela. Then we shall pass on people by people, state by state. . . . New Granada, then Quito, then Peru."

If he was aware that San Martín had also announced his intention of liberating Peru, he did not mention it. As he was lying in the reeds on the day of landing, he had cried out, "We shall climb up Potosí and plant the flag of freedom on the summit of the silver mountain!"

An officer had exclaimed, "My God! The Liberator has gone mad."

Perhaps. But eight years later, it would come to pass.

Bermúdez, Piar, and Mariño refused to recognize Bolívar's leadership and, with other revolters, set up a congress. Bolívar refused to accept it.

Brión and Piar sailed up the Orinoco and seized Angostura, capital of rich Guayana province, a city not yet world-famed for its bitters, a place of parrots and chattering monkeys. Bolívar soon established his headquarters there and set up a provisional and national government.

"It was a piece of bravado," he later said. "I not only proclaimed the independence of Venezuela. I challenged also Spain, Europe, and the world," there in a twilight realm of jungles and semi-illiterate mongrel people alongside one of the greatest rivers of the world. He held little territory, had no army; he simply turned a few officials and soldiers into a council of state.

Piar refused to recognize the new government, skipped out with all the gold he had collected in taxes, and joined Bermúdez, a lieutenant of Mariño, Bolívar's most inveterate enemies.

Bolívar hunted Piar down, court-martialed and shot him. "Soldiers!" he proclaimed, "I speak with heaviness of heart. But he planned not only a republic but anarchy as well. With one hand he dug the grave of the republic, to bury in it the life, happiness, and honor of its brave defenders, our sons, husbands, and fathers. Heaven is watching over your welfare and the government. Your father, your leader who is always with you in hardship, danger, and victory, trusts you. Trust him for he loves you as his sons."

But the execution so impressed Mariño that he fled to Trinidad and from there wrote Bolívar an abject letter of submission.

By mid-1818 the Spaniards controlled all the rest of the country, except for the Orinoco area. They had 25,000 troops, and 10,000 more were on the way from Spain. Yet on August 25, Bolívar sent off a small contingent to fight for New Granada, with flaming words about Spain's oppression.

"The Spanish empire has exhausted its boundless resources and all its reserves against a handful of naked men fired with enthusiasm. . . . The day of America has come. . . . No human power can check the course of what is foreordained by eternal Providence. Unite with your brothers of Venezuela. March with me to liberate yourselves as once you marched to liberate Venezuela. . . ."

Already his secret project was continental liberation, and he saw that the real pivot of power in northern South America was the future Colombia rather than Venezuela, where the bulk of Spanish force was now concentrated.

"Mere bombast," he later remarked, but it "scored a great moral success both inside and outside the country among all who did not know the truth" about his desperate situation.

The following year he issued a weekly paper, which came out on Saturdays, called *El Correo del Orinoco,* for which he wrote many articles and which was circulated all over the world.

He had eliminated Piar. Bermúdez was now cooperating. The big question was Páez up the Orinoco. Bolívar brought up forces for him, a month-long trip, and interviewed "the lion of the llanos" in Hato de Cañastifola.

vii

Páez, perhaps the greatest *guerrillero* in the history of the Americas, was brutal, half-savage, cruel, and astute. Subject to epileptic fits and dark superstitions, he kept a hunchback Negro to carry his lance.

Daniel Florencio O'Leary, a young Irish lad who arrived as a volunteer shortly after this, was fascinated by Páez, for him a rare, never-known animal.

"He was then thirty-four years old," O'Leary later wrote, "of medium height, robust, and well-formed, though the lower part of his body did not match his big torso; chest and shoulders very wide; a short, thick neck held up a bulky head covered with dark chestnut hair, short and kinky, a round beard; lively brown eyes; straight nose with wide apertures, thick lips. . . . His clear white but deeply tanned skin indicated good health. . . .

"In the presence of educated persons he was taciturn, even timid, but with underlings was loquacious and addicted to spoofing. . . . The slightest contradiction or emotion produced strong convulsions, during which he became briefly unconscious, which were followed by physical and moral weakness. . . . Wholly illiterate, he was ignorant of the theory of the military profession which he had followed so long, ignorant of the most elemental terminology of the art. . . . As a guerrilla leader he was unparalleled. Reckless, active, valiant, resourceful, quick to plan, resolute in execution, and rapid of movement, the smaller the force he commanded, the more he was to be feared. A thousand men would have embarrassed him.

"Without method, without knowledge, without moral scruples, he was a nonentity in politics. He was fickle in friendship but prodigal . . . with his confidence with the favorite of the moment and permitted himself to be guided by advice, provided it did not conflict with his interests. Without being bloodthirsty, he did not economize on bloodshed. . . . His ambition was without limits. He wanted power, but absolute power, the power of caprice and abuse. Ambition and greed were his dominant passions."

Between this half savage and the effete, urbanized Bolívar there sprang up a certain mutual respect, periodically broken by quarrels and recriminations, yet for many years, until the final hours of betrayal, Páez was hypnotized by the restless, educated Creole.

"At that time," Bolívar later remarked, "all we wanted were men of courage. . . . Gold was useless, and I had none to give them. The only thing to fire them was rank or title. Hence we had generals and officers of all classes—Negroes, mestizos, mulattoes, white men—most without claim except they had killed their quota of Spaniards."

With Páez he now pursued Spanish General Pablo Morillo to Calabozo, then to Victoria, not far from Caracas.

Once Bolívar exclaimed, as they rode to the river they were to cross, "But where are the boats you promised?"

"Over there," replied Páez calmly, pointing to enemy craft on the opposite bank. He and fifty men plunged into the river, knifed the Spaniards, and brought the boats back.

Bolívar had his own adventures. Once he and Santander, now his chief of staff, were ambushed and escaped into the jungle by a hair. Another plot to kill him all but succeeded. In a hand-to-hand fight he was unhorsed and left for dead.

A Spanish counterattack brought the Spaniards back to the Apure. Páez kept up a hit-and-run operation, and Bolívar returned to Angostura to receive British and Irish recruits being brought in from Europe.

By running the Spanish blockade with shiploads of hides, sugar, cacao, coffee, and tobacco, Brión had been able to get money for the cause, buy arms, and enlist 1,000 Englishmen and Irishmen and a number of officers.

Among the volunteers was the sixteen-year-old O'Leary, destined to play a great role in Latin-American freedom. Not overly imaginative, he was nevertheless a romantic with deep feelings; above all, was practical, energetic, and reliable. Order him to move a mountain, and it would be moved by the day and hour ordered. With an eye to the future, at once he began keeping a record and collecting documents. Eventually, years after his death, his *Memoirs,* three volumes, and his *Documents,* twenty-nine volumes, were published.

Another bunch of Irishmen came from La Plata. Further recruiting was carried on in Dublin and London, until eventually some 6,000 men of these two nationalities were fighting for Bolívar.

Alfonso Rumazo González in his *O'Leary* describes the arrival of the first thousand volunteers in the little 5,000-population city, devoted chiefly to fishing and hunting wild cattle, although rich sugar cane and other plantations spread out on the other side of the river.

The prostrating heat, the mosquitoes, the strange language disconcerted the new arrivals, even though they were attended to with great solicitude. They were wildly cheered. The Negroes opened their eyes wide at their uniforms, "the color of purified blood, and the dogs barked furiously when the blond men marched through the narrow streets toward the plaza with its big colonial palace. It seemed like fiesta time, the church bells speaking out with their loud voice. . . ."

They were sent far up the Orinoco and the Apure Rivers to San Fernando Apure, a cattle mart of egrets and alligators, due south of Caracas. There they met many soldiers driven back after the advance on the capital.

Soon after the arrival of British troops and a dress parade, their commander, Colonel Wilson, Pedro Briceño (brother of the one shot by the Spaniards), and Colombian officer José Concha spoke out at a banquet, proclaiming Páez captain general of Venezuela.

In his later autobiography, Páez stated that he had no part in the conspiracy: he had not been in San Fernando. Immediately he embarked for the city, seized Wilson, and sent him to Bolívar to have him put in some other post.

Bolívar ordered a court-martial, but after four months in

jail Wilson was deported. He published letters in London and Dublin newspapers denouncing Bolívar and the Venezuelan patriots.

Young O'Leary, not able to stomach Wilson's treachery, got leave of absence and returned to Angostura, where he asked to be assigned to a Creole regiment where he could "learn Spanish."

Not long after, he met Bolívar personally. The leader was then thirty-five. "He had a high forehead, black eyes, lively and penetrating; a perfect straight nose . . . an ugly mouth, lips slightly thick; beautiful white teeth; . . . black hair, fine and curly, blond moustache and sideburns; a narrow chest and slender body. His small hands and feet could be the envy of any woman. . . .

"His aspect, when he was in good humor, was tranquil, but terrible when he was irritated. The transformation was unbelievable."

Another observer remarked, "He was the incarnation of the tropics, where peace and the roar of tempests do not obey the seasons but come and go with the winds, the caprice of the clouds, the intense sweating of the burning regions, or the willful melting of the white snows of the volcanoes."

Long afterwards, O'Leary wrote, "I had the good fortune from the outset of my career to merit the friendship and confidence of Simón Bolívar." It was mutual, and it "lasted as long as he lived, until with broken heart, with my face bathed in tears, I saw his mortal remains lowered into an humble grave in the Santa Marta Cathedral."

viii

In Angostura, Bolívar set up the national congress of Venezuela with twenty-nine deputies in a small, seven-windowed house facing the river. He presented to it a proposed constitution, not an imitation of that of the United States but one based on his reading and the philosophy he had worked out in a Jamaica hammock and during his marches through the mangrove swamps.

By this time, Bolívar was well aware that Venezuela was sick of bloodshed and the marching and countermarching of unscrupulous generals, whether Spanish or Venezuelan, through the halls of government, without any programs but their own lust for power and loot.

"Happy the man," he pronounced, "who summons, in the name of the army, a national assembly as the expression and instrument of the will of the people." Out of necessity he had had to undertake the difficult, onerous role of a dictator, but he now returned those tasks "to the representatives of the people." The crucial thing, he added, "is that elections be respected, for nothing is more dangerous than the permanent domination of one man. . . . It is a terrible truth that it costs more strength to maintain freedom than to endure the weight of tyranny. . . . Peoples rather than systems lead to tyranny. . . . Citizens must strengthen their minds before they can digest the wholesome fruit of democracy."

He refused to become provisional president and had Francisco Antonio Zea named. Zea had been imprisoned in Spain for having studied natural history at Bogotá and had been helped to escape to Venezuela by von Humboldt.

Bolívar added a proposal for a life term for the presidency. "In a republic the executive must be strongest, since everything conspires against him; in a monarchy the legislature, since everything conspires for the monarch."

Above all, he urged, for the sake of his own life and the life of the republic, that the congress "confirm and complete the emancipation of the slaves."

He ended with an eloquent picture of the forthcoming union of Venezuela and New Granada, a new nation to be called "Colombia." "In my mind's eye . . . I can see my fatherland, this huge united country, in the heart of the world, along vast rivers, between two oceans with which nature first separated them, linked by long canals. I see it yielding up the gold and silver of its mountains to the four corners of the earth, its healing plants to the weak of the Old World, its precious secrets to the scholar. . . . Gentlemen of the assembly, begin your labors, mine are ended."

During Bolívar's absence from the upper Orinoco, the campaign had gone badly. Morillo had come back relentlessly with 6,000 magnificently equipped royalists. Páez had had to fall back and back, using his usual hit-and-run tactics, retreat, quick sharp jabs, retreat.

One night he rounded up wild horses, tied dried cowhides to their tails and sent them galloping toward Morillo's horses, which stampeded madly across the llano, forever lost. The Spanish general was stripped of all quick mobility.

Bolívar, elected President, got back to the front in March, bringing along 450 more English volunteers—"strange blond creatures on the burning plains, the heat-dancing rivers, the dusk of the jungles." They were amazed, for England was a drop in this cup of vastness; they had never known such limitless expanses, such hot-iron heat, as on these 100,000 square miles of open prairie.

They paraded in their rose-colored uniforms and were left open-mouthed by the show of horsemanship of "the magnificently trained men from Oriente," the brave, indefatigable *llaneros.*

There were no speeches, no proclamations, this day, only orders to go out and hunt down the enemy wherever he might be.

But the Spaniards soon captured San Fernando, and Páez put the bulk of his infantry on a river island, along with a thousand refugees, and moved across the Apure, going downstream with 800 fast-riding *llaneros,* playing hide-and-seek with the increasingly confused enemy.

Morillo finally drew back and dug in at Achaguas, Páez's own town, place of good pasturage, sugar cane, bananas, yuca, and maize.

Bolívar met up with Páez at the juncture of the Arauco and

Orinoco rivers and ordered an immediate attack on Achaguas, but after a thirty-six-hour battle they were forced to retreat in the face of Spanish reinforcements and recross the Apure.

Páez, using his favorite tactic, swam 150 horsemen back across the river and hit the main Spanish force hard, with yells, bullets, and machetes. To his astonishment, the enemy fled.

Fighting stubbornly in retreat, Morillo, fearing disaster when the rains began, set up headquarters in Calabozo to wait out the winter. On the Orinoco, there are, of course, two summers and two winters—if they may be called that.

O'Leary, whose Creole division was back at the front, described that long pursuit across an arid plain. "Worn out by the heat, not even a tree for shade the livelong day, not a drop of water to moisten the lips, hour after hour fooled by mirages . . . the troops arrived late to bivouac, where they could expect only a scanty ration of jerked meat, without salt. There they slept in the open, exposed to the harsh, fickle, unhealthy climate, but never a single word of complaint was ever heard from that valiant suffering army. All were animated by the determination and example of the General in Chief [Bolívar] who dressed as they did; the same flannel jacket, linen trousers, high boots, and an ordinary cloth artillery cap. . . . Incredibly energetic, he scarcely slept because of his concern for the fate of the republic and the welfare of his men."

But to Páez, Bolívar did say, through cracked lips, "Nothing but the blazing sun like fire itself, wind, desert, charcoal, tough steer meat without bread or salt . . . foul muddy water. If I do not desert, it is only because I don't know where to go."

The Englishmen suffered the worst. They considered Bolívar's dirty artillery cap an omen of disaster; when it fell into a stream and was swept away, they cheered loudly, and from then on their morale improved. Bolívar implored Zea, now Vice President, back in Angostura to send shoes. "The Englishmen are barefoot, and they cannot march."

ix

Two months dragged by before they neared the Spanish army at Calabozo. There, Bolívar left Páez to keep an eye on the Spanish army and pushed on westward.

Many of his men were sick with fever, many deserted, all were in a deplorable condition, practically naked except for their ragged ponchos, their only protection for their guns and supplies and themselves in the recurrent deluges, in which they had to sleep, soaked as they were, at night—and nights could be chilly, for the storm-lashed rainy season was now full upon them in ugly fury.

The only enemy they had in sight now was the rain, not the sun; deep sloughs of mud, not dust, and, if anything, the heat during the diluvial flooding was even more suffocating—worse still when the rain turned into days of persistent mortifying drizzle.

The chiefs of the army of about 3,000 men were called together in a ruined hut. Páez rode in for the conference. "There was no table, only the skulls of cattle for chairs. On these skulls, whitened by rain and sun, the chieftains proceeded to decide the fate of America."

A vast campaign plan was mapped out. They would bypass the heavy Spanish forces in Venezuela and invade New Granada, a reverse of Bolívar's first successful campaign.

Messengers raced off to Angostura and to all the republican forces to coordinate the proposed action. Páez was ordered to march in a parallel column to Cúcuta to protect the right flank, the only one threatened, and thus keep the Spaniards in New Grenada glued to the Andean passes.

Páez never moved to Cúcuta, and a whole squadron of mounted hussars from Apure deserted.

"March on! West . . . west . . . west," was Bolívar's only comment.

The going was terrible. What sane man would tackle such a march in rainy weather? Every stream became a torrent. They had to cross these and big Orinoco tributaries, with rawhide boats to carry across the men who could not swim, their arms and ammunition, their cannon. For seven days they toiled through flooded country up to their waists, snatching a bit of sleep on exposed knolls, where the mosquitoes swarmed down like black plagues.

"West . . . west . . . west."

A strange band, half mounted, half on foot, wives and sweethearts, all plodding like dumb beasts through the mud and rain. Never a dry moment. Their rags, their blankets, soaked with water.

They finally reached Tamé, a small town where Santander was bivouacked. "The joyful reunion of the two forces was like the meeting of two torrential streams." It was like paradise just to be able to have a few bananas, a little salt. Already they had covered a thousand kilometers.

Four days of blessed rest! Then, after a few more days of marching, they were at the foot of the Andes towering against the sky. The next day the 3,000 soldiers began toiling up those incredible crags.

The way grew more difficult. Sharp rocks cut bare feet. At each painful step, the men of the plains gazed unbelievingly on the crags, the glaciers, the snow, and murmured, "Is this, too, our country?"

There were three routes by which they might cross. Two were heavily guarded by royalist troops. The third, La Pisaba, was considered almost impassable, even in the dry season. No human being had ever taken it in the rainy season, so Bolívar was informed.

"Where a goat can go, an army can go," was his answer. "We will take the Pisaba pass."

Astonishment gave way to terror as they advanced higher and deeper. "Each summit they believed to be the last and highest, yet it was always the first stage of a yet higher one, till finally the highest ones of all were lost to the earth in cloud and mist."

Santander, in the vanguard, seized the 300-man garrison in lofty Paya. Provisions there heartened the forces. Now came the pass.

In their near nakedness the soldiers shivered and froze; they keeled over from mountain sickness and sudden strokes. The icy water gave them diarrhea. Many dropped in their tracks, gasping for oxygen, and often died quickly from the rarefied cold air. They managed to slap one cavalry colonel back to life with rawhide straps.

The *soldaderas* seemed able to endure more than the men. When pregnant, a woman went off alone to give birth, wrapped the child in her poncho or shawl, and by the next day would catch up and trot along in the line of march.

All the horses died in the first days. A few mules survived, and these presently either dropped dead or tumbled off into the abyss. Their cattle herds fell far behind, and the men had to live on a bite of unsalted jerked beef and wild celery. The Englishmen, like the cattle, lagged four days behind the others. A fourth of them died.

Seventy days after the start of their march across the savannas, the vanguard began to descend to the high Granadan plateau and reached Socha, the first town in Tunja province.

With cries of delight, the overjoyed people showered everything they had on the liberators: bread, tobacco, honey, and *chicha* beer. No one, but no one, they marveled, had ever gotten through La Pisaba in the rainy season. And now these incredible heroes—a whole army—had appeared.

The *llaneros* looked back at the awful heights, crossed themselves piously, and vowed to fight and conquer or die rather than have to retreat by the route they had come.

x

It was now July.

In all New Granada, including Quito, the Spaniards had only 11,000 men, but 3,000 of these were in Tunja, just ahead. The enemy had everything: food, munitions, uniforms, guns, cannon. The naked newcomers had no supplies except what the farmers brought them. But the *paisanos* brought horses, too, and a portion of the patriot force was able to take to the saddle again.

After only four days' rest, Bolívar quick-marched them to Gameza, twenty-five miles west, where the Spanish vanguard had arrived.

For eight hours, until dark, they fought. But more and more peasants were moving up to help, from all sides, with machetes, old guns, or whatever weapons they had, some with only clubs. The Spaniards had to draw back.

Four days later, on July 25, Bolívar crossed the Sogomoso River and fell on the enemy in the Vargas swamp.

Santander's vanguard was beaten back; so were two other battalions, which included the British Legion. Its commander, Colonel Rooke, was wounded and his arm had to be amputated—without anesthetic. He seized up his severed limb in his remaining good hand and waved it in the air, shouting, "Viva la patria!" Three days later, he died from loss of blood and incipient gangrene.

When the Sogomoso River battle seemed lost, Bolívar hurled in on the flank what little cavalry he had—*llaneros* all—and, just as night fell, the Spaniards broke in disorder.

The climactic battle of the whole Independence struggle in northern South America, which definitely assured the eventual liberation of the entire continent—though years of futile fighting would continue—was fought at Boyacá on August 7, 1819.

In the Boyacá valley, south of Tunja, where a small stream meanders down between terraced fields, the main Spanish army, hurrying north to reinforce the Bogotá garrison, moved down the Samanca Road toward a bridge where they expected to water their animals and to cook food, for hot rations were imperative in this eternal highland chill.

Bolívar's cavalry swirled down to seize the bridge, and he sent infantry up behind them from two directions. The little stream became a river of blood.

O'Leary gives the official communique in his *Memoirs*. "The Cazadores of our advance guard sent out a company in scattered guerrilla formation; the rest attacked the enemy riflemen in column formation, drove them to a high wall from which they were dislodged, and back across the bridge."

The main enemy force was in a hollow a mile and a half from the bridge. They attacked on the left flank but were stopped by the "rifles" and a British company. The First Barcelona, the Páez Bravos and a cavalry squadron from the upper plains advanced on the center. The New Granada Line Battalion and the Guías rearguard joined the Cazadores, moved to the left, and the Tunja and Socorro columns were held in reserve. Action began along the entire front. "The enemy's fire was terrible, but our troops, in the most daring but disciplined maneuvers, surrounded every enemy formation. Our Upper Plains Cavalry charged with its usual bravery, and from that moment the Spanish general . . . lost his position."

The enemy's mounted grenadiers (all Spaniards from the Peninsula) were the first to flee the field "in a cowardly manner."

General Santander, who had been mopping up the riflemen of the advance guard, charged in with two line companies and rearguard Guías, crossed the bridge, and completed the victory. "The enemy's entire army fell into our hands." Only fifty escaped. General Barreiro, 1,600 men (half his force were dead), his staff, and nearly all the commanders and officers were captured. The patriots suffered only 66 casualties.

"On that day New Granada became free for all time!"

The great march was over—from the far-off mouth of the muddy Orinoco, across the hot plains, through the driving rainstorms, through the ice of the Andes, across the beautiful highlands of New Granada to this small fertile mountain valley—Boyacá: name to remember forever.

The French general Charles Marie Emmanuel Mangin called Bolívar's crossing of the Cordilleras "the most magnificent episode in the history of war."

Bolívar entered Bogotá in triumph without resistance. The viceroy had fled for his life.

The Liberator threw out a rhapsodic message to his troops. "From the lagoons at the mouth of the Orinoco to the rocky heights of the Andes where the Magdalena rises, you have taken fourteen provinces from the legions of the tyrants, from the robbers who wish to enslave America. . . . There were not two hundred of you when this incomparable campaign began. Now you are thousands, and all America will be the scene of your deeds . . . north and south of this center of the world, you will create a haven of liberty." The next goal, he intimated, would be Peru.

Bolívar sent three monks off to try to arrange for an exchange of prisoners, particularly of Barreiro, and thirty-eight officers he held. Then he hurried back to Angostura, leaving Santander in charge of the army.

Fearing Creole royalist plots and being a man of limited patience, Santander had the prisoners brought to the plaza, where they were forced to kneel and were then shot in the back. He looked on from the palace portals. When the last was killed—General Barreiro—Santander (according to O'Leary, who could never stomach him after that bloody scene) followed a band of musicians and singers, gaily playing and chanting verses about the bloody deed, up and down the tilted Bogotá streets.

The struggle would go on for years. But now the new power of the free countries built up steadily; the foolish Spanish counterefforts became, every day, every week, every month less effective, even though, in blind stupidity, they poured in more and more forces and drained the defeated motherland of blood and treasure. From the day of Boyacá, Spain ceased to be a world power—a nation doomed for a hundred and fifty years thereafter to sink into ever deeper moral and physical disgrace, the cul-de-sac of all imperial power.

Bolívar's hasty trip back to Angostura was made necessary because plotters had been busy against him in his absence; congressmen were denouncing him for having taken the country's soldiers out of the land to free, not Venezuela, but New Granada. But he came back crowned with victory and fame and it did not take him much effort to silence his critics and to win from congress a declaration of full independence for the new unified country of Colombia.

In December he journeyed to Cúcuta, and there on the hill above the cemetery where he had issued his invasion manifesto of freedom, he again proclaimed the imperishable union of Venezuela and New Granada as the new free country of Colombia—"Gran Colombia." Here in Cúcuta, he would build the capital of the united realms, a city which he planned to rename Las Casas, after the great Spanish monk Bartolomé, who had labored all his life to improve the lot of the Indians.

By his side stood tall dark-haired Daniel O'Leary, the Irish boy with the long nose and handsome bony face, whom he had just promoted, at the age of seventeen, to be his chief aide-de-camp, his *edecán*.

Here in Cúcuta on May 6, the joint congress of Venezuela and New Granada assembled to ratify once more the new union as Gran Colombia, with Bolívar as president, with extraordinary powers, and Santander as vice president. But the Spaniards still held Caracas.

9

The Great Encounter

At Cúcuta—as described by O'Leary—the president rose at 6 A.M., dressed, and went out to look over his horses, which he cared for with great devotion, for the horse was the most rapid vehicle and the strongest arm in those days.

Returning to his room, he read until nine—usually Montesquieu or Rousseau—breakfasted, then received his secretary, his minister of war, and the chief of staff. He listened, either pacing the floor or reclining in his hammock, from which he jumped up when anything struck his attention.

A monk who had always been hostile to Independence asked for a favor.

"Go ask it of the king!" Bolívar snapped at him.

A doctor who had looted stores during the anarchy preceding the entry into Bogotá asked to be appointed physician to the general staff.

"Be content with what you have stolen," said Bolívar bluntly.

After lunch he went riding, often with O'Leary. At night he read, lying in his hammock, or dashed off newspaper articles, severe, pungent, sarcastic.

There were troubles. Irish volunteers in northern Colombia demanded their back pay, which they believed their officer was stealing. It was untrue, but they plotted, then burned the town of Rio de Hacha. Bolívar shipped them all off to Jamaica.

In Achaguas five hundred British Legionnaires under Páez refused to obey orders because of the bad food and asked to be repatriated. Páez, who had only eighty Creole cavalrymen with him, rode in and made them prisoners, lined them up, had every officer and ringleader step forward. He ran one through with his sword, then ordered the rest killed and decapitated in front of their comrades. The rest he marched back to their barracks. "If any of you show me a long face over this, he, too, will be beheaded," he warned them.

Bolívar sent orders that henceforth no more English or Irish volunteers were to be accepted.

Santander, discouraged by the constant opposition to the new confederation, resigned three times. Bolívar wrote him, "I have the fate of eighteen provinces in my hands and cannot play at drakes and ducks with them. . . . As regards your misgivings, wipe them out. . . . As regards your resignation, wipe it out. . . . If you resign a fourth time, I shall sentence you to become President of Colombia."

Presently Santander wanted a house confiscated from the royalists. Bolívar replied, "I have no right to dispose of the national property . . . ask me for something worthwhile."

Morillo managed to send a few small expeditions into northern Colombia, but the situation in Venezuela was too shaky for him to risk mounting a full-scale offensive. New rebel forces were hard by on all sides, and Bolívar's men were not far off.

But Bolívar lacked resources, weapons, and money to face the big Spanish army, and so, when Morillo asked for a six-month armistice, he accepted, provided the Spanish general agreed to make it an armistice between Spain and the *sovereign republic* of Colombia. Morillo was obliged to sign on these terms. He then expressed a desire to see the famous Bolívar, and O'Leary was sent to arrange for the meeting in Santa Ana.

With his staff and a platoon of soldiers, Bolívar rode into the little town.

"Which one is Bolívar?" asked Morillo.

O'Leary pointed him out.

"What! That little man!" Morillo stared in amazement at the insignificant figure, riding a mule and clad in a blue cape and dirty campaign hat, but he jumped off his horse, and the two leaders embraced. After dinner, Morillo took Bolívar to his own quarters. They were enchanted with each other, and that night they slept in the same room.

Soon after, Morillo left for Spain with two Colombian emissaries. "Better than a victory!" exclaimed Bolívar. No Spanish officer of similar stature remained.

Meanwhile, he made preparations to invade Ecuador and add it to Gran Colombia, which would then be almost as large as Europe. But Quito was still in Spanish hands. Only Guayaquil, the coast port, had declared itself independent— and remained independent and neutral as between Colombia and Peru, though more inclined to join the latter if San Martín finally drove out the Spaniards.

But within four months, word came that Spain had refused to receive or recognize Bolívar's emissaries.

The news came at the most opportune moment. Bolívar was finding it difficult to feed and pay his troops. Restless at sitting around idle, many were deserting. He now turned the Ecuadorean expedition over to young General Antonio José de Sucre, who for the moment was to take 700 well-equipped men, but who was to make history in the southern continent, and Bolívar himself renewed the Venezuelan campaign. He launched every rebel force toward Caracas from all sides. Bermúdez was near by. Rafael Urdaneta was swinging in from another side. Páez was moving up.

Bermúdez struck into Caracas but was too weak to hold it. However, the Spanish commander, confused by the approach of the enemy from all quarters, made the mistake of dividing his forces. Nearly all the patriot troops converged at Carobobo.

The decisive battle for all Venezuela was fought there on June 24, 1821—and it was over in an hour.

Bolívar entered Caracas again. The triumph was partly ashes, for the city showed the damages not only of the great earthquake but of war, misery, and hunger; it was almost deserted, for most of the people had fled with the Spanish troops. The hero moved through streets lined with the beggared, the sick, and famine-stricken, who scarcely cheered.

"I know you to be patriots, even though you left Caracas," Bolívar proclaimed at their vanishing heels, "could you take flight intentionally before the arms of Colombia? No, no, no!"

On his way back to Cúcuta, on August 23 and 24, he sent two letters to San Martín in Peru, offering help there if needed. He would be able, he wrote, to send 11,000 men in all, 4,000 from Panama, 4,000 from Buenaventura, and 3,000 from Guayaquil. Doubtless he expected to have this many available by the time a reply could get back.

The joint congress met soon after. It believed the situation demanded that Bolívar become dictator. He rejected the idea. "I am resolved to give the example of a great Republican. . . . It is not right that power and opinion should be in the same hands, and that all power be vested in the government." If he commanded only the army, Colombia would always have him at its call, "in the advance guard. If I suffer a defeat, the government can make up the losses. . . . You say history will speak well of me. I believe history will have nothing better to tell of me than my retirement from the ruling power."

ii

Bolívar resumed his plans to take Quito. Sucre would move up from Guayaquil; he himself would lead forces through the passes from the east.

He set out at once for Popayán province, where a holdout force in Pasto was led by the bishop, who was daily issuing anathemas. O'Leary, himself a Catholic, described him as "a Spaniard by birth, a bastard by instinct."

It was difficult terrain; even with his large force, the crushing of the zealous bishop was not going to be easy. Besides, Bolívar had to leave 1,000 men sick in the hospitals of Cali and Coloto. It was not until February, 1822, that he occupied Popayán—all except well-fortified Pasto.

By then Sucre was in bad trouble: revolts in his forces and the countryside, sickness among the troops. He was calling for more aid. In addition, San Martín was sending in forces and threatening to annex Guayaquil.

Bolívar sent O'Leary posthaste to Panama. En route in Buenaventura he was to solicit or seize a fleet of vessels sufficient to transport 1,000 men from the Isthmus to Guayaquil.

O'Leary got hold of the *San Fernando*, a Spanish vessel recently captured by Lord Cochrane, and put aboard all the men he could muster, about 800 in all. Even to get this many, he had to load on all the sick, to get well or to die on the voyage.

Meantime, Sucre, aided by 1,200 men sent him by San Martín under General Gamarra, began the march toward Quito.

Half of O'Leary's men arrived in Guayaquil sick—those who had not died during the voyage. He picked out the best 200 and rushed them to put down revolt in Guarandá province in Sucre's rear, and with the rest hurried on to the latter's side.

Sucre's forces were made up not merely of Colombians (New Granadans and Venezuelans) but Ecuadoreans, Bolivians, Peruvians, Chileans, and Argentines; it was truly an international army. The famous Trujillo Regiment was sent as a token for the Colombian Numancian Regiment remaining in Peru. Among the forces from the south were part of San Martín's original grenadiers, who had already fought through four countries.

A brilliant victory was won in Riobamba, halfway up the Andes.

Sucre's army climbed on up from Latacunga into the *tierra*

negra, the cold black earth country with its sparse stunted grass and its scrub *frailejone* growths. They slithered through the torrential deluges of May. Great lightning bolts blazed and crashed from peak to peak. He led them along the snow slopes of giant Mount Cotopaxi in a human serpentine to meet the Spaniards, who had dug in at Quito at the foot of another icy giant, Pichincha. The ordeal cost a large share of the forces.

Quito is 9,236 feet high, next to La Paz, the highest capital in all South America and third highest in the world. To be able to fall on the city and the Spaniards from above, the army followed treacherous slopes, dragging along munitions and cannon without benefit of trails.

On May 24, 1822, the sun eased over the eastern heights and glistened on the towers and cupolas of this tilted crazy-quilt city of churches, convents, and monasteries. The population was top-heavy with priests and monks, but there were only two or three doctors, ignorant of nearly everything but bleeding people to make them die more quickly. On a prominent hill rising from the heart of the city—Panecillo, Little Loaf—gleamed the Spanish artillery.

The cannon of Sucre spoke out exactly at nine o'clock and were promptly answered. Instead of attacking the patriots from the flank or rear, the brave but thickheaded Spaniards moved straight up and up in frontal assaults.

They were met by a withering fire, and the men on the mountain rolled down huge boulders that crashed through the Spanish ranks. Even so it was an assault in force, and the battle was once thrown in doubt when the courageous Peruvian officers, their ammunition gone, ran away with their forces —the famed Trujillo and Piura Regiments—and hid in caves. Sucre had to draw back and shift ground, but after three hours of fighting and large losses on both sides his men stormed down the mountain and on into the city.

The following day Panecillo surrendered to O'Leary, who rode up with a white flag. According to Torrente, the surrender included "1,100 soldiers, 160 officers, 14 artillery pieces, 1,700 guns, a large quantity of cartridges, bugles, flags, war chests, everything the Spaniards possessed."

Shortly before the Quito battle, Bolívar met the enemy outside Pasto at the Hacienda Bombona, a bloody battle hand-to-hand with bayonets, machetes, and knives. Pasto was won, and the road to Ecuador and Quito was open. Bolívar's advance through the Andes cost him a third of his forces.

iii

On June 16, Bolívar entered Quito in triumph. Rockets burst overhead in blue and red stars; the captured cannon on Panecillo thundered a salute over the massed crowds, over towers and flat roofs and the slanting, red-tiled roofs; the hundreds of bells rolled their clamor through the narrow streets.

All Quito was out, lining the streets, crowding the plazas. The towers were black with spectators. Flags of the republic flew from every rooftop. Every balcony was decorated with bunting, rugs, and brocades and filled with families, from grandparents to tiny children.

Pinned among the hordes of sandled Indians in gray and brown and red ponchos, here and there was a grandee, like some lost glittering emperor, in silver embroidered waistcoat, silver buckle breeches, and tricornered hat. Girls in Regency dresses or still newer French styles—waistlines high under their breasts, low, square necklines edged with velvet ribbon or handmade lace—fluttered along the high cathedral terrace fronting the plaza. Near them, shepherded by white-cowled nuns, swarmed pigtailed Indian girls, dressed as angels with silver-tinseled wings, and carrying batons tipped with gold-tinsel stars.

The Liberator passed under numerous arches of triumph. Since there were no flowers this chill, wintery May, they were decorated with pine and cedar boughs, interspersed with laurel and palm fronds brought up especially from the hot coast. Indian orchestras greeted him, playing curious harps and fiddles, beating their carved drums. Three Indians carried a great bamboo trumpet twenty feet long that boomed and croaked like a giant bullfrog—a boom that could be heard for miles through the winding Andean valleys. Ragged venders sold food and candy and fruit-ades and patriotic songs, hastily printed for this occasion on red and green sheets of coarse paper by Quito's only printing press.

Bolívar's staff was decked in gaudy uniforms, with much lace and plumes and glittering decorations. The hero wore a plain black tunic, with a single medal, and tight white doeskin trousers.

His quick eyes did not miss the crumbled walls, the gaping holes caused by gunfire, nor the rubble from the terrible earthquake that had hit the city in 1797, twenty-five years before.

As he rode past the iron-studded portals of the mansion of wealthy Juan de Larrea, a laurel wreath hit him in the side of the face. He recoiled and looked up in hot irritation. Then he smiled, transfixed with admiration.

It had been tossed by Manuela Sáenz de Thorne, a guest in the house, just arrived from Lima, a twenty-four-year-old *mestiza* beauty with ivory skin, a mass of black hair, and enormous black eyes. Their glances mingled in quick passionate understanding, and that exchange, though neither knew it, was to alter the course of history and the fate of nations.

She, too, wore a medal, the Order of the Sun, the highest decoration of the new independent Peru, bestowed on her by San Martín himself, for her aid to the revolutionary cause.

That night Bolívar met her at the victory ball given in the great salon of the Larrea mansion, with its polished tiled floors, high brocaded walls, stuccoed ceiling with elaborate grape and cherub designs, its enormous dewdrop chandeliers. Here assembled the elite of the city; unlike those of Colombia and Peru, nearly all were ardent supporters of the Independence cause.

Bolívar's whole interest focused on Manuela. He watched her dance the cotillion and the polonaise, a slim lithe girl, but luxuriously shaped, with a lovely classic oval face, perfect features, a passionate full mouth. He knew something about her, already. Her half brother, also an Ecuadorean, had just become a member of his personal staff.

Suddenly she stepped out alone on the floor, her skirts held high, to dance the *ñapanga* before the shocked eyes of the gathering—"Not a dance," remarked one bishop, "but the resurrection of the flesh"—not a ballroom dance but one for hoi polloi, during fiestas and in chicha beer parlors. Manuela held stuffy conventions in little esteem.

After that the Liberator danced with her, and the rest of the evening only with her. He loved dancing; he was adept and insinuating. Sometime before daybreak they vanished. Nobody saw them go, but everybody became aware of it, and the tongues of all Quito, from fine salons to servants' quarters, the plazas to the markets, buzzed.

iv

Manuela was an illegitimate child by wealthy Creole Simón Sáenz y Vegara and Joaquina Aispurú, member of an exclusive family, a fact as well known in the city as were some of Manuela's earlier madcap doings. Now she had come back to Quito in order to sue the Aispurú clan for 10,000 pesos awarded to her by her mother's will, which had been stolen by the relatives. This, too, was enough to revive old scandal.

Years before this, her father, Simón Sáenz, because of complicity in a revolutionary plot, had had to flee to Panama with his wife and children. Manuela was left behind in a leading Quito convent school. At seventeen she was expelled in disgrace for a love affair and was deported to Panama.

There she met James Thorne, affluent British merchant and shipping magnate, hand in glove in lucrative deals with the viceroy of Peru. A mysterious, taciturn, coldly aloof individual, he was twenty years her senior. She brought him an 8,000-peso dowry which, according to signed contract, was to be recoverable by her with interest should he die.

In Lima she moved in the highest court circles but was soon involved with the revolutionists. She distributed revolutionary leaflets and served as messenger, even managing to get her hands on arms.

She was aided by the Peruvian dress style, an elastic, fluid, multi-pleated *sayo* and a *manta* or shawl worn covering all the face except one eye that made the wearer almost unidentifiable. It was marvelous for love assigations in that thoroughly corrupt city; it concealed whatever a woman wished concealed, including her virtue, if any, and it concealed Manuela's incendiary materials.

Naturally her husband found out. He ordered her to desist —it would ruin his business; besides, he was insanely jealous of the young men with whom she was plotting. He might have known better. He had already learned that he could not give orders to Manuela; she was a law unto herself. This was painful to him, since he set tremendous store by the proprieties and liked a well-ordered, respectable ménage, being a strait-laced, puritanical man.

Her half brother, later to become Bolívar's aide, was an officer in the Numancia Regiment, made up of Ecuadorians and Colombians brought in to Lima to help save the day against San Martín. Through him she met and subverted the officers, so that on their first sally against San Martín the entire regiment deserted to his cause. It was chiefly for this achievement that San Martín had decorated her, when he entered the capital with his forces.

Shortly after, she went north on a British vessel with her two female black slaves, Jonotás and Natán, and her husband. While he went on to Panama, she made the difficult horseback trip to Quito, just in time for Bolívar's triumphal entry.

Her own entry was also a triumph. She had left Quito an illegitimate girl, a wanton madcap in disgrace. Now she was back, a wealthy guest of the richest Creole family in the city. She became doubly a target of gossip.

Bolívar, after their fateful night of love, went to the palace without sleeping. A thousand details awaited him: caring for his troops; reorganizing the Ecuadorian government; conducting a voluminous correspondence across a whole continent; planning for his forthcoming trip to Guayaquil, a trip that might decide the fate of the continent. He worked like a demon all day and far into the night.

It was midnight when he sank into a chair, weary unto death but without desire for sleep. His eyes, deeply sunk in his face now, were feverish with incipient tuberculosis, but his unhealthy, yellowed skin strangely enough seemed to glitter. He sipped a glass of wine, snatched up his quill, and wrote to Manuela, "Come to me. Come. Come now."

He sent the note off with his lifetime servant and bodyguard, José Palacios, a Goliath of a man whom Bolívar's mother long ago had assigned to watch over her son, a duty he fulfilled faithfully. A mixture of three races, or maybe more, he was Spanish, Indian, Negro, but had red hair and gray eyes. When he slept no one knew. He was awake when Bolívar was awake, and he was wakeful every moment the Liberator slept. His fearsomeness was enhanced by two great half-savage mastiffs he kept on leash. Sometimes he was asked to sit in the corner of the salon when Bolívar was interviewed, the two mastiffs growling until quieted, which often added to the nervousness of generals or cabinet ministers. On the narrow streets, when he walked abroad with the animals, people gave him a wide berth.

José took the dogs with him on the night's mission, lighting his way with a *sereno* watchman's lantern, for there were no street lights. At the Larrea mansion he hammered the door with the big brass knocker to awake the porter sleeping on a straw mat on the tiles just inside. He waited until Manuela appeared, then led her back through the empty hill-climbing streets, pitch black except for the occasional flickers of the *serenos* lanterns, silent except for their occasional calls, "Ave Maria. One o'clock, all is well!" She was dressed in her Peruvian clothes, her voluminous shawl covering her head and face except for one eye.

Manuela was with Bolívar every night he was in Quito. Never had he found a woman so exquisite, so adept at love-making, or so clever. His passion for her seemed insatiable.

It was not wholly activity in bed. To her he poured out all his grandiose hopes and fears, his plans.

"I have to reach Guayaquil before San Martín," he told her. "The city still refuses to accept the Quito government. It has a strong pro-Peruvian party. We cannot permit a divided Ecuador, half of it Colombian, half of it Peruvian. But they are stubborn people in Guayaquil. It's a trading port, and they have always distrusted the people of Quito."

"And if they resist?"

"I have instructed my agents to prepare for my entry. I shall enter as Liberator and Emancipator. But how it will turn out, it is too soon to tell. If necessary I shall use force. I shall have a long hard march, and our troops are tired and we have so few supplies. But I have sent word to Bogotá to Santander that I intend to use force if necessary. I am taking other measures."

From her first day in Quito, Manuela began nursing the wounded soldiers, and, knowing of Bolívar's needs, she prodded the women of the city to work and sew for the patriot cause. She went from house to house, getting cloth for uniforms, old blankets, money, jewels.

Everywhere she was accompanied by her slave Jonotás, a big, bouncing, bubbling, black girl who wore a soldier's uniform, red turban, and bright jangling earrings. She was a great mimic, and Manuela and others were convulsed by her satiric take-offs of the society dames and prominent personages of the capital. Often her pantomime was cruel indeed, and this did not endear her or her mistress to aristocratic families in the *casas grandes*.

Manuela sent Jonotás out to the Aispurú hacienda with an order for eight mules, which she claimed belonged to her. Whatever the facts, the owners were not going to go against the mistress of Bolívar—not yet—and Jonotás came back, bouncing on the lead mule, and turned them over to Sucre.

Sucre sent Manuela a grateful thank-you note: it meant much to him and his men to know "there are heroines such as yourself, with whom one can share your generosity."

There is a hint or two that Bolívar was uneasy at the quick, sure way in which Manuela acquired a hold on him. Since the death of his wife, though he had long dallied with Fanny de Villars, he had let no woman get any real claim on his affections or his life. He had had many women; he sought them in the busiest moments, even during the worst disasters. The sex act seemed to augment his vitality, not diminish it; he was spurred to more intense efforts. But Manuela was a woman such as he had never known. He hungered for her every moment. She seemed to grasp his feelings and thoughts better than anybody else; her responses were instantaneous and perceptive; her advice was good, based on a far-reaching knowledge of events and particularly of people; and she also shared his revolutionary aspirations.

At this juncture her information was especially valuable to him, for she knew the Peruvian leaders inside and out. He asked her innumerable questions about San Martín, whom he would soon be meeting in Guayaquil and with whom he would have to measure wits, and perhaps swords. San Martín seemed to have so little desire for the sort of glory which Bolívar craved. Nourished by glory, Bolívar was a drunken god. His hunger for fame, for the plaudits of the multitude, was insatiable. But San Martín had simple habits, an absolute integrity, asked nothing for himself, not even glory, and yet he inspired unshakable loyalty. Few men had betrayed him, as so many had tried to do with Bolívar.

Manuela had been a close friend not merely of San Martín but particularly of his mistress, Rosita Campuzano. San Martín, it was clear, was primarily a soldier—methodical, sure, even relentless, but having no great flare or imagination. His military drive seemed to have weakened. He had shifted ground politically, now advocating that the new countries should be set up, not as representative republics, but as monarchies with kings imported from European royalty.

Already looking ahead to the day when he would not only get to Guayaquil but would go on to complete the liberation of Peru, Bolívar asked about other outstanding Peruvians.

Marqués de Torre Tagle was a schemer and turncoat; José de la Riva Agüero was sinister and capricious, inordinately ambitious, but chiefly to appease his vanity and not for power or money; Peru's minister of war, Argentine Bernardo Monteagudo, head of the Lautaro Lodge since its founding and more than anybody else the architect and intellectual of the continental revolution, was Jesuitical, without scruples, fanatical in his purposes, as ruthless as Robespierre, a man who worked behind the scenes rather than in the open, and in appearance so much the perfect dandy that his enemies questioned his sexual habits.

But Bolívar kept coming back to San Martín. San Martín. San Martín. Soon they would meet in Guayaquil. And what were the real conditions in Peru?

v

The Peruvian campaign was dragging. While San Martín sat lethargically in Lima, royalist troops ringed the capital; there was fighting all through the sierras, and the Spaniards mostly were getting the better of it. A strange trancelike immobility seemed to have come over San Martín. He seemed to shrink from completing the task he had set himself to do, to draw back from the great effort and sacrifices required.

Things had gone from bad to worse and still worse. Royalist General Canterac had taken Ica on the south with a brilliant deployment of his forces. The Numancia Regiment in Lima soon revolted for lack of pay and the failure of the government to repatriate them as promised. Lima royalists plotted a *coup*.

Monteagudo answered with police terror. Spaniards were yanked out of their houses at night, clad only in nightshirts. Torrente described them: "Respectable ecclesiastics, venerable eighty-year-old well-deserving heads of families, wealthy persons accustomed to every comfort, civil and military officials— all, without regard for their age, were obliged to walk in the dead of night six miles to Callao." There they were thrust on board the frigate *Milagro* to be deported to Chile. Similar prisoners were marched in from the interior and a large number, the royalists claimed, were shot or died en route.

Some thirty prisoners were allowed to buy their liberty for from 1,000 to 10,000 pesos, but even so they were promptly deported on an English boat bound for Brazil. However, a few days out, they took the captain prisoner and forced him to head for the Peruvian shore beyond Quilca, the point furthest south recently taken by patriot *guerrillero* Colonel Belford Wilson, an Englishman, whose fast-riding men had borne the brunt of the struggle in the interior. But the captain and his officers managed to regain command, and they dumped the prisoners into two small boats in a tempestuous sea. Their provisions were soon gone, with no sign of land, and they began eating those who died. By the time the surviving boat drifted on shore, one died on landing, and the patriot soldiers found only two prisoners lying insensible on the sand—the only ones to come through alive.

It was shortly after this that San Martín, leaving Torre Tagle in charge of the government, set out in a small schooner, the *Macedonia*, to meet Bolívar in Guayaquil.

Two great revolutionary personalities, the two mightiest forces in South America, were to come face to face. Both were crowned by a hundred victories. Both had crossed the Andes in unbelievable marches. Both wore a major decisive battle as symbol of success: the glory of Chacabuco, the glory of Boyacá. Those two battles had won the independence of South America, all except Peru. In a few days the two giants would be together in the disputed Ecuadorian port.

vi

On the afternoon of July 11, 1822, Bolívar rode into Guayaquil along the river-front Malecón under a great floral arch bearing the words TO THE SON OF WAR, THE RAINBOW OF PEACE. Joyous crowds greeted him as the Liberator.

He had feared trouble. Guayaquil had been stubbornly independent, and he feared the strong pro-Peruvian party. Before setting out, he had written Bogotá. "The Protector of Peru is proposing to meddle in the internal affairs of Colombia. He has offered to Guayaquil that it should remain independent. . . . We believe ourselves authorized, should it become necessary, to use force to keep Peru within her boundaries and oblige Guayaquil to form part of Colombia—and as soon as possible."

He had prepared the way in very plausible manner, even circularizing forged letters from Páez and Zea and from the Spanish commander, still a thorn in the flesh in Venezuela, to the effect that full independence had been granted. Yes, Guayaquil, the only good port on the Pacific for more than a thousand miles, was important, not only to round out the Ecuadorian annexation, the enlarging of the Colombian confederation, but as the gate, the one gate, through which he could move on to Peru.

Now the issue was being decided by Bolívar's entry; he had beaten San Martín to the punch. But though the crowds cheered him, there were also shouts of "Viva el Peru!" "Viva Guayaquil Independiente!" Even now the junta, at least partly pro-Peruvian, rejected the proposal that the local province be incorporated into Ecuador and Gran Colombia. Involved was not merely the new independence and the power politics of the two great leaders, but an ancient feud between coast and highland Quito that went back centuries before the Spanish Conquest, still persisted, and persists still.

Two days later, Bolívar arbitrarily declared himself head of Guayaquil province, informing the junta that the step was necessary "to save the Guayaquil people from their present frightful state of anarchy and avoid the evil consequences." The announcement read, "His Excellency, the Liberator of Colombia, in response to the general clamor, takes the people of Guayaquil under the protection of the Republic of Colombia. His Excellency assumes political and military command of this city, without, however, in any way curtailing the absolute liberty of its people." He was ever, from the time of his Jamaica proclamation, a master of double talk.

Though Bolívar kept reassuring the junta and the public that they would have full and untrammeled choice to decide their destiny, the junta disbanded and its members boarded a Peruvian vessel in port. He sent repeated messages to Olmedo, the head of the junta, to remain, but the poet-statesman's reply was, "It is sweeter to be part of an honorable failure than a triumph." He made it clear he wanted no part of an arbitrary decision imposed by the Liberator. "To avoid evils and disasters to my people, I do not wish to oppose your resolution. My country does not need me now."

Many people had considered the junta oppressive, and the saying ran from lip to lip, "The last day of despotism and the first day of the same!"

Nor could Bolívar wrench a clear-cut decision out of any of the other governing bodies. Not until July 31, after San Martín had visited the port and had departed (without uttering one word regarding the status of the port), did the provincial assembly declare: ". . . From this moment, Guayaquil is forever integrated as part of the Colombian republic."

The Argentine leader arrived on the *Macedonia* on July 26.

A magnificent welcome was prepared: palm- and flower-decked arches, music, parading troops, people in fiesta costumes. Everywhere the flags of Peru and Gran Colombia flew side by side. Whatever the fate of Guayaquil, even the humblest citizen was aware of the momentous importance of the day when the two greatest men of the continent, perhaps at that moment of the entire world, were being joined under the laurel of triumph. The crowds were delirious with excitement, with vast patriotic pride that this meeting should take place in Guayaquil. It was a great moment of truth for everybody, a universal awareness of historic destiny—the long vista of the past, the long vista of the future, opened up and illuminated by a flash of glory and greatness.

Bolívar and his aides in splendid uniforms met the Argentine hero as he stepped off the little coastal schooner.

"Welcome, my general, to the soil of Gran Colombia," were Bolívar's first words.

San Martín must have realized at that instant, if not before, that the annexation of Guayaquil to Colombia was a *fait accompli*, that thereby Bolívar held all the high cards, that he himself had been maneuvered into the position, not of meeting the northern hero on equal terms, but as a guest in his house. But if any differences or doubts existed, it was not revealed by the warm greeting exchanged by the two leaders. What the humblest citizen sensed was that this was one of the great highlights of all human experience on earth, that on the restraint and wisdom and decisions of these two leaders rested the fate of Independence, the destiny of all South America, the future of nations, the fate of millions upon millions of human beings.

At times the forces of history move obscurely, the minds of men are confused, events seem haphazard, deeds seem devoid of reason or purpose. But here in Guayaquil that day in July, 1822, the whole Independence movement was brought to a white focus of truth and splendor. Here was the climax of fifteen years of struggle and sacrifice.

For the thirty-six hours that San Martín remained in Guayaquil, the people celebrated joyously and the authorities showered honors on both heroes. After a formal banquet, the two
generals retired, completely alone. What went on there and
during their two other meetings can never be known, though
from the later writings of both men, and of those close to them,
something of a picture has emerged.

vii

In temperament, the two leaders were poles apart. San Martín, puritanical in his adherence to his purposes and principles,
was a child of the cold south, a temperate-zone man, austere
and reticent, a careful, persevering planner who prepared
every move painstakingly—a perfectionist. Above all else, he
was primarily a soldier, not a thinker or statesman; but he
was handsome and, in spite of his severity, his charm, sim-
plicity, and undeniable integrity brought everyone he met
under his spell.

Since he did not wear his heart on his sleeve and had infinite
patience, San Martín was able to wait for the right moment
to strike. In his feud with the Carreras, he bided his time for
years, made his final moves deftly, and in the end—not for
reasons of personal vengeance, but as part of his grand design
for Independence—the three brothers were executed. He was
never bloodthirsty, not even cruel, rarely arbitrary. A magnificent avenue of tolerance ran through his nature. He could
never have slaughtered nearly a thousand prisoners as Bolívar
did in La Guayra.

Nor could San Martín ever have repeatedly deserted his
comrades in moments of disaster, as Bolívar did. He suffered
a few defeats, but he planned too carefully ever to have been
caught in the overwhelming disasters that struck Bolívar. San
Martín would never have gotten on a ship bound to sink in
the first place; Bolívar did many times. (Had he gone down
with the ship, of course, he would never have learned how

to command a ship; he would have sailed no more ships; he would not have liberated a continent.) Bolívar, often isolated, often penniless, had to conjure confidence and victory out of his own soul, in a manner never required of San Martín.

The differences in their temperaments and methods were revealed by their respective crossings of the Andes. San Martín spent years getting ready and prepared every detail down to the last horseshoe nail. Bolívar stormed across the llanos and the icy pass with half-naked men and with whatever human or material resources he could lay hands on in a hurry. Partly it was the mania for motion which Fanny had observed in Paris. Haste was a built-in part of him. The dreams were great, and life was short.

Unlike San Martín, Bolívar was a true child of the tropics—impetuous, capricious, whimsical, supremely imaginative, his head bursting with romantic concepts, with poetry, with visionary projects. He had never known San Martín's mental or military discipline. The Argentine moved within rigid bounds; Bolívar knew no bounds, put no limits on what he believed he could accomplish.

Above all, Bolívar loved this New World and its people. As he trampled through it in triumph with the sweetness of popular applause in his ears, he came to love it almost as he loved the flesh of women—not any particular woman, just love for love's sake. He embraced this vast world, this mighty universe, and felt it yield to his passion and joy. He was transformed to dizzy bliss—it colors nearly everything he wrote—by the vast Andes, the million square miles of forests, the endless burning plains, the mighty rivers, the broiling sun and the swirling snows of the heights, above all by the ready submission of Nature and Man to his every exploit, the glad submission of the people as his fame and power and knowledge increased. He could hear the maize creak as it leapt toward the warm skies; the brown Indians were like the earth he loved; the Negro was sinuous, lithe, a creature of inspiring dark mystery and sleek beauty. Bolívar was a blue-blooded Creole of the wealthy clans—"his blue blood could have served for litmus paper"—but actually his inner being had absorbed and fused with the instincts and thoughts, ways and mores, of all the races and classes of South America. He was a virile synthesis of the people, the epitome of the "Cosmic Race," and he was planting the seeds of new birth, of new flowering, all across the continent.

The turmoil of this unborn world was within his own soul; his inner chaos represented the fetal stirrings of a world being born. In mind, spirit, and emotions, he was a universe in himself, a swirling cosmos from which shot new stars of ideas and aspirations and wild comets of poorly disciplined impulses. San Martín was never able to produce such flamboyant and gilded proclamations, illogical, flaming, often defying reasonable analysis to the point of near idiocy, yet instinct with the awareness of the glimmerings in untrained minds, the unexpressed suffering and hopes of the people. Those outpourings were often contradictory from sentence to sentence; they shot off in a dozen different directions; they zigzagged; they swung from pole to pole; they were childishly frank and naïve, yet often instinctively cunning. And yet for all his disorganized fury, somehow Bolívar always swung to a central balance, an unshakable position, to be less vacillating in the long run than the more prosaic San Martín. The very core of Bolívar's belief was independence—freedom for all men, equal opportunities for all men—and the unifying power of justice, and a hope for eventual constructive peace as a basis for the confederation of all the countries of the continent. More than any other man, he created the enduring, undying dream of Latin America.

There was, it is true, a streak of schizophrenia: his nature was split. He loved glory, power, authority (his Napoleonic complex), yet he shied away from imposing his power and sought always to build representative governments. He craved personal aggrandizement, yet he craved popular freedom just as strongly. The world, of course, has known many enlightened

dictators and many democratic tyrannies. Nothing is more ter-
rifying than demos run amok. Without full tolerance, majority
rule is one of the cruelest forms of government.

Bolívar had the advantage over San Martín when they met,
not simply because he had moved faster into Guayaquil but
because he was at the height of his powers and because his
achievements already were so great. He had driven out the
Spaniards, and he had created Gran Colombia with incredible
rapidity. He was mightily bemused by his dreams of freedom,
democracy, representative republican government, and continental unity. He was still bemused, also, by his vast yearning
for Napoleonic grandeur. Bolívar at this moment was a
drunken god, moved by all the passions and glories of this
hour of history, still flushed with brilliant victories. He wanted
new worlds to conquer, not so much for the sake of conquest
as to extend the pattern he had devised over the continent;
his whole dream was continental—not regional, not national,
nor entirely of this earth.

In San Martín the fire had begun to die down. Chacabuco
already seemed ancient history; Maipú and Chile seemed far
behind. Peru, it was true, was still an uncompleted enterprise,
and possible disaster still threatened there. In Bolívar there
had been signs of the forthcoming breakdown of his health,
but San Martín had been a sick man during most of his greatest achievements. The pain in his chest, in his stomach, in his
joints was worse now, and he had to resort more and more to
opium to quiet it. Peru was really too much for him. He had
never measured Peru correctly, this temperate-zone man in a
lush semitropical climate, and a subtle disintegration had
taken place in him, which clouded his judgment. Lima was
rich and corrupt, a city of filthy intrigues, and he was caught
in the jungle of sordid pettyfogging politics which was its
major characteristic then and still is today. As he had deteriorated, in Peru, so had the whole military and political situation. The situation was explosive, aside from the presence of
pro-royalist forces just outside Lima, their strength consoli-

dated with 10,000 well-trained, well-armed troops, that held most of the highlands and were a growing menace to the Independence government.

A change of viewpoint had grown in San Martín; a growing distrust of the people was taking him outside the main revolutionary current into a stagnant eddy. He now believed that the new countries should become limited monarchies, more or less in the British style, rather than having representative governments.

He had wished the Peruvians to free themselves, but there had been little of the popular response that had marked his campaigns in Argentina and Chile. He became more aware every day that Peru was a deeply divided land—geographically, ethnically, culturally, and in its class distinctions—a division more ancient and irrevocable than, for instance, the Gaucho-urban struggle in Argentina.

Lima was a city wholly apart from the people it ruled, a Conquistador city that still retained all the imperialistic and arrogant attitude of the Conquest. Its Creoles were greedy, corrupt, unenlightened, even ignorant of history and social realities, utterly faithless except for their fanatic religiosity. They were pro-royalist to the core and had accepted Independence chiefly because it was preferable to exertion and they hoped by cunning to salvage their wealth, properties, and ruling positions.

The Creoles of the highlands were even more ignorant and cruel, and the Indians of the Andean plateaus and valleys, who comprised 95 per cent of the population, could see little difference between the Spaniards and the Creole "liberators" who had slaughtered them not so long before in the Tupac Amarú war, committing the most barbarous savagery. All Spaniards and all Creoles were whites; all were oppressors and exploiters. Indeed the Indians, as did the Negroes and mestizos or Cholos, seemed at times more inclined to embrace the Godos rather than the Creole oppressors they knew so well from first-hand experience.

Thus the failure of the masses to respond to San Martín's call had isolated him in Lima, and Lima was a rancid, reactionary city—an unfriendly, almost hostile, city—anxious chiefly to preserve its sensuous luxuries and vice (the counterpart, in an earlier day, of Havana just before the Castro revolution). In one despondent moment, San Martín had exlaimed, "Not even God could liberate this disgraceful land!"

And so, despite his own glory and success, he was bringing Bolívar a failure, whereas Bolívar was fired by full success.

viii

The two great men, alone, measured each other as they discussed the problems of the new worlds they had created. Ecuador's fate was decided, for the moment at any rate, and it is doubtful if San Martín even broached the ticklish question. Ecuadorean historian Oscar Efrén Reyes states categorically, "There was not the slightest discussion of it in their interview."

The fate of the New World had moved beyond Ecuador to Peru. For the nonce, apparently, they also avoided that issue, the who-how-when of its salvation. Instead they discussed the geography, the shape, the nature, the hopes of the independent world being forged under the hammer blows of war and destiny.

All commentators agree that they discussed fully the forms of government that could or should be established, particularly in Peru. According to Ricardo Levene in his *Historia Argentina*, San Martín told Bolívar, "Consider the scant civilization of the Spanish colonies, the heterogeneity of races, the way in which property is divided, the unity of religion, the aristocracy of the high clergy, the ignorance of the majority of the priests, the military spirit of the masses, and the consequences of prolonged civil wars, . . . the unhappy anarchy that will be precipitated by all the demands once the war of

Independence is completed." And he concluded, "The Creoles have always lived under absolute monarchy."

Bolívar's conclusions were quite contrary. "I consider the epoch of monarchy past. Thrones will not come back into fashion as long as there are men who love freedom and feel repelled by false glamor of that sort." As he was to write Santander not much later, "My three colleagues, San Martín, O'Higgins, and Iturbide of Mexico have experienced a terrible end because they did not love freedom."

The theme song of San Martín, even before the Spanish were fully dislodged, had become "peace and order," a reflection of the thinking of Lima's privileged elite. The reactionary Creoles embedded in the revolutionary juntas everywhere feared that the day victory came the lower orders, having gained military experience, would proceed to take over the new governments and impose a juster social order. They wished to maintain all the abuses of colonialism without the Spaniards; all they prayed for was a smooth transition of power without any change in the economic structure.

Under the now-vanishing absolutism that had been practiced for so many centuries, the law-and-order system of yesterday, the Creoles had forfeited some rights in order to be assured of the right to hang onto their vast estates, originally stolen from the people, and to be able to exploit the lower classes. In the new absolutism which they hoped to establish, they wished to retain all the old privileges and add new ones, or at least take over those possessed by Spain and her bureaucrats and soldiers and priests. The movement for Independence also included many counterrevolutionists fighting against the 1812 liberalism of Ferdinand, against the French revolutionary doctrines of equality, and against Napoleonism which was striking such terrible blows against feudalism. For the struggle for Independence, all they wanted of Indians and Cholos was cannon fodder—and docility. They expected the submerged people to make the biggest sacrifices for an independence which promised them few rewards.

Already the mestizos had risen to positions of power in the army, especially in Venezuela (Páez), in Uruguay (Artigas), and in Argentina, where the Gaucho heroes were all men of mixed blood. And there was Gamarra in Peru, whom San Martín had hoped would be able to lead the campaign against the Spaniards of Quito and take over Ecuador. The conflicts that were bound to ensue could be voided only by the establishment, if not of real revolution, at least of far-reaching changes in the social structure which the Creoles, holding the keys of economic power and seeking to gain all the reins of political power, would never willingly permit.

Bolívar knew well that Peace would not bring peace, that stormy days lay ahead. He even expressed the hope that the Spaniards might be able to hang onto Puerto Cabello in Venezuela, as they were still doing, for decades to come. "I fear peace more than war," he remarked more than once, as have politicians from that day to this.

But he found little to praise in San Martín's new emphasis on law and order; it smacked too much of the long deadly silence that had been brutally imposed on South America for three centuries.

This was the hour of change, of revolution, the birth throes of new nations, inevitably a bloody process. San Martín himself had been a major creator of revolution. He now feared his own handiwork. Surfeited with violence and war even before he had won peace, he was now doubling back toward the dying past.

Bolívar was positive that, first of all, peace and order could not be re-established until every possibility of restoration of Spanish power was destroyed. Nor could there be any peace and order on the basis of *diminishing* the liberties already won. The cure for disorder was more liberty, not less. He had not fought for the imposition of a meaningless state of peace and order that would steal away the victory—nor for the Creoles alone.

It was, he intimated, the custom of the powerful and the ancient enjoyers of privileges to make a fetish of law and order in times of crisis and revolution. It was a smoke screen to save their power and to maintain existing abuses. The Romans had called it the status quo.

The true law of nature, of man, of societies was change. The status quo was ever the cowardly refuge of men afraid of change, who desired comfortable security and were weary or terrified of the struggle for existence. The status quo was a childish way of death, not of life; of decay, not of progress. Since it violated the processes of nature, it merely meant that violence and disorder would be that much greater when they finally struck. This was particularly true in a predominantly revolutionary epoch; dam the flood back, and the breakthrough would be overwhelming.

Bolívar was well aware of the clouds on the horizon, aware that his grandiose system might collapse. Already there was the treachery of his late allies—of Santander in Colombia, of Páez in Venezuela, of the petty caudillos of Ecuador. They would try to smash his great scheme with their narrower concepts, their provincial ignorance, their regional limitations, their avarice and insatiable ambition. The fires of petty nationalisms, the patria chica, were already flickering on the horizon, threatening to set ablaze the temporary unity in the countries and among the countries and destroy it. Already baser men were stirring up social and racial antagonisms and low passions. In his heart, though he remained exalted, hopeful and determined, Bolívar had no illusions.

Even so, the true road lay not in reverting to monarchy so contrary to the spirit of the age; it did not lie in curtailing the rights the revolution had promised to all citizens. The New World, at whatever cost, had to move forward bravely to representative governments and free republics, regardless of the dangers of war and chaos. One had to move toward the light, not shrink back into the false safety of darkness.

San Martín and Bolívar came at last to the immediate deep concern of both: the saving of Peru. Without victory there, San Martín's whole career would be swallowed up in ignominy and catastrophic failure. The persistence of the Spanish strength in Peru, the constant possibility of their recovering the ramparts of the Andes, of bringing back Spanish absolutism and colonialism, made independence doubtful even in the north, in Gran Colombia. Serious reaction in Peru could also destroy Bolívar's work; the whole movement of freedom might be wiped out.

Bolívar knew this. He wished to save Peru, but he also craved to be its savior, not for the monarchy which San Martín now favored, nor for the promotion of San Martín's glory; he wanted to save it on his own terms, in his own way—in short, for the greater glory of Bolívar and, more than that, to promote his concepts of free representative government and his grandiose overall plan for the continent. He could not conceive of all this being accomplished except as an enterprise conducted by himself. Furthermore, the intrigues and uprisings already springing up in Colombia would be quieted if the northern confederation could be aroused to back a Peruvian crusade.

Bolívar was well-informed as to Peru's plight. He was well-primed about Lima; the patriot army was cooped up there, mostly idle, its morale disintegrating. Manuela had told him of the lack of money and trade, the lack of patriotism, the Creole intrigues. He knew that the matter was urgent.

But he played his cards close to his chest. He affected indifference, speaking of his own pressing duties in Colombia. He could not possibly get away, nor could he send much assistance. He thus made San Martín the supplicant and, since the latter was caught in the middle of the disintegration like a fly on sticky paper, he had to plead for Bolívar's help.

Previously, in a still dark hour in Colombia on the rocky road to Cúcuta, Bolívar had offered to send a whole army, but now he suggested only a token force of 1,062 men, the precise number San Martín had lately sent to Ecuador to aid Sucre.

San Martín insisted that Bolívar's whole army was needed to save the day. Not only forces; Bolívar was needed in person at the head of them.

The Venezuelan's eyes flickered and brightened, and San Martín added, "You must come yourself with every soldier you can bring."

"I have no authority from the congress to leave Colombian soil. . . ."

"You, the president! The head of its army! Surely your congress will grant you the privilege of completing your life's work."

Bolívar continued to shake his head. His eyes were veiled, his face transfigured by some inner ecstasy that did not come from opium—not San Martín's kind of opium.

San Martín, studying his fellow liberator, saw that only the supreme personal command of the Peruvian enterprise would be acceptable to Bolívar. He did not hesitate. "I myself will gladly serve under your orders." The salvation of the country was more important than personal status.

In thus downgrading his own importance and showing his willingness to humble himself to bring about the triumph of the Independence cause, San Martín was, in his way, a far greater patriot than Bolívar. Already he had proved his own distaste for personal glory. In Chile he had constantly sought to give all power and glory to O'Higgins, not to himself. In Peru, unable to find a single Peruvian unflinchingly dedicated to Independence and seeing that the few men of ability were devoid of moral integrity and self-abnegation, he had agreed to assume command of the state for a single year, but within four months he had handed over the reins to Monteagudo, who, whatever his tortuous methods and slyness, was a relentless revolutionist, and to Torre Tagle, a doubtful pillar at best, in the hopes that this dual control might shake down into a workable pattern. Torre Tagle, the greedy Creole and aristocrat, and the insinuating revolutionary mulatto, Monteagudo, perhaps would keep each other in line—perhaps.

Bolívar, with a gesture of great magnanimity, refused to accept San Martín's self-humiliating offer; quite likely San Martín, however sincere, knew such would be the response.

They came to no final decisions and parted, a bit stiffly. There was a duel here, carried on by both men, in the most subtle fashion.

San Martín was well aware that Bolívar could not possibly let Peru go by default; this would shake him from his Gran Colombian throne. The Argentine leader worked late that night with his entourage, considering possibilities, drafting plans Bolívar might be obliged to accept.

Bolívar gaily danced the night away. Rumors of his conduct reached Manuela in Quito.

ix

The next day the Argentine presented a rock-bottom list of what was needed to liberate Peru and the continent. It was almost, though not so phrased, an ultimatum. Unless it were fulfilled, Peru would be lost, Bolívar's whole cloud-built castle of continental unity would melt away, and the north, too, would crumble.

Bolívar waved it aside and without comment laid before San Martín a letter from his ambassador in Lima that had come the same morning. Despite the threat of a royalist take-over, there had been a palace *coup* in Lima. Riva Agüero had persuaded other members of the government to seize Monteagudo and deport him to Panama, and congress had chosen Riva Agüero as Peru's first president.

Without Monteagudo—even though he no longer sympathized with his ideas—San Martín was lost. He could never govern with men like Riva Agüero, concerned only over personal property and selfish advantage, intrinsically unreliable, treacherous to the marrow, perhaps secretly pro-royalist, pro-Spanish, ready to sell out at any moment. The one consideration of such types was to save their great landed estates, not to save Peru. San Martín had no intention of going back and knuckling under to the petty breed of self-seeking Lima politicos. It would be a lonely struggle, with enemies within and a powerful enemy without. San Martín choked up, turned abruptly, and stalked out of the room.

There was a grand ball that evening for the two leaders. Bolívar, never gayer, flirted outrageously with the three Guaraycoa sisters. Two of them had had husbands murdered by the royalists. The youngest, Joaquina, responded to Bolívar, it is said, "with passionate adoration," a relationship which lasted for many years.

But San Martín remained aloof, hiding his agony of body and spirit behind a set smile. Those who spoke to him found his terseness almost rude. He danced several times, the minimum required by etiquette, gathered his cape about him, and slipped out into the night.

Bolívar rushed his partner to a seat and darted after him. They talked things over on the dark river pier. There San Martín told him simply, "I am returning to Lima, where I shall pack up and leave at once for Mendoza, then for Europe. I shall live the rest of my days in exile. I have finished my public life. . . ." And he added, "Time alone will tell which of us has foreseen the future more clearly."

As he left he may also have said, "Only your great prestige can hold the Peruvians together. They will obey you as they will no longer obey me. Don't delay. Time is running out."

Sometime before daybreak he boarded his vessel, slipping away without farewells or ceremonies. He had dumped the whole fate of Peru and the continent into Bolívar's lap.

Even before the little vessel vanished into the dark jungle of the looping river, Bolívar must have known that he had won a most dangerous diplomatic victory. With this lowering of San Martín's prestige, Peru itself would be weakened. What was worse, nothing could be done about it with lightning rapidity. It was going to take time. Before he could come to the rescue, greedy, petty rivalries—typical Lima products—might cause all Peru to collapse and bring about Spanish restoration, a collapse that still might engulf the continent. The struggle then would be even more prolonged and terrible.

10

The Eagles of Ayacucho

/v.v. Arriving in Lima August 19, San Martín resumed supreme command and brought a semblance of order to the city. He recalled the congress, dissolved by Riva Agüero, to meet September 20, and appeared before it in a splendid uniform, with great pomp and ceremony. In front of the assembly he removed his insignia, renounced his high position, gave up all rank and titles and position, all authority in the army and in the government, and retired to his Magdalena villa.

Two hours later a congressional delegation came to offer him the rank of general in chief of the army.

He accepted the honor, but without command, and that same night he embarked in Callao for Chile, abandoning Peru, abandoning the whole revolutionary struggle, abandoning, too, his Rosita.

A three-man junta was named to carry on the government. It included General José de La Mar, presently to become president. But already the fear and greed of the Creoles had flung Lima into confusion. Everything was being undermined.

Nevertheless, the new junta worked hard to whip together a new army. A levy of 400,000 pesos was imposed. The English merchants refused to obey, saying that foreigners had always been immune from such impositions, and they were backed up by the British frigate *Aurora* in Callao.

On their side, the Spaniards had ample money. For years they had received a minimum of 33,000 pesos a month, merely from the Potosí silver mines in Bolivia.

Even so, the junta managed to get together a force of 5,000, under Argentine general Rudesindo Alvarado, that put ashore at Tacna. Several small battles were fought. General Canterac then brought royalist forces down from Puna, and a tremendous engagement, featured by his usual brilliant deployment of troops, was fought at Moquegua.

It was a major disaster for the patriots: only 800 survived. Now, except for Lima and Trujillo and the small force of the wide-roving, extraordinary British Colonel Wilson and his hard-riding *guerrilleros,* the patriots were stripped bare. The Spaniards were well consolidated throughout the country.

ii

In spite of these mounting disasters, Bolívar, after four months, still had made no move. Perhaps he wished the Peruvians to reach the complete abyss of despair.

Certainly he faced a tremendous task, the most difficult undertaking of his career, and was well aware of the numerous pitfalls that could ensnare and destroy him. Even his own exalted position was a threat to his success. As he put it, "The higher I rise, the deeper the abyss yawns at my feet." His march into Peru would be "a wonderful plunge." Yet "the bread might burn the oven door"; Peru might also be called, he noted, "a terrible cavern where possessions, freedom, and courage would be swallowed up."

He was forty; this would probably be his last great effort. If it was to be the crowning glory of his career, he could not afford failure. Something of the patience and dedication to details that had featured San Martín's enterprises now marked his own preparations. His every move was cautious.

First the affairs of Colombia had to be put on a stable basis. If he were to succeed, he had to have Colombia firmly behind him just as San Martín had been supported by Chile and

Argentina. One worry was Vice President Santander, carrying
on as president in Bogotá (for Cúcuta had been abandoned
for the time being). While Santander never openly flouted
Bolívar's orders, he was known to be much opposed to the
Peruvian enterprise; his imagination had never been able to
rise much above his own village.

On November 10, Bolívar hurried back to Quito. Manuela,
to whom he had not written once, tongue-lashed him as he
had never been tongue-lashed—she knew of his dalliances in
Guayaquil—but she came back into his arms.

For his part, Manuela's husband knew, by now, of her affair
with the Liberator. Thorne had written that he would never
grant her a divorce; besides, he still loved her; for the sake of
appearances, if nothing else, she must give up Bolívar and become a respectable wife. Her reply was a sharp No! Over the
years, she wrote him about the situation. She always gave him
full credit for his fine qualities and admitted how much she
owed to him, but she grew increasingly more sarcastic about
his cold aloofness, his excessive love of respectability, his rigid
rules of life, saying that he had ice water in his veins, not
blood.

Now Manuela had Bolívar back. And though savage quarrels characterized their nightly meetings, their passion grew
more intense. The bond between them was closer than ever;
they were more necessary for each other than before. He promised—though she brought it up reluctantly—that her suit
against the Aispurús would be settled promptly. Now that a
break with Thorne threatened, she would really need the
money.

But Pasto revolted under the leadership of Tomás Boves,
nephew of the terrible royalist *llanero* of an earlier day who
had taken over all Venezuela and sent Bolívar flying into exile.
Tomás was backed by the governor of the province and aided
by the ineptitude (or the treachery) of Colonel Antonio
Obando. The matter was serious.

Bolívar sent Sucre out at once with a flying column of lancers and brought up the foot soldiers himself, five hundred miles across the snow-swept upland.

He left so precipitately he had no time to say good-bye to Manuela, and he wrote her—perhaps his first real letter to her —in a leaky thatched hut in the village of Yacán, by candle-light that guttered and almost went out from the gusts through the wattled walls and his own icy breath. It reached her when, thanks to his absence, a tricky judge was prevailed upon to decide against her and in favor of the Aispurús.

Her letter to him in reply said that the battle for Pasto, still to come, had cost her dearly since it had taken him from her side. "You will say that I am no patriot."

Pasto was captured by Sucre on Christmas day before Bolívar's troops caught up. The patron saint of Pasto, Santiago (also that of Spain), had been put in front of the church as protector of the Boves forces in the fight. According to O'Leary, when the royalists had to gallop away they threw the image down and angrily trampled on it, cursing poor Santiago for having failed them. Boves fled down the Marañón to Brazil, and Bolívar made a triumphal entry.

iii

The Liberator came back to Quito in February (with Colonel Obando added to his retinue), a sick man, worn out by his ordeal but too keyed up to rest. Manuela took over with a stern hand and saw to it that he obeyed the doctor's orders. She gave him his medicine and stayed by his bedside day and night, becoming not only his nurse but his private secretary, decreeing whom he would see and bossing his staff, the dominant personality of his official inner circle.

Sometimes he shouted against her dictatorship, but she held him to his needed rest and his medicine and threw out the chaff of less pressing duties.

"There has arrived," she told him, "a man I despise but whom you must see. Even though he is out of power, he controls the secret revolutionary apparatus over the continent."

He was "pock-marked, cat-faced" Bernardo Monteagudo, a dandy wearing the latest London-style suit and waistcoat, diamonds on his cambric shirts, diamonds in his ring, his jeweled watch held by a gold chain on which dangled a gold nugget in its original quartz setting. He came in smelling of eau de cologne (various slurs had been made about his sexual habits). He was small but had a heavy torso and square shoulders, a gray complexion, thick lips, and kinky hair that hinted at Negro blood.

But regardless of his unprepossessing appearance, Monteagudo had a razor-sharp passion for independence, and he was one of the few men in all South America who knew that if Independence was to have any valid meaning a new social order had to be created. As had happened in the French Revolution, the Creole aristocrats—not merely the Spaniards—had to be cast out and "made to eat *caca*." Monteagudo had confiscated their estates, jailed them, exiled them, killed them. He ran Spanish priests and bishops out of the continent. His weapons were terror, espionage, defamation, and assassination, legal or otherwise. Even when holding high office, he was always, as he had been in three countries, the *deus ex machina,* always manipulating things through his powerful secret Lautaro Lodge and exerting adroit influence, by fear or cajolery, over generals, police, and, above all, the civil and military judiciary. His dark-night cliques carried clubs and knives and struck from hidden corners.

Though San Martín, with whom he had been associated from the time of the latter's arrival in Buenos Aires in 1812, had come to dislike his ideas and his methods—most likely he did not know the ins and outs of all he did—Monteagudo had shown a lifelong loyalty and had been able to turn the tide at every dangerous juncture, getting needed results when no one else could.

Monteagudo had thus become the revolutionary "boss" of the continent. He had pushed governments out in Buenos

Aires. He had integrated the forces behind O'Higgins in Chile, relentlessly wiping out all clerical and royalist intriguers and destroying all lukewarm supporters. But he had never been able to outsmart the tricky turncoat, Rodríguez Aldea, who in time became O'Higgins' most sinister adviser and who, as much as anybody, brought about his downfall—by deliberately making a breech between O'Higgins and Ramón Freire, O'Higgins' best general. (Later, when Monteagudo had gone to Peru with San Martín, O'Higgins warned the liberator that they had to blame themselves for many of their troubles. They had given too much power to persons such as Monteagudo.)

Bolívar, lying half sick in Quito, was now entranced by Monteagudo's vast knowledge, his astuteness, and his agile ideas. He recognized his unflagging devotion to the Independence cause, his passionate determination to further it in every way. Monteagudo was both a Jesuit and a Robespierre; no matter, he had a mind, and most of Bolívar's generals and advisers, except Sucre, were little better than turnips or pumpkin heads. Here was a man, not only ruthless but endowed with tremendous flights of imagination regarding the new order.

He, too, believed in a continent-wide system. And he wanted to save Peru. He urged Bolívar to lead his whole army to Lima forthwith. "Under your leadership, and only under your leadership, will all unite. One great battle, such as Boyacá, will end Spanish rule there forever. The continent will be won. It will be secure for the revolution. As it is, everything is going to pieces."

Hardly had this conversation taken place and Monteagudo been made part of Bolívar's entourage than a Peruvian delegation arrived, informing him that their government was too weak to resist the royalists any longer. They, too, said that only Bolívar, with his great renown, could save Peru's tenuous independence.

Bolívar did not trust them and sent them off, merely saying he would consider the matter. But hardly had the door closed on their heels than he took up his quill pen and wrote to the one member of the government whom, according to Manuela, he could trust, "I have decided to save your country from the tyrants." At once Riva Agüero was informed and sent ships to carry the Colombian troops.

iv

All spring and summer, men and supplies poured into Guayaquil: Venezuelan lancers in jaguar-skin caps; galloping barefoot *llaneros* able to survive on a sliver of dried meat or a handful of parched corn; remains of the foreign legion, Englishmen, Scotchmen, Irishmen, Germans, Russians, many of them veterans of Waterloo. Andean-tested Colombian veterans were whipped into better efficiency. New Ecuadorean regiments were recruited and clothed in green, red-trimmed homespun uniforms. Preparations were feverish; time was of the essence.

Few vessels were available, but several piratical English freebooters were commissioned to bring in Spanish prizes and did. Among them was Juan Illingworth, whose corvette *Rosa de los Andes* was the terror of the South Seas. The Spanish crews were made to walk the plank or were strung up on the yardarms. But ships were obtained. (Illingworth, off and on, also fought in the patriot armies and won many laurels.)

Bolívar hurried to Guayaquil to press matters. He put up at the Guaraycoa hacienda. He walked into his quarters where Joaquina was putting things in order, and she flew into his arms. Over his shoulder she saw his new aide, Obando.

She flared up. "Simón! Simón! Why didn't you shoot this rascal? He's a trouble-maker and a traitor."

"Men make political mistakes."

"Can't you see it in his tricky eyes? He who makes one basket of snakes will make a hundred."

Obando turned on his heel and the following day went back to Pasto.

Vast supplies were accumulated: food, weapons, munitions,

uniforms—everything except money. There was no money, and Bolívar was determined that his men and officers should be promptly paid. He wrenched a million pesos out of Guayaquil in a few days. It was not enough.

He wrote Sucre (February, 1823), who had been left in Quito as *intendente,* to send more money and men. "Do it *flying, flying,* without losing a minute. . . . I am determined to take 6,000 men at one whack. . . ." He gave the numbers to be conscripted in various localities. "Get 800 men in Cuenca at once and outfit them however you can."

To Santander he wrote, "I have exhausted the fountain of my strength getting together men and money for the expedition. . . . Violence on violence. The fields, the cities, have been left as deserts to get 3,000 men and 200,000 pesos. I know better than anybody how far violence can be used, and I have used it. In Quito and Guayaquil we have taken all the men, in the temples, in the streets. Money we have taken at the point of the bayonet."

Even before the expedition got under way, the current phrase in Ecuador came to be, "How do we liberate ourselves from the Liberators?"

Once the vice president wrote back. "Your letter came today, and today there is not one cent in the treasury, not even for our current expenses. What do we do now, my general?" He urged Bolívar to return and carry on the necessary tasks at home.

Bolívar replied, "I no longer belong to the Colombians . . . nor to Caracas, but to the whole nation now; besides, the royalist army exists and wants to conquer Peru. . . ."

He had asked congress for permission to lead the forces there, but his request was held up. He suspected Santander of blocking it. He wanted his personal departure put on unquestionable legal footing. This would reinforce the principles of constitutional and representative government; it would prevent future charges of disobedience that might serve as a pretext for Santander or others to seize power; it would create a moral obligation for congress and Gran Colombia as a whole to lend further money and aid as needed.

But congress or no congress, he intended to dispatch the expedition. Until he could obtain his personal license, he put Sucre in full charge.

Sucre was a short-tempered, arbitrary soul, a maker of personal enemies, but he had drive, he had military genius, he was dedicated to the cause of Independence on the basis of justice, equity, and free government. In addition, he was probably the brainiest, most competent officer in Bolívar's entire army, in most respects the noblest of all the great leaders.

And so, all summer, troops were floated south—a ten-day voyage—3,000 at first, 6,000 in all.

Sucre reached Lima in April, 1823. He was appalled by the chaotic situation: the brazenly greedy politics, the crumbling loyalties, the undisciplined troops. As things stood, he wrote Bolívar, any military campaign would probably be unsuccessful, and he urged him to come at once.

But another revolt broke out in Pasto, and insurrectionary forces advanced toward Quito. Pretending weakness—indeed, there were few troops left in Quito—Bolívar retreated before the advance and led them into a trap in a narrow valley, where the patriots charged down with drawn sabers and smashed them. A lesson had to be taught to the people of this hotbed of persistent revolt. He ordered Pasto depopulated of all but well-known patriot families. Those arrested—men, women, and children—were deported to Guayaquil, a world away. Those who resisted were shot on the spot. More than ever, this uprising made congress reluctant to permit Bolívar to take troops out of Colombia. He was needed at home.

In Peru, meanwhile, Riva Agüero, encouraged by Colombian help, managed to get together 5,500 men under General Andrés Santa Cruz. These, too, were sent to Tacna and Arica by sea.

Sucre opposed the move, saying the Spaniards were too near

Lima for comfort, and would not budge his 3,000 men. Actually, he wished first to see the political situation clarified and to gain command of the entire military establishment; a single authority was needed to integrate the effort.

As Sucre had foreseen, 9,000 royalists moved on Lima, and the patriots had to retire to Callao in the shadow of the forts. There went the remnants of congress, those who had not fled elsewhere. There went Riva Agüero, but he soon fled to Trujillo, with the million pesos of the national treasury, and set up a rival congress. There were now two patriot governments in the tragic land.

The congress in Callao gave Sucre supreme command of all Peruvian forces. The first thing necessary, he realized, was a big patriot victory, and he went south with 2,500 men to help Santa Cruz, but the Peruvian angrily refused to recognize his authority and would not cooperate with him, and, as a result, the campaign was utterly disastrous.

More than ever, Bolívar was urgently needed, but the enabling act did not come. Finally, since the situation in Peru was now intolerable, he decided to leave regardless of legality and ordered the frigate *Chimborazo* made ready, sending aboard his personal battalion of hussars and his staff. Manuela was determined to go along, but he put his foot down flatly.

Just as the anchor chain was being drawn up, a mule-riding, mud-spattered courier galloped onto the river pier and handed Bolívar the enabling act signed and sealed.

v

Twenty-two guns roared out from the ancient Callao fortress as the *Chimborazo* moved toward shore that bright day of September 2, 1823. A dazzling sun followed along the tawny rainless coast of Peru for a thousand miles and swept the snowy heights with shimmering fire.

As the landing boat put Bolívar ashore, he was met by the

mayor of Lima, wearing a red coat. They rolled toward Lima almost as if nothing had changed, in a six-wheeled blue-and-gold coach that had belonged to the viceroy, its lackeys in powdered perukes and silk knee breeches—strange attire in a presumed republic.

Though Lima is merely an oasis in the desert, better said a gem—"the city of palaces"—thanks to artificial irrigation, it was a bower of green and cascading flowers.

The jungle heat of Guayaquil was behind; here was a warm perpetual spring, a city draped with luxuriant vegetation—palm trees and oleanders, bougainvillea and mimosas—next to Rio, the handsomest city of the Americas.

The seven-mile avenue to the capital was lined by majestic trees and also by Sucre's green-uniformed Colombian soldiers and by a cheering multitude. The crowd grew denser as they went smartly through the great gate of the walled city, curiously enough still bearing the Spanish coat of arms.

From the boat, Bolívar had been able to see the vast Andean snow ridge, more continuous than in Ecuador; then, as he neared the beautiful city of gold and blue *talevera* cupolas, of tall towers and carved balconies, the great snow wall vanished, shut off by the foothills that reach to the very edge of Lima, sear brown outcroppings, mountains themselves, steep, utterly barren, forbiddingly impregnable. Closest at hand was tall San Cristóbal hill, surmounted by a huge cross—for the Limeños, though their practices were so corrupt, were as fanatically religious as the Quiteños.

But unlike Quito, Lima, except for a slight dip toward the trickle known as the Rimac River, was a level city, laid out in severe right angles. The streets, however, were narrow and lined with convents and the ornate, roccoco facades of an incredible number of churches. Each mansion had its elaborate, jalousielike carved balcony. But much of the magnificence of a few years previous had vanished. There were few fine carriages. Numerous great mansions had been abandoned; some were falling into ruin. The streets were heaped with filth, and the center gutters of water were choked with garbage and litter.

The carriage rolled on to the viceregal palace on the Plaza de Armas, flanked by arcades in front of the main stores and by the cathedral, less impressive than those in Bogotá or Quito. Bolívar found the palace dilapidated, dirty, and gloomy, scarcely up to the grandeurs of imperial Lima, and he soon moved out to the viceregal villa in the Magdalena suburb, a charming little town drenched with all-year flowers. His new residence fronted a small plaza, and he took over an adjacent house to stable the horses of his aides and couriers.

A week after Bolívar's arrival, a big state banquet was held. Among the guests was General Bernardo O'Higgins, who had been overthrown and was now in exile. He offered his sword to Bolívar, but his services could not be accepted lest the new Chilean government under Freire—who had stripped O'Higgins of offical rank, decorations, pay, and pensions—be so vengeful toward its erstwhile liberator that it might sever relations. Bolívar hoped to get aid and troops from Chile; O'Leary was sent off on that fruitless mission.

Royalist General Canterac was leaving tracks of blood and smoking ruins all across Peru. Two patriot forces had already been wiped out. In the south, General Santa Cruz went down the drain. To the north, Riva Agüero was pulling his own chestnuts out of the fire, acting as an independent government. He wrote to San Martín, who had reached Argentina on his way to Europe, to come back and save the country. He believed if he could get San Martín back the two leaders would have a falling out, and his own importance would be enhanced.

Torre Tagle was now seated in his place in Lima—at best an equivocal and bankrupt government, both morally and financially.

For days and weeks after Bolívar's arrival, the situation was discussed endlessly at the viceregal villa with Sucre (after his return), government officials, and army officers. Even the discussions seemed to get nowhere and sunk little by little into the quagmire of dalliance, intrigue, laxity, and halfheartedness.

In spite of the depressing situation, Bolívar was enamored of Lima. "More delighted every day. . . . The men respect me, the women love me, the food is excellent, the theater only so-so but adorned with beautiful eyes, . . . the carriages, horses, bullfights, *Te Deums*. . . . Nothing is lacking here except money."

Lima was a paradise of lascivity. Bolívar's worldly wise secretary, Colonel Juan Santana, called it "a Babylon where all the beautiful women . . . conspire to turn our heads. . . . A giddy succession of . . . beauties and flirtations."

vi

Bolívar's own wings were clipped a bit when Manuela arrived toward the middle of September with her two slaves and her trunks of clothes and settled in a house she owned only two blocks from the Liberator's Magdalena headquarters. At the moment her husband was in Chile on business.

In answer to Bolívar's upbraiding, she replied airily, "I had no money to keep on in Quito. I have always lived in Magdalena. This is my home." After a furious quarrel, followed by reconciliation, she was back in the Liberator's bed.

She drove about the city in a small *calesa,* renewing old friendships and creating much gossip and speculation.

Bolívar soon found her indispensable. She knew Lima intrigue inside and out. She knew people and officers. Things he found mysterious, intricate, or irritating were clear as water to her. Furthermore she knew all the hidden scandals, the intimate social, political, and amatory affairs, past and present. For, if Bolívar had Manuela to tell him about these things, Manuela had Jonotás, and Jonotás had the knack of obtaining information about anybody, even military officers and their schemes. She was, even now, having an affair with a soldier in the Callao fort.

Within a month, Manuela was able to wheedle Bolívar into making her a permanent member of his staff, in charge of his personal archives. Her post would fool nobody but would maintain appearances of a sort, now that Thorne was due to return. She gave herself the title of Colonel and designed a trim blue uniform with silver-leaf insignia, epaulettes and scarlet cuffs and collar.

General Jacinto Lara, furious with the ostentatious arrangement and fearing the effect on public opinion, stormed in to protest to Bolívar and was told to mind his own business. (After some years of huffiness, Lara became a good friend and helped Manuela in many ways.)

Above all, Secretary Santana approved of her, worshiped her, became her devoted ally. For years, when she was not with Bolívar, he wrote her intimate news about the man she wanted to be near.

One man was ready to lay down his life for her, Majordomo José Palacios, who had brought Manuela to the Quito palace that first time. His two big mastiffs recognized her at once, and, with Palacios and the dogs, she often went about Lima on her duties or strolls. During the day, the two animals lay on the polished tan tiles of her office, dozing with their muzzles in their paws but ever alert to spring to her defense.

The day after the banquet, Bolívar had demanded full powers from the congress. "I promise you victory," he told them, "and I promise that my authority will not exceed beyond the time necessary to prepare for and win victory."

His first serious trouble came from Riva Agüero in Trujillo, whose traitorous correspondence with the Viceroy de la Serna had been intercepted. He offered the Spaniards an armistice, one secret provision being that he would eject Bolívar and all foreign troops from Peruvian soil. Manuela knew Riva Agüero well, from the days when he had been a Spanish gen-

eral; she had helped recruit him for San Martín, so that Trujillo had been won without a fight. More recently, high in the
Lima government, he had conspired to oust Monteagudo and
thereby San Martín.

Bolívar moved against him by sea and land, departing from
Lima November 15, but before he reached Trujillo, Riva
Agüero's own officers, informed of his treachery, seized him.
Bolívar deported him to Guayaquil and sometime later per-
mitted him to go to Belgium.

vii

In Bolívar's absence, Manuela became virtually dictatress of
the Magdalena villa. This shocked the elite, and no one worse
than the wife of the all-powerful Marqués de Torre Tagle.
One minister of state was furious because she refused, as she
did to everybody, to turn over to him one of the Liberator's
documents which he felt should be published.

Manuela wrote her Simón voluminously about affairs in the
capital. Her only reply came from Secretary Santana. Bolívar
would be returning in five days and would spend the entire
summer at the villa.

The Liberator was not well. While in the northern coast
city, he began vomiting and coughing blood and was put
aboard ship more dead than alive. So bad did his condition
become, the captain put him ashore at Pativilca, a miserable
little shore village near the Paramonga ruins. There for a week
he hovered between life and death.

Manuela and others wrote him that Torre Tagle (having
learned nothing from the downfall of Riva Agüero) was in
turn communicating with the Spaniards. The fact was, his
wife Josefa loathed Manuela. A prudish religious fanatic, she
hated the Independence cause and wanted to undermine
Bolívar.

Bolívar lifted himself from his bed and wrote the acting
head of government. "Believe me, believe me, the country will

not be saved in this way"—by seeking to compromise with the Spaniards—"but by unity and discipline. . . . The bloody war in Venezuela lasted fourteen years, yet you complain of black bread for four years."

On February 4, the Callao fortress was betrayed by the Argentine Negro regiment. They released all Spanish prisoners and ran up the Spanish flag.

As the situation deteriorated, Bolívar observed, as San Martín had so many times before him, "There is much corruption in Peru; it seems impossible that this country ever be a republic."

On February 29, Torre Tagle, issuing a hateful and disgusting proclamation against Bolívar, opened the gates of Lima to the royalists. They began a house-to-house search to seize and shoot republicans.

Already, thanks to Jonotás' contacts, Manuela had begun boxing up Bolívar's precious archives. When the Callao blow came, all the guards at the villa fled, taking off their uniforms and donning peasant rags. Palacios was with Bolívar. She was practically alone, but she continued to pack up the documents, silver and gold plate, and clothes and arranged for mules to transport everything.

English *guerrillero* William Miller rallied a few troops and galloped up to guard the villa until she could depart.

He was the most amazing man of the whole Independence struggle, a battle-scarred veteran of incredible exploits. One hand had been permanently disabled by a bullet, and he limped from another wound. His face was deeply scarred, having been blown half off by an explosion of Congreve rockets he was firing at the Spanish fleet in Callao. For weeks he had writhed in torment under a plaster cast, with only an aperture for a silver tube to feed him. He had started out from Buenos Aires with San Martín's grenadiers, had been with San Martín on the Pampa, in Cuyo, through the Andes, at Chacabuco, at Maipú, all through Chile. He had fired the first shots at the landing below Ica. Years later he provided historian William Prescott with vivid descriptions of the Andes for *The Conquest of Peru.*

He now led the toughest band of patriot *guerrilleros* in all Peru—the Montañeros. They included the three hundred male survivors of the Spanish slaughter of the population of Reyes on Lake Junín in 1821. The two requirements for enlistment with Miller were hate for the Spaniards and ability to ride a horse skillfully. Strangely enough, though many of his men were pure-blooded Indians, they were fanatically devoted to the tiny, blue-eyed, blond Englishman named "Meeyér."

Those who escaped the royalist dragnet assembled for refuge at the villa: General Lara, Monteagudo, Bolívar's cabinet. Some of the latter, dreadfully frightened, urged immediate flight, but Miller refused to depart until Manuela's mules were duly loaded.

They rode off in the dark, eluding the Spaniards, and reached the desert outside the city. To avoid showing their silhouettes (it was a vivid moonlit night), Miller kept them to the hollows, serpentining in and out among the larger dunes.

Hours later they were climbing up the Andean foothills and soon were tracking their way over yawning abysses, up and up, until they were two miles high. They debouched onto the frozen plains between snow peaks. Here they were joined by the tough Reyes fighters.

It was a wild crew, in bright ponchos and bobbing felt hats. But with them were many suffering civilians, among them a few obese politicians, and the little pock-marked Monteagudo, in spite of the hardships still looking like a dandy, still exuding eau de cologne. Manuela brought her black slaves and her string of slow-plodding mules.

General Lara was in a great stew. He wanted to get rid of the civilians, particularly Monteagudo, whom he loathed. He was irritated by Manuela and her pack mules. But though he was Miller's superior, the Englishman paid no attention to him. These were his men, this was his command, and he knew the mountains better than Lara or anyone else in Peru.

It was a bleak, icy world. Since this was midsummer, they

did not encounter snow blizzards, but often the trails were solid ice and packed snow underfoot, and several times they were whipped by dreadful sleet and hailstorms. The sharp ice cut hands on the bridles to bloody strings. Yet at midday sometimes the temperature shot up to 90°; occasionally men went permanently blind from the sun's glare. Food was scant; the Indians had little. But cattle ran wild and could be hunted down. There were several deaths from mountain sickness—*soroche.*

Miller was trying to meet up with Bolívar, who was scouting through the mountains trying to get supplies and more recruits to save Trujillo, the only foothold the patriots now had in all Peru.

It was a major disaster; these raw crags could not support an army. So long as they held Lima, they could enjoy trade and obtain money and food. Now, nearly all was lost.

As Bolívar had risen from his bed to go to Trujillo, he was asked, "What will you do now?"

"I? I? Why, I will triumph."

Miller led the way to the red-tiled roofs of Huarás, a small village in a protected valley under great snow and glacier peaks, where they found Bolívar and his little band of troops. He was busy with paperwork in the townhouse on the plaza.

Lara expressed his bitterness about Manuela and her mules and Monteagudo. "Some day," he growled, "somebody is going to kill that little creature."

Bolívar reared up in fury. "Just let anybody touch one hair of his head!"

viii

Manuela and her mules had put up in neighboring Huamachuco. Bolívar wrote her of his delight that she had come through safely. He did not suggest she come on to Huarás but said he would come to Huamachuco, for he was bedded down with a pretty eighteen-year-old of the village. Manuela learned about it and was heartsick and furious.

But when he finally showed up, she did not upbraid him. The whole situation was too dreadful, the burdens almost too great for his small, sick body. They were reunited in terror and ecstasy.

Then he was gone again. Manuela kept trailing after him through the Sierra, dragging along the many boxes of archives across the terrible chasms of the Andes. She was still a colonel and still the archivist.

Bolívar was building up his force and accumulating supplies in Huarás and planned once more to march through the snow passes of the higher Andes. He laid out a march through three lofty passes, and this time he prepared well. He had the soldiers put Indians to work building stout sheds all the way through the passes, as refuges for the soldiers. In nearby caves supplies were cached: ammunition, food, dried llama, rice, corn, tobacco, salt, coca leaves. *Champas,* a thick mountain peat, was cut up for fuel.

The Indian workers were kept under guard so that no word could leak out to the Spaniards. Just before the march, they were taken to the coast temporarily, for the same reason.

Bolívar led one wing of the forces through the pass. Manuela remained behind in Huarás, with a rear guard, and did much to keep up the spirits of the men and officers. She threw wild parties, for which she dressed with as much care as for a stately ball in Lima itself. She served drinks and luxuries seized from a Spanish supply train. Jonotás danced the suggestive Ecuadorian *ñapanga* and then beat the drum for Manuela to dance the whirling Peruvian *honda,* an Africanized bolero.

All through June—it was winter now—the dreadful march continued. Bolívar had 9,000 troops by this time, three infantry divisions and two cavalry divisions; a tremendous supply problem. They drove before them—Bolívar this time did not let them lag behind—6,000 head of cattle. Miller's *guerrilleros* went ahead to guard the defiles and prevent attacks at dangerous points.

Manuela, clad in her colonel's uniform and a red-and-blue poncho, in due time took up the march with her mules, her archives, the gold and silver plate, her own trunks.

It was a terrible odyssey, even though well planned, for this was twice as high as the Colombian crossing. Every mile a soldier died from fatigue, cold, or *soroche*. Mules rolled to their death.

But the entire army, minus the casualties, successfully emerged onto the bleak black plateau, the so-called *puna*. There they faced hit-and-run attacks by royalist cavalry who seemed to swarm everywhere.

Bolívar made his headquarters at Huánuco—the Eyebrow of the Mountain—a beautiful spot of eternal spring climate, on the inner face of the Andes overlooking the Montaña. He ordered Manuela to take up residence in an adjacent town.

She did not see him, but Santana wrote her frequently, referring to him as the Colonel so as to avoid disclosures should the letters be intercepted.

On July 28, Santana wrote, "We go on to Cerro de Pasco, and on August 10, the whole army will be reunited, and we shall start operations. . . . I shall not speak to you now of snow, gratitude, or duty. . . ."

On July 18, he wrote from twelve-thousand foot Huriaca, where Bolívar reviewed his assembled troops from a hilltop. Monteagudo was at his side. At his back were the jagged crags; below him on the plain of Junín was a frozen lake, the highest source of the Amazon River.

Though Bolívar's whole force had not yet united, even so that army was a great spectacle: veterans from the battles of all America, veterans from the wars in Europe. Miller, in charge of the cavalry, led them at a gallop, guiding his wiry horse with his one good hand; they thundered by, raising a fine powdery dust—the best horsemen on earth: Argentine Gauchos, Chilean *huasos;* Venezuelan *llaneros,* Peruvian *montañeros.*

The whole royalist army began converging on the plain,

after a long, hard, double-paced march on the east side of the lake. Bolívar sent a fast-moving force around the longer side of the lake to try to cut them off. The first royalist comers were startled to see such a big array of forces. After some fighting, they fell back some ten miles to more advantageous positions.

A hard-riding band of patriot cavalry charged right in with their twelve-foot lances—the longest lances in the Americas— a deadly innovation introduced by San Martín back in Argentine days.

Though it was late, and the long shadows of the tall mountains stretched far across the plain, Bolívar set his whole army in motion.

The royalists by then had swung their cavalry into a front position. The two main mounted forces met with a terrific impact, and the galloping patriots hurtled right on through. The battle changed into a crazy melee of flashing sabers, horses and riders, horses crazed with fear, unhorsed men, in a mishmash of steel, of blood and screams. The patriots fell back, then rallied, as mounted reserves were hurled into the fight.

This fresh onslaught broke the Godos. They began fleeing. Bolívar pursued them relentlessly, hacking and slashing and killing.

The battle of Junín was won. The dead and wounded lay in great heaps. The royalists had lost six times as many men as the patriots.

Before the dead could be sorted over, Indians, who had watched the fray from the heights, rushed down to loot the battlefield and strip the dead and injured of their uniforms. Many wounded perished from the cold, not from their wounds, before rescuers arrived.

Bolívar met with his officers hastily in a windy hut to assess the victory.

"Enough," he finally said. "Follow the enemy. Pick a suitable place and there fight the final decisive battle."

They drank a toast. An English officer, veteran of Napoleon's retreat from Moscow, failed to lift his glass. "I wish to rectify your record of the number of officers killed. The number is not seven but eight." He slid to the floor. He had been quietly bleeding to death during the talks.

Manuela, following the main march, reached the Indian church of Carahuamayo on the plains of Junín and there arranged for the burial of the brave Englishman, putting up the marker with her own hands.

Near the end of August, Santana wrote Manuela again, not knowing where she was—Bolívar wanted to know—"We are six leagues from Ayacucho (Huamanga), and tomorrow we shall enter the city, the second largest of Peru. [It has since fallen into sad decay.] The Spaniards are still fleeing; we are pursuing them."

Manuela had already followed the Liberator with the archives, the plate, and her clothes for a thousand miles, with only several glimpses of him. She settled finally in lovely Jauja, not far from his latest headquarters. Spring was nearly there. Already the hard rains were beginning, when the Andes become gloomier than ever. But Jauja was nice.

It was October when Bolívar finally rode to see her. He was preoccupied and morose. It was not her charms that were at fault; Santander had forced the Colombian congress to strip him of active command. He was now forbidden to lead the army into battle. Santander gave as the reason that Bolívar would ruin himself and his reputation. This, after the great battle of Junín!

Santander had not taken this arbitrary step so long as Bolívar seemed to be losing the fight, for it meant he himself could take over Colombia unobstructed. The victory of Junín came as a shock to his schemes.

Manuela told Bolívar he should ignore the orders and have Santander hanged as a traitor. But looking far ahead, he decided to obey and so put the command into Sucre's hands. A

few of his officers said they would serve under no one but the
Liberator. He told them that meant they had to serve under
Sucre—he was "The Liberator."

He gave his last instructions to the new commander. "Maneuver for one big successful battle, then all other battles will
be easy. Above all, avoid marching too much. Feet spared
Peru, feet saved Peru, and feet can lose Peru again. Since we
cannot fly to our enemies, we must conserve our energies. . . .
Sooner or later they will stop running, and we shall defeat
them."

He turned on his heel. Many of his officers were weeping.
In a few minutes he was flying off to Lima, but he delayed en
route to recruit more men for Sucre. Thus Manuela arrived
before he did.

After Junín, the Spaniards had evacuated Lima except for
a small token force to maintain order. Manuela was not
bothered, and when Bolívar arrived on December 7, 1824, the
royalists themselves flung open the gates for his entry.

ix

The following day—clear and bitterly cold up in the Andes
—Sucre's army was bivouacked above Ayacucho beyond the
Indian village of Quinúa, on the bleak jumbled inner table-
land, flanked on either side by deep rugged ravines.

Near the top of a bulky height across the valley to the east,
on Condorcanqui—Condor's Neck—was encamped the royalist
army.

In spite of Bolívar's injunctions, there had been considerable marching and countermarching. In spite of the Junín victory, partly because of the absence of Bolívar's dynamic presence, there had been considerable desertion and also much
sickness and death. The force had shrunk to 5,000 men, and
the royalists had twice as many.

All night Sucre's men huddled around their meager fires
under the diamond-sharp stars, preparing for the morrow's

THE EAGLES OF AYACUCHO

battle, sharpening their bayonets, casting lead into bullet molds, mending their gear. Few tried to sleep.

During the night, Sucre sent a company to the foot of Condorcanqui to keep up a fire to pin the royalists to their positions till he could deploy his army.

At daybreak—a sparkling clear morning—the royalists moved artillery along an adjacent ravine and at nine o'clock began coming down the steep descent, in two columns with cavalry in between. It was so precipitous the horses had to be led.

A small cavalry unit, commanded by a Spanish general, galloped toward the patriots with a white flag. He merely wanted to chat before the engagement; he was a believer in medieval etiquette.

The bulk of the patriot forces, Sucre in the center of the line, began moving across the valley floor in the face of a withering fire.

Patriot General José María Córdoba dismounted and killed his horse with a single knife thrust. "I want no horse on which to escape from this battle," he said, and raised his wide sombrero on the tip of his saber. "Forward!"

"At what step?" a wounded officer shouted.

"What step? Why the step of conquerors!"

In that charge, the dead mounted in heaps. The patriots kept right on over their own dead and bit deep into the royalist lines.

Miller and his *montañeros* rode into the breach, swinging sabers. They struck toward the artillery, captured it, turned it against the enemy.

The royalists drew back, presently fled in wild rout, but were trapped under the cliffs. Those who tried to climb up were picked off by sharpshooters, and their bodies, said General Miller, rolled down till "arrested by the brushwood or some jutting crag." The slaughter was worse than at Junín: 1400 were killed, 700 wounded.

Viceroy de la Serna, his gray hair matted with blood, was captured, along with sixteen generals and sixteen colonels. He signed a complete capitulation, handing over all Peru. At that very moment, the king in Spain was naming him Count of the Andes.

It was the final important battle of the Americas. There was no doubt now but that all the freed republics would remain free.

Before anything else, Sucre dashed off the tidings to Bolívar, using the end of an uptilted brandy keg as a desk.

His message reached the Magdalena villa late at night. Bolívar had been coughing blood all day and was wrapped in a large blue cape, his unshod feet on a brazier for, though it was midsummer, the night was chilly. Manuela was reading to him.

Juan Santana burst into the room without shoes, his clothes unbuttoned, still tugging on his jacket. At his heels came Captain Alarcón, the messenger, his uniform thick with dust.

"News! News!" yelled Santana.

Bolívar read the message in stunned silence, once, twice; then, waving it in his hands, he raced around the room, jumping over chairs, landed on the table, and danced madly, shouting joyously, "Victory! Victory! Victory!"

11

Dictator of Gran Colombia

/\/\/\ At Bolívar's urging, the Peruvian congress made Sucre a field marshal, with the title of Liberator of Peru, and awarded him 200,000 pesos. But in everybody's eyes, Ayacucho was Bolívar's victory; he was the real liberator. Congress awarded him the title of Father and Savior of Peru, ordered that a statue of him be erected, tablets of stone put up in all public buildings, his picture displayed in all *cabildos,* and medals struck off, bearing his likeness and the motto, Liberator of Peru. It voted him a million pesos. He told them it would be a breach of self-respect for him to accept it. "I have always believed that the only reward for a man's devotion to freedom and glory should be freedom and glory." He sent the money to promote education and social welfare in Colombia.

His stature increased immeasurably when he handed back to congress the supreme power he had been granted. "Allow me to felicitate the people on their release from the two worst things the world knows: from war, by victory; from despotism, by my resignation." Congress insisted he continue, not with the title of dictator but as president for life.

The Spaniards under General Ramón Rodil still held Callao, six miles from Lima. The first white-flag messenger, sent to demand surrender, came back with a defiant refusal pinned to his flesh with a knife. The second emissary was thrown into the sea.

Bolívar set up a siege with 4,000 men. The guns pounded day and night. Casualties mounted. New fears took hold of volatile Lima. Robbery increased. Hens stopped laying. The churches were jammed with the fanatic fearful. One day, according to Victor von Hagen, the hangman, obliged to work overtime, slipped the noose over his own neck and jumped.

To break the hysterical tension, Bolívar ordered bullfights, cockfights, and reopened the old Comedy Theater where famous Perrichole had held forth.

Then, on the night of January 28, Bernardo Monteagudo, who had been working to organize Bolívar's proposed amphictyonic congress in Panama, was stabbed in a narrow street near the San Juan Plazuela. Bolívar was called from a ball celebrating the Ayacucho victory to view the body. None of Monteagudo's ostentatious diamond jewelry had been taken.

Bolívar ordered wholesale arrests, among them slaves of Count San Isidro, who had often denounced Monteagudo and his revolutionary ideas. Convinced it was the work of widespread conspiracy, Bolívar seized the private papers of Creole aristocrats, but nothing was discovered. Finally three known cutthroats "confessed" and were hung. Few people believed they had done it.

The siege went on. The relentless cannonading went on. Presently the city was stricken by yellow fever and smallpox epidemics.

Bolívar's nerves were frayed; after a prolonged session, marked by harsh irritability, his secretary Santana would reel out like a wet rag. He quarreled frequently with Manuela, picking on her for her smoking—a habit she had acquired in Panama, where all women smoked. Thus far she had been the only person, thanks to Bolívar's sensitive throat, allowed to smoke in his presence. She refused to stop.

Manuela, for her part, accused Bolívar of carrying on with other women. One night, the story was told, when she came to the villa unexpectedly, she found an earring in his bed and scratched his face so badly he had to stay in his room with "la grippe" for a week. Whether true or not, she cared for him zealously during that time.

There was plenty of discord also in public affairs. Bolívar wrote Santander, "Here they compare me to Mercury's staff which had the power to link in friendship all the snakes which might have devoured each other. Nobody here gets along with anybody, but everyone gets along with me."

ii

In April, Bolívar set out on a triumphal tour of all Peru, with a new, smartly uniformed Colombian cavalry unit. Palacios and the two mastiffs went along, but not Manuela.

He told her bluntly their affair had ended. In his present position he could not afford scandal; the time had come to preserve appearances. He advised her to return to Thorne, who was coming back to Peru, and be a good wife. This she tried to do, but kept on writing to him of her devotion and love. Occasionally he replied; increasingly, as he missed her and felt the need for her affection and advice.

His trip was leisurely. They first went south along the coastal desert to Mataratones, Pisco, Ica, and other towns. After the hot, desolate miles—sterile desert or utterly barren mountains—each of these places was a little dot of green perched on the banks of an Andean river; each seemed a little paradise.

As they turned toward the sierra the villages became more Indian, and the Indians greeted Bolívar with love and enthusiasm; the fiestas—music, fireworks, dancing—were prolonged and jubilant.

"They wore their richest, most showy costumes," said O'Leary, "the same as the ones their ancestors had used." They believed that the new order, now that the Spanish slave-owners were gone, would wipe out the abuses they had suffered for so long and would bring them justice. (To appreciate how badly they were defrauded, one need but look at present-day Peru.)

It took twenty-eight days to reach Arequipa, where Bolívar remained twenty-five days. It was a grand entry. The Andean veterans of freedom were lined up in new parade uniforms, with tears in their eyes; there the last Spanish viceroy and field marshal, wealthy Pío Tristán, exchanged his titles for that of general of the republic and thereby saved his vast possessions, though he and other big landowners had to cough up heavy imposed levies.

Bolívar put into effect new decrees regarding popular rights and sovereignty, freedom and equality of opportunity. He reorganized the economy, cut down on the number of bureaucrats, founded schools. The local authorities cooperated—at least while he was there—wholeheartedly.

Fifteen more leisurely days up and up the *cordillera*, through historic Quechua ruins and towns old before the Spaniards had come, brought him to Cuzco, the massive Inca capital, to this day the most interesting—in its way, the most impressive—city of the Americas. Bolívar rode past the vast llama and alpaca herds, between the colossal Inca walls, to the Joy Plaza and the Plaza of Tears, both laid out ages ago by the Incas. From the Spanish balconies of the birdcage Spanish houses imposed on the ancient structures were showered down flowers and laurel wreaths and handfuls of coins for the people crowding the streets. He was presented with the gold keys of the city and a fine horse with gold-encrusted saddle and bridle. A thousand girls and women presented him with a gold crown, dazzling with diamonds and rubies, emeralds and pearls. He accepted it in the name of Sucre, to whom the Liberator sent all his gifts except the gold keys, which he gave to O'Leary.

"The city of Cuzco," remarked O'Leary, "could truly be called the Rome of America. Its history, its legends, its ruins were an enchantment. The enormous fortress to the north is the capitol; the Temple of the Sun, the Coliseum; Manco Capac was its Romulo; Viracocha, its Augustin; Huáscar its Pompey, and Atahualpa its Caesar. . . . The Spanish Conquerors, Pizarro, Almagro, Valdivia, Toledo, were the Huns and Goths and Christians who destroyed it."

Its one hope since those earlier days, he remarked, had been a quarter of a century before this when Tupac Amarú led a revolt of 60,000 Quechuas and Aimaras to re-establish the old empire and almost drove the Spaniards out of the land. Everybody in this upland country still spoke the native languages; only a few spoke Spanish.

Now here was Bolívar, who had succeeded where Tupac Amarú had failed. Looking at the ruined temples and palaces, the great walls and gardens, he exclaimed, "A people who, without the aid of modern civilizations, had done such great things, would reach an honorable position under a good government!"

O'Leary, a profound Catholic, wrote, "The official *corregidor*, the priest, the landowner, the mine owner, the factory owner, each and all have been oppressors of the Indian, obliging him to fulfill the most onerous and fraudulent contracts; life for the Indians was a curse under exploitation of such magnitude; even the consolation of religion could be bought only with gold."

Bolívar, "made desperate by such physical and moral degradation," issued decrees, decrees, decrees—decrees that became a dead letter the day he left Peru to return to Colombia, and which have remained a dead letter until this day.

He reduced the number of monasteries and convents and used the added income to found and support schools. He distributed lands to the Indians and suppressed serfdom, especially the forced domestic service in rich homes.

And so, for a whole month, the jubilant fiestas went on day and night: banquets, fireworks, barbecues (*pachacamacas*), *chicha* drinking, and music, music, all the time.

On he went into the cold *puna*, 14,000 feet or more above the sea, and in the village of Choquehuanca the Indian mayor told him, "Your glory will grow through all the centuries just as the shadow grows when the sun declines." There he heard that in Alto Peru, an assembly in Chuquisaca, the capital, had declared independence and formed a new state comprising the four highland and jungle provinces, previously annexed to Argentina and Peru. It had called itself Bolivia, in his honor.

iii

Sucre was already in Bolivia, mopping up the last puddles of Spanish resistance. The two leaders met in La Paz, a city in a slot of a lofty canyon under the awe-inspiring crests of some of the grandest snow mountains of the Andes. As Sucre dismounted to embrace Bolívar, his sword fell.

"That's a bad sign," remarked O'Leary.

The next day Sucre broke his sword when he hit an insolent aide with the flat blade.

O'Leary, who had found Sucre's sudden spurts of anger difficult, remarked, "That's an even worse omen than that of yesterday. From this day on, your disgrace and troubles begin."

"That's exactly what I've been thinking," said Sucre glumly.

At the request of the congress, Bolívar wrote a constitution for the new country. It was a product of his studies, his dreams, and his battles in five countries, a document heralded the world over for its high intelligence and progressive republicanism.

Here in La Paz, as elsewhere, he was concerned for the Indians, first and foremost, and promptly abolished slavery and other abuses and made them full-fledged citizens.

He called a conference of a hundred better-prepared Indians and had them speak out concerning their grievances and government abuses and draw up proper reforms. That body soon turned into an exclusive and obstructive clique, and he dissolved it.

He was implacable in his squaring of old accounts, even among his own followers. In Mendoza, San Martín—who had established the death penalty for any defalcation of army funds —was approached by a colonel, paymaster in one of the barracks, who had lost the regimental funds gambling. The Argentine leader replaced the money and told the trembling officer, "Just don't tell your commander in chief [San Martín himself] about it, or he will have to have you shot." But in La Paz, Bolívar promptly put a thieving military commander, who had stolen funds, before the firing squad and made the officer who had appointed him restore the stolen money.

Not all was smooth. The eastern Bolivian province of Chiquitos, under the leadership of Colonel Sebastián Ramos, refused to recognize the new government or Sucre or Bolívar. "The province of Chiquitos puts itself under his Imperial Majesty of Brazil, until either Spanish America or Peru is evacuated by the revolutionary power commanded by the seditious Simón Bolívar and Antonio José de Sucre and is reconquered by the arms of his Catholic Majesty of Spain."

The Brazilians, who had already seized Uruguay, sent troops into the province, but on the advance of Bolívar's forces they withdrew. Subsequently, Sucre exacted a formal apology from Brazil.

Argentine emissaries arrived, offering Bolívar the political union of Argentina, Bolivia, and Peru, and asked for aid to free Uruguay. He was tempted, but he agreed to try to get the Brazilians out of Uruguay by diplomatic pressures.

However, the new Argentine navy and the Argentine army soon thoroughly whipped the Brazilians. The Uruguayan patriots, particularly the wild Gaucho leader, José Artigas, then refused to recognize Argentine rule. By an 1828 treaty between the two larger countries, Uruguay became an independent republic, the last in Latin America to achieve that status, though Ecuador and Venezuela subsequently broke away from Gran Colombia and, still later, thanks to the United States if the word thanks is appropriate, Panama also.

Bolívar went on to Chuquisaca, the Bolivian capital, to see Sucre elected and inaugurated as life president. There an emissary from Peru arrived and presented each general with a sword, encrusted with thousands of diamonds. "This sword," said Bolívar, "will always remind me forever that the city of Lima is worthy of being the capital of the most grateful nation in the universe."

iv

Meanwhile, in Lima, Manuela was having her troubles. After she had dutifully returned to Thorne, things became ugly. He tried to keep her shut up in the house and block her correspondence with Bolívar, but without success; it was being conducted through the hunchback police chief of Lima, Cayetano Freire, devoted to both Manuela and Bolívar.

Freire wrote to Santana, explaining why letters from Manuela had been delayed. "I do not go much to her house, because of that brute of a husband. . . . I am a friend of the Liberator, and every time I go there he gives me looks that would singe the dead."

Manuela laughed at Thorne and at herself. He had warned her that she would suffer in heaven. She retorted she would suffer quite as much in England or Constantinople if he required her to go there. "You are more jealous than a Portuguese. That is why I don't love you." He beat her, and she left, vowing she would never live with him again. "You are a Catholic, I am an atheist. . . . Aside from that religious obstacle, I have a still stronger reason. . . . I am in love with someone else."

Thorne left Lima on business, but wrote her imploring letters. She replied to one, "Do you think for one moment that, after being the beloved of the general for years, I should choose to be a wife even of the Father, the Son, or the Holy Ghost, or all three? . . . I do not live for the laws of society, invented only to torture one another. . . . You love without pleasure. You converse without grace. You walk unhurriedly. You sit down with caution. You do not laugh even at your own jokes."

Bolívar wrote her, "I am desperate to return to Lima." And,

as though he had never forced her from his side for reasons of state, he added, "I think constantly day and night of your loveliness and of my love for you, and all we shall do when we meet again."

He returned on February 10, 1826—a ten-month absence—a few days after the Callao fortress, with only a few hundred defenders left alive, surrendered. The last Spanish bulwark in the Americas had crumbled. Torre Tagle, "the traitor," had died the previous month. His wife Josefa died that same year.

Once more Bolívar was at the Magdalena villa. O'Leary remarked, "Though he lives with less ostentation than any aristocrat, he has more influence and more absolute power in a large part of South America and in the entire continent than the most outstanding monarch of Europe in his domains."

Again congress showered him with gifts: a gold service, the former viceregal carriage repainted with his own coat of arms, a uniform so richly embroidered he was ashamed to wear it. Now in all the churches, the priests—who mostly had denounced him—prayed fervently for his well-being. To the patriot leader of Ecuador, Olmedo, author of a flattering poem about Junín, Bolívar wrote, "You have extolled me to such a degree that we are cast down into the abyss of oblivion."

Honors came from all over the world: from the United States, a miniature of George Washington with a likeness painted by Gilbert Stuart containing a lock of his hair. Lafayette called him "the second Washington of the New World." In the Senate, Henry Clay extolled him as the hero of a new Iliad. Bolívar hats were worn in Paris. Lord Byron sailed to glory and death in Greece on the *Bolívar*.

v

But peace saw also the rebirth of ugly passions and ambitions, all the nasty place-seeking of petty, cowardly men who had been afraid to sacrifice themselves in the struggle for Independence. In this greedy scramble, Bolívar soon became the prime target of abuse. Even the stiff-necked United States Consul, Bostonian William Tudor, sent home ugly reports, especially about the Liberator's relations with Manuela. "Some authentic anecdotes, if they could be told, would seem incredible," he wrote Secretary of State Clay.

Manuela had Tudor's correspondence intercepted and came out in public against him. He had said Bolívar had "no characters of weight and dignity about him," and sneered at O'Leary, Fergusson, and Wilson, the young Englishmen, his closest advisers. (Tudor, incidentally, was the nephew of the wealthy New England Ice King who shipped ice at fancy prices to the West Indies.)

As for Manuela, Bolívar now realized he could not live without her. It was too late for any clandestine arrangement; attempted concealment would be more damaging than open acceptance. He made her the complete mistress of the Magdalena villa, and she was his hostess at state dinners. The elite no longer dared snub her, but she was still the prime target of rumors and secret pasquinades.

Presently there were violent outbursts against Bolívar and against the continued presence of Colombian troops. He broke up one Creole plot, arresting some sixty prominent persons. Tudor reported that they would probably be executed. He pictured Bolívar as a bloodthirsty tyrant. (He did have the original betrayers of Callao—Torre Tagle had already died—executed.)

Bolívar calmly ordered the general in command of the Colombian forces to prepare to abandon Peru and announced he was leaving the country. Consternation shook everybody. Delegations from all over the country, even the leading women of the city, came to plead that he remain.

He then let it be known that marching orders had been rescinded and announced postponement of congressional elections for one year, "at the request of a majority of the deputies." He proposed a federation of Colombia, Peru, and Bolivia. The immediate response was that he should be crowned king of the three countries.

His sister wrote him in anguish from Venezuela, "Don't accept. Your greatest crown is the title of Liberator."

Bolívar was also sending off delegates to the inter-American Congress at Panama, of which he had dreamed for nearly twenty years. Its purpose was to lay plans for the joint construction of a canal by all New World nations, to further international cooperation as well as world trade, and be a symbol of continental unity.

Presently worrisome news came from Bolivia, where Sucre was being described as a foreign dictator and the Colombian troops as conquering oppressors. Partly his troubles were due to Bolívar's old tutor Simón Rodríguez (now Robinson).

While in Lima, before his trans-country tour, Bolívar had heard that his beloved friend had arrived in Colombia, where he and twelve other apostles, all of them carpenters, had set up a school of woodwork to emulate Christ and to implant ideas of modern "naturalist" education. He was, in short, partly a forerunner of Thomas Mann and John Dewey.

Bolívar invited him on to Lima with a letter, good for travel expenses from Santander. Not very flatteringly for Manuela, he wrote his old friend, "Instead of a mistress, I need a philosopher. For the present I prefer Socrates to Aspasia. Come!"

Robinson, still a strong disciple of Rousseau, had always been a misfit, unable to conform to ordinary staid society. He had wandered all over the world and tried his hand at everything, translating in Jamaica, setting type in Baltimore, tutoring in Paris; he had joined the circus in Russia, made candles in Germany, sold books in London. In Bogotá, besides his teaching, he had distilled and peddled liqueurs. Now, nearly sixty, he had a young French wife, "a very nice girl and a good laundress." She died en route to Peru.

He was met at the Magdalena villa by Manuela. He told her, "I wanted to make this world into a paradise, but I made it into a hell for myself." She adored him, and for the moment he was in clover. He took up his residence at Magdalena in grand style with a delightful café-au-lait mistress.

Bolívar called him on to La Paz. He mule-backed out of
Lima with his mistress, his books and instruments, and letters
from Manuela to the Liberator. Bolívar promptly made him
Bolivia's minister of education, in which post he remained
after Bolívar departed.

But Robinson's "naturalistic" pedagogy and his novel ideas
scarcely appealed to a deeply religious community. He founded
a special "nature school" which soon created a furore. He believed in the body beautiful and, though his own body was
scarcely beautiful any longer, he walked naked in the class-
room in order "to accustom the pupils to the naked body and
to teach them anatomy." The priests and the good Catholic
ladies wanted him run out of Bolivia as an immoral fiend.

Also, he believed in free love and, though his hair was now
white as snow, he practiced it. His rosy, angelic face was as
innocent as a babe's and he had no sense of wrong-doing by
making love to every woman he met. Finally, "by force of cir-
cumstance," he was obliged to marry tiny teen-aged Manuela
Gómez, and the outraged citizens of the capital sent him and
his girl bride scampering back to Peru. In Lima he set up a
school with the motto Light and Virtue of America and made
candles on the side.

Manuela, still at the peak of her glory, did not know that
the day would come when, exiled in poverty in a tiny village,
confined for years to her hammock because of a broken hip,
Rodríguez, at the age of eighty, would appear from nowhere
and live in an abandoned hut nearby to become her neighbor,
friend, companion, and solace until her last hour.

vi

Even more disturbing news came from Gran Colombia.

There were uprisings in Ecuador, and Bolívar hastened a
trusted aide there "to gather men together and maintain the
peace."

Joaquín Mosquera, a senator in whose judgment Bolívar

had great faith, wrote, "You are much needed here. . . .
Fraud is corrupting every channel; disorder is multiplying the
misery of the state. Army salaries have been reduced thirty
per cent, creating visible uneasiness. Even the clergy feel their
interests have been injured."

Another informant remarked, "Men are everything, institutions nothing. A spark would be enough to blow up everything. Anarchy and disintegration are increasing."

Páez, accused in congress of brutal methods of enforcing the
new conscription law and conspiring with separationists, had
been removed from his command of the army. He refused to
get out and wrote Bolívar in Lima, "You cannot imagine all
the damage that intrigue causes in this country," adding that
the Spanish general, Morillo, was right in saying, in Santa Ana,
that "he had done the republic a great favor by killing the
lawyers."

Santander, Bolívar knew, hated Páez, who had once put him
under arrest during the Orinoco campaign. What was the
truth of the conflict and Venezuelan disobedience?

He sent O'Leary to look over the ground and talk with Páez,
to try to smooth things over and report back to Bogotá, where
he would now have to go himself. More uprisings were occurring, and the country was in financial ruin. Santander had
gone through a thirty-million-peso foreign loan like a hot knife
through butter. If Bolívar did not return promptly, Gran Colombia would soon break up.

When he again announced he was leaving Peru, the consternation was even greater than before. Once more, delegations arrived at Magdalena. Once more, outstanding society
ladies came in a long cavalcade of open carriages, to add their
entreaties; one recited a special poem of adulation. He seemed
to waver, but hardly had the door closed on their heels than
he said, "I'm going to Colombia."

He feared leaving Manuela behind but did not wish to take
her on this new, dangerous, and delicate enterprise. Yet if he
abandoned her, she would be the target of female fury, merely

his "discarded mistress." He charged his minister of war, the
Argentine Las Heras, and chief of police, Freire, to take good
care of her. She did not appear at his two farewell banquets.

vii

In uptorn Ecuador—first in Guayaquil, where he saw Joaquina, then in Quito—he was given another hero's welcome,
more exuberant even than he had received four years earlier,
and was asked to become president of an independent Ecuador.
He made it clear he was already president of Gran Colombia.

Traveling on to Bogotá, he rode over the trails where he
had once led his revolutionary troops and, though this was
spring and even the higher slopes were vivid with wild flowers
and the purple flowers of the potato plants, he was over-
whelmed with sadness. His major mission, whatever came to
pass in the new nations, was over. The great glorious days of
reckless and courageous enterprise were ended.

At lofty Ibarra, he wrote (October 6, 1826), yearning to have
Manuela in his arms. "Charming Manuela: Everything in you
is love. I, too, am suffering from this fiery fever which con-
sumes us like two children. . . . *I love no one else but you.*
. . . The shrine which is yours will never be desecrated by
another idol or image, unless it be by God himself. . . . I am
so tired with all this traveling and all the troubles of your
country. . . ."

Meanwhile, O'Leary, who had left Lima June 3, 1826, more
than three months before Bolívar, talked his mission to Páez
over with various Independence leaders and army officers. He
was greatly influenced by General Carlos Soublette (his future
brother-in-law—O'Leary was courting his sister Soledad), who
was bitter toward Páez, a bitterness that also went back to
Orinoco days. And Santander completely twisted O'Leary
around his fingers. Páez had violated the constitution; he had
to be eliminated—so was O'Leary's mind made up, even before
he went on to Venezuela. In Valencia, he made threats to

Páez's closest advisers and to the head of the *cabildo* there which had called for Venezuelan independence.

Páez had warily retired to his home town of Achaguas on the Apure for, there among his *llaneros,* he was impregnable, and to Achaguas—a long hard trip—O'Leary had to travel. They did not meet until August 19. Páez received him courteously; there were long talks for a week. O'Leary remained wholly unreasonable. His formal message was an ultimatum which Páez disdained, and he left in a huff.

Bolívar already knew the score before he reached Bogotá. He had not used merely the one arrow of O'Leary for his bow; he had sent another emissary, Antonio Lacadio Guzmán, but Santander had arrested Lacadio en route, in Panama, "to avoid any contradiction in the two commissions."

O'Leary rode out from Bogotá to La Plata to greet Bolívar as he approached Bogotá, in November. He was still boiling with indignation at the way Páez had rejected all his proposals.

Bolívar received him coldly and intimated he was not pleased with the way O'Leary had conducted his mission. "You did not carry my ideas and wishes to him."

O'Leary exploded. "The only ones who wish Páez pardoned are your enemies. Your disapproval of his rebellious attitude will sweep aside those who are causing disturbances. If you compromise with Páez and his faction, from now on out you will have to humiliate yourself in order to satisfy all his demands, his insolence, and his ambition."

Bolívar's reply was tart. "I did not send you there to threaten Páez or to frighten his supporters, but to prevent civil war." He raked O'Leary over the coals and dismissed him brusquely.

O'Leary was wild with fury and deeply hurt. Another aide tried to cool him off by saying Bolívar was ill and tired.

"Tell him," raged O'Leary, "that he has killed his own daughter: the constitution."

On reaching Bogotá, Bolívar dismissed O'Leary from his staff and wrote Páez, "I have declared an amnesty for everybody. You had every reason, and I have said so in a loud voice, to resist injustice with justice, and to resist abuse of power with disobedience. I am surrounded by calumnies and enemies, but I have not come here to serve as the vile instrument of their vengeance." He deeply regretted O'Leary's abusive threats. "I am so angry with him I do not mean to see him or hear from him. He did not carry my ideas to you, but those of others. Instead of taking to you my love for Venezuela and my friendship with you, he carried passions unworthy of an emissary and mediator of mine." It was too bad, he added, that Lacadio Guzmán had not arrived; he would "have revealed to you the very depths of my heart."

Later Bolívar wrote General Lara, "Colonel O'Leary upset my plans by making himself the instrument of Santander's hate and vengeance and endeavoring to start a civil war in a land where rest the ashes of my forefathers."

The Liberator remained in Bogotá only twelve days to set urgent matters aright, not even bothering to go before congress to resume his title as actual president, and set out for the interior on a trip that carried him on the month-long journey to Venezuela.

He quickly scotched all trouble and on January 12, 1827, made his entry into Caracas—his first visit in six years—side by side with General Páez. The apotheistic welcome surpassed any he had ever received. There was no doubt of the overwhelming popularity of both leaders; there was no doubt that, if they stood together, they could keep peace in the country.

By setting aside all charges against Páez, Bolívar slapped Santander in the face. He expressed open condemnation of both his own followers and those of Santander who, though at each other's throats, were opposing Páez, but he postponed the possibility of civil war, for he put a quietus on all parties advocating immediate independence from Colombia. He gave Páez a mandate to maintain order, and Páez was the one man in Venezuela who could do so.

But it meant that, in the end, Venezuela would break away. Something similar was happening in Ecuador; even while Bolívar was settling things in Venezuela, in the extreme eastern end of the country, in Ecuador, a separatist movement, promoted by the Quito *cabildo* itself, was suppressed bloodily, the leader being cut down with sabers beside his cannon. This occurred on January 27.

viii

Simultaneously came betrayal by Santander, who struck treacherously in Bolívar's rear, suborning Colonel José Bustamente in Lima to take over control of the Colombian forces there and arrest all Bolívar's officers. Clearly the vice president was scheming to get the threads of military power into his own hands.

Bustamente struck on January 25, 1827, by rounding up all trusted Bolívar officers except Argentine General Las Heras, minister of war, who happened to be out of the city. Bustamente filled the Plaza de Armas with his rebellious troops at daybreak and harangued them, saying Santander would support their liberties, see that they were paid, and he himself would repatriate them at once as their "general."

The mask was off, for in Bogotá Santander fired off cannon salutes and had the church bells rung to celebrate Bustamente's treacherous *coup*.

The embarkation began promptly, and Peruvian troops moved in to take over the vacuum. The last few thousand Colombian troops were actually moved aboard transports under Peruvian bayonets, though this was sometime later.

The United States consul, William Tudor, rejoiced. "We never expected to get rid of them without battle."

The only one who tried to stem the tide was Manuela. She attempted to arouse barracks troops against Bustamente and strode to and fro before them in her red hussar's uniform,

waving her drawn sword. She was seized and held incommunicado in the Nazarene convent; only Jonotás was permitted to see her.

Jonotás carried out a letter hidden in her turban addressed
to the Colombian attaché, Cristóbal Azüero, demanding that
he act in her behalf. From then on Jonotás smuggled out letters to him and to Colombians and Peruvians loyal to Bolívar.
Azüero had to be cautious but was backing her play; presently
Tudor was denouncing him as a menace. "Like most all of the
agents of Bolívar," he informed his government, "he is a man
of unprincipled character."

Jonotás' activities were discovered, and she was thrown into
terrible Casa Matas, women's prison for prostitutes and sexual
perverts. Manuela's other slave, Natán, disguised as a nun,
took up the work of smuggling out messages. Presently also,
Manuela was visited by high Peruvian officials, whose admit-
tance could not be denied. The supporters of Bolívar were
beginning to be a threat to the actual Peruvian regime.

On April 14 she was released and ordered to leave the
country within twenty-four hours. She was allowed to take
along with her Jonotás, Natán, and her faithful servant Juana
Rosa. She also took with her Bolívar's archives, his abandoned
personal effects, and her own trunks. Deported along with her
were Generals Lara and Córdoba, the hero of Ayacucho, and
other arrested Colombian officers.

She had long since quarreled with Córdoba, and now, on
board the *Bluecher*, she upbraided him so violently before
the other officers for his failure to have shown resoluteness
against the enemies of Bolívar in the Colombian forces that
he stepped forward to strike her. No human being was more
touchy and vain than Córdoba, and her stinging words in
front of his colleagues put him in a ridiculous light. A mere
lieutenant stepped in to prevent physical violence.

They were being deported to Guayaquil, now under the
control of rebels against Bolívar's authority. The city was in
miserable condition, half in ruins, full of filth, bogholes, sick-

ness, drunk soldiers, and bald gray-black vultures. The deported officers and Manuela and her slaves were confined to their quarters until they left the city.

Having no funds, Manuela put her belongings in safekeeping, picked four handsome soldiers as a bodyguard, and set out on foot with her slaves and servant for Quito. It took them ten days. There she put up at the home of her half brother, José María Sáenz, now a general, and sent for the archives and her possessions. She was completely ostracized by Quito society.

ix

Where was Bolívar? At the moment he was still in Venezuela, waiting, watching.

O'Leary, who had cooled off, realized he had been gulled by the vice president, whom he had never liked since the assassinations of prisoners in Bogotá, and now sat in Soublette's home and bombarded the press with articles defending Bolívar and attacking Santander and his followers. He was a great polemicist. One letter was a scathing exposé of the pro-Santander senators—their intrigues, their thefts, their shady deals—with devastating word pictures of their appearance and mannerisms. Every description was a reason for a duel, but apparently none of the pettifogging legislators, scarcely any of whom had a clean record with respect to the revolution, wished to face the fiery young Irishman. He also exposed the secret *"Círculos"* fomented by Santander to discredit Bolívar.

On March 19, Bolívar sent word from Venezuela to Santander, breaking with him completely and "forever" and ordering him not even to communicate with him. Shortly thereafter, an aide of Bolívar came to see O'Leary with an astonishing request. "The Liberator is sending his resignation to congress and wishes you to deliver it with appropriate remarks."

"For fourteen years," the resignation stated, "I have been the supreme chief and president of the republic; the many dangers forced me to fulfill this duty; they no longer exist, and I can retire to enjoy private life. . . ." Jealous republicans had become unable to look at him without secret fear, because history had taught them that such as he were ambitious. "In vain, the example of Washington tries to defend me." He admitted he was ambitious, that he feared his own love of power. "With such sentiments, I resign, once, a thousand times, a million times, the presidency of the republic. I implore congress and the people the favor of permitting me to be a simple citizen."

Before presenting the document, O'Leary published twenty-four reasons why it should be accepted. It was a brilliant summation of the Liberator's whole career and his exploits in freeing half a continent, from his first battle for freedom in Venezuela to Boyacá; how he had driven the Spaniards out of Peru and had created three new nations: Gran Colombia, Peru, and Bolivia. His efforts had brought order out of chaos. Doubtless, added O'Leary sarcastically, there were many other men who could match these achievements and for this reason the resignation should be accepted forthwith.

Congress was shamed into voting overwhelmingly to reject it.

x

Bolívar did not get back to Bogotá until September 10. He did not fail to note the chilly manner in which he was received by the crowds in the streets. He rode directly to Santo Domingo Church where congress was in session, and there took the oath as acting president.

The legislators, without great enthusiasm, did his bidding and voted him extraordinary powers. They also dutifully passed a law stripping vice president Santander of all authority, and they ordered the calling of a constitutional convention to write a new magna charta, what Bolívar said was to be "a social contract. . . . The people must recover their sovereignty." The date was set for the following April, 1828.

"Dictatorship," Santander remarked savagely.

"Or chaos," rejoined Bolívar.

He had a thousand things to do. The nation was bankrupt. Commerce was at a standstill, the ruined haciendas idle. He flung himself into solving the pressing problems of agriculture, manufacturing, trade, education, hospitals, veterans' care. And why had slavery been restored, he demanded? It had to be abolished once and for all.

Bolívar's second act, that day of his return to Bogotá, was to write Manuela in Quito. He wrote her he was far from well. "I cannot live without you. Come. Come to me. Come now."

It was the same refrain that had brought her to the palace in Quito that first time. But he had dropped her by the wayside too many times. She wrote back, "I, too, am ill—and very, very angry." She doubted the sincerity of his love. Even so, she said she would leave for Bogotá in December, "because you call me." But unless she received proper assurances, she would return to Quito at once "to die rather than be taken for some shameless trull."

She rode out of Quito, with her three servitors, mules bearing Bolívar's archives and belongings, and her own trunks. She wore her hussar's uniform, bright red black-braided trousers, black boots, gold spurs, and a brace of Turkish pistols. A thousand miles lay before her through a devastated land, and she was escorted—at Bolívar's explicit command—by a strong escort of lancers, for demobilized soldiers, finding no way to make a living, had turned into marauders, looting homes and falling upon unwary travelers.

At last, late one night, she rode through the sad, cold city of Bogotá, blue-veiled with mist, past the massive monasteries and convents and churches, along winding Calle de Florián to the great plaza and the San Carlos Palace. Bolívar was at the villa—his Quinta—just north of the city on an eminence below Monserrate. It had been a gift to him by the nation the year after Boyacá.

She rode on across the Carmen bridge that spans the San Agostín River and up the steep northern streets, arriving at the Quinta travel-worn and disheveled. She passed the sentries, entered through French doors to the big salon, and, to her dismay, stepped into a reunion of the cabinet and Bolívar's most trusted officers, waiting for Bolívar to wind up business in his study.

Nearly all knew her, and she was greeted with shouts of glad affection. They insisted on drinking to her health, making such an uproar that Secretary Santana came out to see what was the matter. He led her at once to Bolívar's study. It is related that he was delayed even longer in meeting his councilors.

Bolívar made Manuela complete mistress of the villa, with the proviso that she was not to attend public affairs and was to avoid making herself conspicuous in the city. But when she rode abroad in her hussar's uniform, or went on shopping jaunts or social calls in her open landau, the only one in the city, she was all too conspicuous, and her doings were on every tongue. "This Madame duBarry," they called her.

By now Bolívar was fighting for his political life, trying to restore order and authority, productive life and trade, and to prepare for the April constitutional convention he had promised on accepting extraordinary powers. This was to be held in the remote mountain town of Ocaña, forty-eight miles from the Magdalena River and a similar distance this side of Cúcuta, where the delegates would not be subjected to the intrigues of the capital.

There were plenty of intrigues, and the conspiracies against Bolívar were formidable. Their pivot was Santander, who would also be a delegate at the Ocaña convention. He was backing federalism, a program for breaking up the country into practically autonomous provinces which, at this juncture, would mean the end of the confederation and, perhaps worse, most probably anarchy and chaos. Ironically, Páez of Venezuela in joining the ranks of the federalists, was cooperating with Santander.

In March, 1828, Bolívar set out on horseback for the sessions, but en route he learned that a Spanish flotilla was menacing the north coast and that revolt was threatened in Cartagena, five hundred miles to the north. He stopped in Bucaramanga.

"If I go north," he commented, "the south will go to pieces. If I go south, the north will revolt." So he sat tight in Bucaramanga and sent O'Leary, restored as his chief aide since the end of December, to be an observer at the forthcoming Ocaña convention.

Just before the opening of the Ocaña congress, Admiral José Padilla, a huge, kinky-haired, mulatto partisan of Santander, revolted. His force was quickly crushed, and he fled to Ocaña, where Santander rushed through a resolution praising his brave fighters for freedom in Cartagena.

The delegates soon reversed this, however, and Padilla fled on, only to be captured at Mompós. He was taken to Bogotá for trial.

Manuela wrote Bolívar, "Those devils on two stakes: Santander, Padilla, and Páez should be killed. It will be a great day when these vermin are exterminated."

O'Leary was not happy about being away from Bogotá, either at the convention or in Bucaramanga. He had just married Soledad Soublette, and his honeymoon was interrupted. He was reduced to writing her jealous letters, ordering her not to go to parties and public affairs in his absence.

When he arrived at Ocaña, Santander said in an audible aside, "Here comes that Englishman, Bolívar's spy." He kept O'Leary and all his servants and visitors under close surveillance.

O'Leary wrote to Soledad, "In all my life I've never seen a more contemptible bug." He began writing savage articles about Santander and his delegates and the work of the congress. The vice president had a majority (not wholly secure) of twenty-five against twenty-one determined Bolívarists. One such article appeared in the Bucaramanga paper.

Bolívar said, chuckling, "O'Leary's the bee in the flowers. Touch him, and you get stung." He sent two messages to be delivered at the proper moment to the congress, "whenever

we have a clear-cut majority." One was an acid attack on Santander's maladministration: "Chaos envelopes us." The other
laid out what he expected of congress. The new constitution
could not be federalist, as Santander proposed—that is, the
creation of four or five autonomous regional governments—for
at this hour that would be the death knell for Gran Colombia.
Local powers could not be increased without running grave
danger; the country would soon be dismembered. He called for
greater centralization and asked for "force without which there
is no virtue. Anarchy destroys freedom, unity preserves it. . . .
If the convention does not conduct itself with wisdom . . .
there will be civil war."

At the same time, secretly he proposed certain regional concessions to Páez to reassure him in his position in Venezuela
and wean him from the federalists.

Bolívar waited in Bucaramanga, taking it easy, putting on
weight, but often raging as the congress wrangled and quibbled for two months. Bolívar's own man, Finance Minister—
"the turtle"—Castillo y Rada, had been put in as president of
the sessions, but his majority was too vacillating and flimsy
to pull what he needed out of the pot. Every proposal was
whittled away, watered down.

"Those wretched creatures!" he exclaimed to his French
aide. "To me they owe even the air they breathe . . . and
they have the effrontery to suspect me." Once more he threatened to resign.

It became evident that the compromise document being produced would be worse than no document at all.

"I'm going back to Bogotá," he wrote Manuela. "I love you
with all my soul."

He left Bucaramanga with his entire staff, including
O'Leary, on June 9. His delegates, per his instructions, withdrew from the convention the following day. Lacking a quo-
rum the convention collapsed. A share of them joined him and
rode back to the capital together.

xi

As for Manuela, she had become the target of scandal, abuse, and pasquinades pasted up on the street walls. No insult was too terrible to be hurled at her; no lie too monstrous to be used. But she had been having a magnificent time. Every night she held balls and dances and banquets.

She held the center of social life, even if the ladies snubbed her. She appeared at her gatherings in gowns of the latest French and British styles, with daring decolleté and glittering jewelry. Her behavior at these gatherings was often shocking to many; certainly her conduct and her tongue were both free-wheeling.

One of her fervent admirers, the young French scientist, Jean Baptiste Boussingault, later wrote five volumes of memoirs, of which the only copy in the United States is in the Harvard library, in which he said, "She has a lot of animation and is gay but uses risqué expressions."

Jonotás, always present in her soldier's costume, enlivened the reunions with take-offs of Manuela's enemies; she mimicked an anti-Bolívar monk reciting the passion; the turtlelike minister of the treasury, Castillo y Rada, who had refused to pay Manuela the amounts ordered by Bolívar; and Ana Pombo, member of a very wealthy clan and the cream of Bogotá society, for being such a brood mare (the bronx cheers of successively issuing progeny, as practiced by Jonotás, was scarcely a savory show).

Even Boussingault was often shocked. In a letter to his brother, he described Jonotás as, "the mulatress slave of Manuela from whom she is never separated, . . . a young Negress with woolly hair, a striking woman, always dressed as a soldier, . . . also supposed to be her mistress' lover, but it conforms to a vice common in Peru. . . . Jonotás is a comedian, a mime. With an impassive face and outward seriousness, she says the funniest things."

At an intimate *tertulia,* "The mulatress changed into the

clothes of her sex, the costume for dancing the Quito ñapanga. She performed to our great satisfaction that most lascivious dance. She pivoted first with great rapidity, then lowered herself, her petticoat inflated with air, and did a *fromage,* as our children at home call it. With great writhing and lascivious movements, she lowered herself on the floor for a moment, then . . . pirouetted out of sight."

Manuela used sterner methods than ridicule against some of her detractors. Old Vicente Agüero, a vitriolic editor, was knocked down and trampled by a lancer. Colonel William Fergusson pounded young Florentino González, a lawyer and editor, into insensibility and wrecked his printing press. Perhaps the fact that young González was married to one of the Soublette sisters, said to have been Bolívar's mistress in Jamaica, added vitriol to his pen. He paid dearly.

Bolívar's return to the Quinta put a brief quietus on Manuela's splurging. His entry into the city produced a popular demonstration previously unparalleled. The fear of anarchy and consequent civil war, wrote Posada Gutiérrez, in his *Memorias,* dominated all classes of society, and all rallied around Bolívar, seeing in him the only hope of unity and salvation from shipwreck. "The enthusiasm was great and sincere, and the same occurred throughout the republic."

He mobilized the entire army and, on July 13, with his generals in full dress in Cathedral Plaza, took the oath of office before congress as absolute dictator, though at the same time he denounced dictatorship, saying he merely intended to put an end to growing chaos. He was given full powers in every sphere "to reorganize every branch of government in the way he considered best to care for internal evils, conserve the union, and establish foreign credit."

He moved into San Carlos Palace and named Santander minister to the United States—except that the plotting vice president found excuses to postpone his departure. Nobody for the moment, dared oppose Bolívar's imperious wishes. But the blows came fast.

12

The Silver Mountain

/\\.V.V.\ Manuela held a magnificent garden party at the Quinta on July 24 to celebrate Bolívar's birthday. He did not attend, but his entire cabinet—the council, it was now called—did so. The highlight was when Jonotás dressed up an old sack of sawdust labeled "Santander, killed for treason." The black eyes and long moustachios were unmistakable. Soldiers dragged it by a rope and propped it against a wall, a leading Catholic dean gave it last rites, then Colonel Richard Crofston of the British legion gave the command to fire.

A Colombian officer refused to take part "in such an undignified farce," and Crofston arrested him on the spot. Drawing his sword, he repeated the command, and the sawdust sack that was Santander was blown to smithereens.

It created public furor. General Córdoba protested angrily to Bolívar. The latter was shocked, considered it decidedly imprudent, and wrote that though it had not been "a public crime," it had been "a despicable and stupid one," and he would suspend Crofston and send him elsewhere. "He alone is guilty." As for Manuela, "the lovable fool," he would have to use "more determination, . . . if need be, force her to leave the country."

He gave her harsh new orders to avoid such publicity. Instead, she defied him by moving into an apartment across from his quarters in San Carlos Palace. He ordered her back to the Quinta, banishing her from the city, and threatened to send her back to Quito.

She laid down her own ultimatum. She would stay in the city. He could send her back to Quito, but in placating his enemies he would bring about his own assassination. He must take the initiative and kill them if they so much as lifted their heads.

She had her way and decorated her new quarters with extravagant luxury and the most elaborate furnishings settling there with her slaves, servants, swarms of cats and a black bear cub. She entertained recklessly—*tertulias* every night. More than social affairs, gay though they were, by them she knit Bolívar's best friends into a close loyal group and kept close tab on political currents, the intrigues, and the hidden moves in the nasty game of power-seeking. She had spies besides Jonotás and Natán, and she learned much about the schemings by his enemies.

Calling on her one morning, the hour when she received close friends in negligee, Boussingault heard snarls from her bedroom and found her still in bed, the bear on top of her, his unsheathed paws on her breasts.

"Don Juan," she told the Frenchman, "this devilish bear won't let go of me. Get a bowl of milk for him."

The Frenchman finally enticed the creature away and took it down to the patio where an Englishman killed it.

"But see," said Manuela, when Boussingault returned, exposing her breasts, "I'm not wounded at all."

Because of the growing atmosphere of danger for Bolívar, she urged him never to go out of the palace without an armed escort. He refused to take precautions, though he did double the small palace guard and had Palacios bring the two mastiffs in from the Quinta.

Santander was the arch villain. He still put off leaving for

Washington, and Bolívar issued a peremptory order that he leave the country by September 5.

This was a bombshell, for a plot to assassinate Bolívar and stage an uprising was well advanced. Bolívar, Manuela, and General Urdaneta, among others, were to be killed during the celebration of Bolívar's saint's day, October 28. The plotters were royalists and rich Creoles, and also students and professors demanding "liberty" and calling Bolívar a dictator, which he now was. A Major Pedro Carujo and a member of Bolívar's own staff, Colonel Ramón Guerrera, were brought into the conspiracy.

But the ultimatum to Santander forced the assassins to advance the date for their *coup*. It was to be staged in mid-August at a masked ball in the old Coliseo Theater across from San Carlos Palace. Bolívar was expected to attend.

Manuela and Jonotás arrived first, at half past eleven. They crossed the foyer and, at the entrance stairs, Manuela heard a guest, clad in Spanish armor, tell another masked man, "Within half an hour, when the clock strikes twelve, death to the tyrant." He displayed the knife in his doublet.

Inside, Manuela could see the masked dancers doing the wild *cachucha*. Not knowing whether Bolívar had arrived yet, she started to rush in, but the Mayor of Bogotá blocked their passage. "No woman in male attire can attend this ball."

"I am Manuela Sáenz, and this is a costume ball," she answered imperiously.

"I don't care if you are Saint Manuela, you can't go in."

She raised a scandalous disturbance, Jonotás helping her.

Bolívar, just arriving, took in the scene. Angered by the spectacle, he turned on his heel, his face livid. For days he would not speak to her. He never did learn the reasons for her conduct, though he relented somewhat toward her when his favorite nephew arrived via Venezuela from the United States, where Bolívar had sent him to school.

ii

On September 25, a drunk captain, shouting, "Death to the tyrant," was arrested and confessed the plot. Perhaps to escape the police dragnet, the conspirators, numbering about thirty, decided to act at once, and they set out that same night in a driving cold rain to seize the palace.

Some hours before their incursion, Palacios went across the street to Manuela's apartment with his two mastiffs to tell her Bolívar was ill and wanted her.

She refused, saying, "I, too, am ill."

Palacios soon returned with a folded note. "Please come."

She ran out into the rain with Jonotás. Bolívar was sitting in a warm bath. "I'm delighted you have come. There's to be a revolution tonight."

She read to him until he fell asleep.

The attackers struck at midnight, surprising the guards and bursting in. The dogs barked, and Manuela raced to Bolívar's room. He caught up a pistol and sword.

She laughed. "Get dressed. Put on your uniform."

He dressed quickly. By then the shouts of the attackers were close by. She raised the window. It was a nine-foot drop to the street. He embraced her and let himself down. Unobserved, he raced to the river bridge.

When the attackers burst in, she faced them with his sword. "Where is Bolívar?"

"In the council room."

They seized her and pulled her there. It was empty. They rampaged through the entire palace.

In the excitement she managed to whisper to Palacios, who had stuck close to her side through it all, "He slipped out to the river. Go."

The would-be assassins pushed her along the tiled corridor. She heard cannon and rifle fire from a nearby barracks. At the stairs she came upon an officer, young Andrés Ibarra, who had tried to bar their first passage, lying in a pool of blood.

She wrenched free from her captors and knelt beside him. He was still alive. She ripped off part of her petticoat and stanched the blood.

He barely whispered, before sinking back into unconsciousness, "Is the Liberator dead?"

"No, Ibarra, he's alive."

The leader of the conspirators, Pedro Carujo, struck her with his fist, knocking her down. The others crowded around her with lifted knives.

From the floor, she screamed, "Kill me! Kill me, you miserable cowards!"

A Frenchman, one of their number, jumped in front of them. "We are not here to murder women."

Carujo kicked her in the head, and she was carried into Bolívar's room and put under guard.

Meanwhile, the Vargas battalion under an English officer reached the palace and drove off the attackers, most of whom were killed. Soon General Urdaneta arrived with additional troops.

During the excitement, Bolívar was crouched with Palacios and the dogs under the bridge in the stinking sewage of Bogotá. They heard running feet, then shouts and cheers. "Long live the Liberator!"

He crawled out, embraced his men, got a horse, changed into a clean uniform at the barracks, and rode to the palace. Already Urdaneta had hundreds of suspects lined up in handcuffs.

There were cheers and more cheers for Bolívar. All the generals and officers rode up to congratulate him. Even Santander appeared. Bolívar cut him off with brittle contempt.

At dawn he rode across the plaza to the palace, entered, and embraced Manuela. He was too dazed even to notice the wound in her head or her cut, bruised hand.

"Manuela! My Manuela, the liberatress of the Liberator!"
She helped him undress, but almost at once he sprang up
and paced. "Tell me what happened—everything."

His aide, Colonel William Fergusson, a favorite of Manuela's, had been killed.

The following day, sick unto death, Bolívar appointed
Urdaneta to run the government and shut himself up in the
villa above the city. As a result of his exposure, tuberculosis
raced through his body with fever and hemorrhages.

A gallows was erected in front of the cathedral, and a few
soldiers were hung at once. For four days, depositions were
taken.

Bolívar was badly shaken by the findings. A large share of
the culprits belonged to the best families. He wanted to declare an amnesty but gave way before Urdaneta's vehement
protests.

A trial court of four other officers and four civilians was
set up.

The first executions began before a large crowd. Venders
sold cakes, bread, fruit, and blue-gold-red cockades of the republic. The drums sounded, and Colonel Ramón Guerrera was
marched in, hands bound in front grasping a huge crucifix.
Next came big black Admiral Padilla and four others.

General Urdaneta, in gold-braid uniform, read the sentences
and yanked off the insignia and epaulettes. Gray hoods were
thrown over the prisoners' heads. Nooses were placed about
their necks. The muffled drums sounded. One by one the
stools were kicked from under their feet.

Guerrera died after a brief macabre dance. But Padilla's
bull neck did not break. He burst his thongs and tore at the
rope. Soldiers rushed up and fired point-blank into his body.

The hangings went on for weeks. Many others were jailed,
many exiled. Santander, arrested September 30, was awaiting
trial. Carujo, the most despicable of the lot, won a reprieve
from death and a promise of perpetual exile, by turning state's
evidence. The ex-vice president, clearly involved, was given a

long, detailed trial and condemned to death. The foreign lega-
tions pleaded for clemency, and Bolívar reduced his sentence
to perpetual exile.

Slowly the Liberator mended, and on October 28 was able
to attend briefly his saint's day celebration at the palace, the
most elaborate ball ever celebrated in Colombia. It was attended by the entire diplomatic corps. Bolívar escorted Manuela in on his arm. He was in full dress and wore the George
Washington medallion on a blue silk ribbon. She was in decolleté, wearing an emerald and diamond necklace.

The party was marred by one unfortunate incident. Colonel
Leandro Miranda, illegitimate son of Venezuela's first liberator, overheard Dutch consul Stewart make a sneering re-
mark about Manuela and slapped his face.

At the duel, Stewart, a fine marksman, clipped off a corner
of Miranda's bearskin hat. The latter put his pistol under his
arm, saluted his adversary, and turned away.

Livid with anger, Stewart shouted, "Shoot! If you don't, I'll
kill you like a dog!"

Miranda aimed, pulled the trigger, and shot him through
the head. He fled from the city to the corps of lancers he
commanded. But a few weeks later they revolted and hacked
him to mincemeat.

iii

President José de La Mar of Peru, who had fought at Ayacucho, not finding anything better to do with the newly won
independence gained for his country by Bolívar and the Colombian army—certainly not by Peru's efforts—now invaded
Ecuador (actually he was an Ecuadorian by birth) to wrench
it away from Gran Colombia and restore it to Peruvian rule.
His invasion was preceded by an Ecuadorian revolt led by
Colonel Obando, in traitorous contact with de La Mar, to
whom he had written, "I await your orders and reiterate the
urgency for your occupation of this bulwark, whose inhabi-

tants are ready to die in an eternal war against the Sultan of Colombia."

General Córdoba easily smashed the traitorous uprising. To his disgust, Bolívar proclaimed an amnesty and refused to execute the culprits. Obando escaped once more. Briefly, later, he was to seize the presidency of Colombia. From that moment, in spite of the clemency shown him, his hatred of Bolívar knew no limits. He plotted with General Mosquera, secretary of the navy, to throw Bolívar out.

Though up to this time Bolívar had been unable to spend more than two hours in the saddle, he immediately rode off across the Andes and ordered Sucre, no longer president of Bolivia but back in Ecuador in retirement from all political and military activities, to head up the defense forces against de La Mar.

Sucre, embittered by his experiences in Bolivia, which the Peruvians had also invaded, and embittered even more by the conduct of his adultress wife, a Marquesa, had dedicated himself to his daughter alone and had no desire to return to active life. He refused, saying he was an invalid, *hors de combat.*

He had had great dreams for a free, democratic, progressive Bolivia, but soon after he was named president, an insurrection broke out against the Colombian troops, a fracas stirred up by the Peruvians. Sucre was wounded in one arm, which was rendered useless for life. Generals Santa Cruz and Agustín Gamarra then invaded—"to restore order and protect Sucre."

Sucre resigned, hoping his departure would bring peace. He made his farewell address in 1828, to the assembled congress.

"I take leave, gentlemen, of you and Bolivia . . . forever. . . . I believe you will . . . be guided by dignity, firmness, and patriotism . . . wisdom, moderation, and generosity."

He begged them not to destroy his work. He had defended Bolivia's independence, and wished them "to prefer all misfortunes and the death of her children to the loss of the sovereignty of the republic which was proclaimed by the people

. . . obtained as a reward for their unstinted sacrifices in the revolution."

He told in a few words of his own efforts and personal sacrifices in behalf of America's freedom, and of his original arrival in Bolivia. "I crossed the Desaguadero to find a group of men divided into murderers and victims, slaves and tyrants, eaten by hatred and thirsty for vengeance. I reconciled all those spirits. I have formed a country which has its own laws, which is reforming its colonial education and customs, which is recognized by its neighbors, which has no foreign debt, which has only a small domestic debt acquired for its benefit, and which will be happy if a wise government rules it."

He spoke of his clemency to all. He had caused no "suffering to any Bolivian. . . . Perhaps this mildness has been the cause of my own wounds; but I am glad of them if my successors with equal kindness will accustom Bolivians to follow the law without any need that bayonets constantly threaten life and put snares in the way of freedom." He would never be sorry for his scars for they would remind him that "in order to create Bolivia I preferred the empire of law to the tyranny of the sword."

He led the Colombian troops back to Ecuador. Bolivia was never again to have a ruler of his nobility and decency. (Santa Cruz, a ridiculously pompous officer, who had lost every previous battle, took over until he was finally thrown out in 1839. Gamarra seized Peru, which thereafter would be run by his epileptic wife who strode about in uniforms doused with gold, slashing generals and cabinet ministers across the face with her riding crop.)

Bolívar was too ill to head up a campaign. Moved by his plight, Sucre finally agreed to carry on the war. Gathering all available forces, he moved down to meet the invading army in late February, 1829, his useless arm dangling. As at Ayacucho, he was badly outnumbered, but he knew the terrain, he knew his people, and his soldiers were equipped with new rifle sights just adopted by the Colombian army.

"Today," he commented, "a bullet is born with an education and knows precisely where it is going. This is progress. All the rest is folderol."

So the Peruvians discovered. At Tarqui on February 27, after a long night's march, the Colombians attacked at dawn. Two hours later, at seven o'clock, when the sun had come up over the Andes in glorious splendor, not a Peruvian—except for the 1,500 dead—remained on the field. Tarqui was an overwhelming victory. O'Leary's bravery at the head of the Cedeño battalion won him the rank of general.

Gamarra deposed La Mar, sent him off to Central America where in time he died, and sued for an armistice which included prompt evacuation of Guayaquil.

Bolívar journeyed to the port, where he saw Joaquina. Her sister Francisca had married Jaime Vivero, a friend of Bolívar, hero of Junín and Ayacucho. They now had a child, Pepito.

"What is he learning?" asked Bolívar. He frowned at the textbook they showed him. "He won't learn a blessed thing from this."

He turned to the poet Olmedo, who was present, having long since returned from Peru, where he and the Liberator had become good friends. "The boy needs an alphabet book," he said. "You get one up."

And so Olmedo, hero of the first independence of Guayaquil, wrote his famous *Alfabeto para un Nino,* rhymes still used in Ecuadorian schools.

"*Amor de patria,*" it begins.

> A love of country shines
> To the degree a man loves
> Its God, its laws, his home,
> And defends them with honor . . .
>
> Honor is in the first place
>   The soul of the citizen;
> Without honor, a man is nothing,
>   And evil is the State . . .

Tyranny and oppression
Sound and mean the same;
To get out of the abyss
Any action is honorable.

iv

Meanwhile, in Bogotá, battle-scarred United States Minister
William Henry Harrison, aching from old wounds, irritable
at all times, and hating Colombia, conspired with General
Córdoba to overthrow Bolívar. The minister's attitude was
revealed at a banquet celebrating the Boyacá battle. A gracious toast was given to the two illustrious liberators, Bolívar
and Washington. Harrison blazed back, waving his glass,
"Washington dead is worth more than Bolívar alive."

It shocked even Bolívar's foes. Manuela became Harrison's
avowed enemy and did a great deal to embarrass his mission.

Córdoba's schemes were known not only to Harrison but to
British Consul Henderson, to whose daughter Fanny the general was engaged. Córdoba, a touchy, intemperate soul, felt
he had not been properly recognized and rewarded for his
revolutionary services. Of him Bolívar had written, "General
Córdoba has rare military valor, but also a hard unbending
character, ridiculous arrogance, and excessive vanity. These
are virtues on the battlefield but otherwise are dangerous."

The uprising took place in the Cauca Valley. Bolívar was
then in Guayaquil.

Before moving against the revolt, War Minister Urdaneta
tried to conciliate Córdoba by bringing him into the cabinet.
Instead of accepting, the general occupied Medellín.

A mud-spattered courier brought Urdaneta the bad news in
September when Manuela had been dining with him. She had
already done much to acquaint him with Córdoba's secret
activities, also those of the United States minister.

"I can handle the general easily," said Urdaneta confidently.

He sent O'Leary, back from Tarqui, at the head of 900

picked troops, with orders to liquidate the revolt completely.

O'Leary outsmarted Córdoba. Most of the seditious forces ran away; the remainder were easily trapped. Córdoba, badly wounded, crawled into a house where he lay in blood, sword in hand, prepared to die rather than surrender.

To his Scotch aide, Colonel Rupert Hand, a confirmed alcoholic who had once been intimate with Córdoba but now detested him, O'Leary is reported to have said, "If he's in there, kill him."

Hand sunk his knife into Córdoba three times. It aroused considerable horror. O'Leary denied having given any such order. Nevertheless, he made Hand governor of Choco province. (Later, after Bolívar had died and O'Leary had been sent into exile, Hand was court-martialed, thanks to a forged letter allegedly from O'Leary, and sentenced to ten years.)

Near the new year, Bolívar started slowly back for Bogotá, sicker than ever. (Rumazo González has described him as "a skeleton, a Don Quixote in march.") During the long hard trip, he wrote, "My grief knows no bounds. Slander strangles me as the serpents strangled Laocoön. I cannot stand it any longer. I am tired. I have had enough. I cannot bear more. A hundred times a day, my heart tells me so."

To another friend, he wrote he could do no more. He had suffered over twenty years. "A country which depends on the life of one man runs as much risk as a man who depends every day on the luck of the dice."

He reached Bogotá January 15, 1830, once more as the savior of his country, victor over the Peruvians. The city was lavishly decorated with bunting, the colors of the republic. Once more laurel-decked arches bore the sign, LONG LIVE THE LIBERATOR. Cannon, church bells, gala troops, officers in brilliant uniforms, school children with flowers.

But people mostly stood silent; no one cheered except, according to cynical-eyed Boussingault, knots of Indian peasants behind whom were stationed soldiers with whips.

A few days later, a new constituent assembly, presided over by Sucre, began its sessions.

Diplomatic troubles loomed. The cabinet had ordered Harrison to leave the country. He shouted at the protocol emissary, "I will not leave my post except by force!" Fortunately, the Washington government had enough sense to yank him out immediately. (Twelve years later he was elected president, but died a month after inauguration.)

British Consul Henderson was also told to get out and left with his not-overly-grieving daughter.

Bolívar soon quarreled with his cabinet, which resigned en masse. He retired to the Quinta, coughing blood. Manuela nursed him back to a modicum of health.

The Admirable Congress being presided over by Sucre, so-called because it was made up of the most illustrious men of three countries, continued its sessions preparing a new constitution. When the new magna charta had been hammered out, Bolívar appeared before it on March 1 to tender his resignation.

Posada Gutiérrez, a contemporary, described the occasion. "Pale, haggard; his eyes, so brilliant and expressive in his days of luster, now dead; his deep voice scarcely audible—everything announced . . . the coming dissolution of his body and his near approach to immortality." His message: My public functions are over forever."

Many delegates wept. With a last effort and in a clear ringing voice he concluded, "I implore, I demand, in the name of Gran Colombia, that you remain united!"

Actually his resignation, this time irrevocable, was a signal heard from the Orinoco to the slopes of Pichincha for the break up of the Colombian confederation. He had created it; it endured only a few months after he left office.

Backed by Páez, Venezuela declared itself independent. A constituent assembly adopted a constitution and denied Bolívar the right to cross the frontier. It ordered his name erased from the list of heroes and from all public places. Páez became the first president.

Before this, at the first announcement of secession, Bolívar had risen like a lion out of his sick bed and put on his uniform. He called in the cabinet and demanded he be restored to office so as to carry on the campaign to bring Venezuela back into the confederation.

Unable to face his imperiousness, the cabinet members hemmed and hawed and withdrew; then they informed him by letter that Venezuela could not be retained, nor Ecuador either.

There, in May, a convention of notables declared the country independent and set up a provisional government, which included the treacherous Obando. Youthful general Juan José Flores, a friend of Bolívar and ironically a Venezuelan but married into one of the wealthiest families of the country, was named chief of administration. Olmedo was chosen vice administrator after he refused to accept the top post.

In view of these separatist trends, the cabinet wrote Bolívar that Colombia should accept reality and set up its own strong independent government—without Bolívar. General Joaquín Mosquera was named president of New Granada. Even the old colonial name was chosen, as if further to destroy the last vestiges of Bolívar's dream.

The Liberator exploded in a paroxysm of rage and bloody coughing. A few days later, walking in the garden and leaning on Manuela's arm, he received the order to leave the country.

v

Bolívar gave his villa, pictures, battle mementoes, and other personal effects to faithful friends. He had no money. Palacios was able to sell his silver and gold plate for 17,000 pesos. Congress voted him 30,000 pesos a year for life, but he refused to accept it.

Friends called to say farewell. Posada Gutiérrez told about those last hours:

"Bolívar walked across the beautiful Quinta meadow. His gait was slow, his voice scarcely audible. For a while he looked at the little brook and said, 'How much time it takes for this water to mingle with the infinity of the ocean, even as man rotting in the grave mixes with the earth from which he came. . . .' "

He pressed his hands to his temples. "My glory! My glory! Why do they destroy it? Why do they calumniate me?"

Several regiments loyal to him had already revolted, and his friends feared he would be assassinated, not allowed to leave quietly. He stayed awake all night with Manuela, listening to the tread of the guard.

She had fought against his going into exile. People would rally to him. He should insist on remaining, should fight and die if necessary. But he was too ill to undergo the ardors of a long military struggle which would drench the country in blood.

She insisted then that she be allowed to accompany him, to be by his side, to care for him. She knew—and told him so—that if he left her behind once more, she would face a bitterly hostile world, more hostile than ever now that he would be gone forever. All the wolves would be upon her; they would make her the chief target of their spleen against Bolívar.

Worse, he said, would be poverty-stricken exile. He did promise that when he was definitely settled, and had made arrangements to make a living, he would send for her.

She left the villa late on the night of May 7 in a drenching storm. The morning was clear and sunny. A file of horsemen rode up, leading citizens and most of the diplomatic corps. They cheered when he emerged from the house. Palacios helped him to mount his horse.

Followed by Palacios and the cavalcade of horsemen, he rode down through the narrow, tilted streets of Bogotá. The news spread as the sound of horses' hoofs drew people to the barred windows. Soon the streets were lined with people. They cheered. Many wept. Others mounted their horses and joined the cavalcade on out into the sunny, smiling countryside.

But the sun faded, and a dense fog closed in about them. The cavalcade became ghostly, phantomlike. Voices took on the quality of lost, muffled echoes. Between Chipalo and Piedras, on high ground, Bolívar drew rein.

"I shall see you soon again," he said, embracing them one by one.

"I knew differently," wrote Boussingault to a friend. "His face carried the stamp of death."

The Liberator rode off into the mist with Palacios and his favorite nephew. A few invited friends went along behind them.

Sucre, considered the most likely successor of Bolívar, had left Bogotá when congress closed and had started back for Quito. He was assassinated in the Berruecos mountains on June 4, 1830, by officers and soldiers of the army of liberation under the command of General Obando, who was believed to be personally responsible.

"My God!" cried the Liberator when the news finally reached him. "They have shed the blood of Abel! It is impossible to live in a land where famous generals, the very men to whom America owes its freedom, are cruelly and brutally murdered. I can no longer serve such a country." And in still deeper sadness, he added, "He was the son whom Providence sent me as recompense for not having given me sons of my own."

Over in Ecuador, Olmedo resigned from the government. "When Flores embraced Obando after that killing, I could no longer remain at my post." O'Leary left Ecuador forever and in disgust. José María Sáenz, Manuela's half brother, by this time a general, raised a revolt against Flores.

Hardly had Bolívar left Bogotá than the nasty venom of nasty little men—and that of society women, of course—was poured on Manuela's head: newspaper attacks, ugly screeds, lampoons, pamphlets, slanderous pasquinades on the walls.

Almost singlehanded, Manuela fought back. She and Jonotás went out at night, tore down the pasquinades, pasted up their own counterattacks. She defied the people of Bogotá and she defied the government as though she had an army at her back. One night, fiesta fireworks were to be displayed in the plaza. The *piéce de résistance* was two castle towers ridiculing Bolívar and Manuela. With Jonotás and Natán, she galloped into the plaza and hacked them to pieces—three women against an army, a government, a people, a whole world. One of their horses was bayoneted. Jonotás and Natán were arrested but quickly freed.

Manuela's courage so impressed even the women of the first families that they issued a protest against her continued persecution, which had "its origin in base and ignoble passions. What heroism she has shown! What magnanimity! . . . Those qualities have served as an example for all of us." But when an anonymous pamphlet, the *Tower of Babel*, attacked the government for ineptitude and lawless conduct, the police tortured the printer till he confessed that Manuela was the author.

A warrant for her arrest was issued by a judge who detested her, but when the district alderman and his bailiffs came to arrest her, she feigned sickness, and they withdrew.

The judge angrily sent them back with stern orders to take her to a prison hospital. This time she met them at the head of the staircase in her red hussar's uniform, her Turkish pistols, and a drawn saber, and the fat alderman tumbled down the stairs when she made a pass at him.

He came back, bringing the Lord Mayor of Bogotá, the judge, ten soldiers, and eight convicts. A big crowd was on hand to watch the *opéra bouffe*, the spectacle—as one paper put it—of "a whole army to arrest a lone defenceless woman." Considerably embarrassed by the presence of so many onlookers, the officials and soldiers barged in, found the door locked, broke it down, and rushed in, but recoiled before Manuela's Turkish pistols.

The Lord Mayor and the judge could scarcely sneak out and let the others take her by force, but her demeanor convinced them she would kill them before she gave up. If they took another step forward, they would be dead.

Talking did no good. Finally a friend, hastily summoned, arrived, the one to whom Bolívar had given his villa, influential in high government circles. After some more give-and-take, the authorities accepted his compromise that Manuela would submit to arrest on condition she would be immediately released on her own recognizance.

Before further legal action could be taken, Venezuelan troops in Bogotá revolted, and the Mosquera government toppled, partly as a result of Sucre's earlier assassination, which had aroused universal shame and dismay. Urdaneta took over, announcing the new regime as merely a caretaker government until Bolívar resumed command.

But the Liberator replied to no appeals. For a moment on receiving one urgent supplication, he had felt exaltation, then sank back. "There is no salvation . . . no solution. . . . If I were to accept, I would have to begin shooting—and shoot so many!"

Urdaneta had sent him the truth. "We cannot preserve our authority and our lives except by killing our opponents, and even then this sacrifice will not bring peace or happiness, honor even less."

Bolívar could not have returned even had he so decided. He was deathly ill, first in Barranquilla, then in Santa Marta, where he was moved by boat; there he lay, under heavy blankets in that steaming lowland port, coughing blood, often only half-conscious, attended only by Palacios, his nephew, a few loyal friends. They took him by oxcart, hoping a change of air would benefit him, out to the Alejandrino San Pedro plantation where, irony of ironies, a former royalist provided him with every possible comfort.

Bolívar asked his French doctor why he had come to America.

"For the sake of liberty, your Excellency."

"And you found it here?"

"Most certainly, your Excellency."

"You have been more fortunate than I."

At another time he said, "The greatest fools of history have been Jesus Christ, Don Quixote, and I."

He died December 17, 1830. Manuela's name was on his lips, tears in his eyes.

The church bells rang out the sad tidings. His last proclamation read: "If death can contribute anything toward reconciling of conflicting parties for the unification of the country, I shall go to my grave in peace."

He was "lowered into an humble grave," wearing a borrowed nightshirt, in the Santa Marta churchyard. O'Leary, despite his sentiments on this occasion as told in his *Memoirs,* actually never arrived in Santa Marta until December 21, one day too late to participate in the funeral rites.

The Liberator was allowed no honors. Instead, the governor thundered that the hero's only claim to historical attention was having been "the spirit of evil, the author of all our misfortunes, the oppressor of the nation." He ordered Bolívar's name expunged from human memory.

vi

Shortly before his death, Bolívar wrote sadly, "He who dedicates his services to revolution plows the sea."

What was the state of the Americas when he died? All South America except the Guianas and the off-coast islands had been liberated. Spain did not have a toehold left anywhere. All her colonies of Central America, Mexico, and the West Indies had also been liberated. Cuba would have been freed also had not the United States exerted such stern pressure on the revolutionary governments not to help the Cuban revolters; it even offered Spain military aid to help her hang on to the island.

Everywhere the liberation had released a struggle for power. The fight for independence had temporarily united all social classes, except the elements favoring Spain's continued rule—the die-hards—in a great nationalistic upsurge. The aims and hopes of these groups were not identical, often were diametrically opposed. The Creole's idea of freedom did not include freedom for the Indians, and Creoles or mestizos controlled all the governments. The attempts to reconcile the many divergent interests, classes, and races led to violence and civil war.

As Alfredo Pareja Diezcanseco put it in his history of Ecuador, "The peace of America began to disappear the same days in which we were born to a free life." Since peace had not existed for two decades previously, this was scarcely surprising.

In this unfortunate process, greedy and ambitious chieftains seized the opportunity to gain power and wealth, as did baser elements who had contributed nothing to the cause of freedom.

That same year of 1830, as noted, Gran Colombia broke into fragments. It was too vast an empire to be bound together by only primitive communications. Bolívar repeatedly wailed that geography—mountains, morasses, vast plains, impenetrable jungles, deserts—was his greatest enemy. The Gran Colombia of that day simply could not be effectively ruled from a single center, even had there not been such powerful regional patriotisms, differences, and jealousies.

Venezuela, in the hands of strongman Páez, started out reasonably tranquil. Ecuador, from the outset, was plagued with continuous revolutionary disturbances, apart from the revolt of Juan José Flores and that of Manuela's half brother Sáenz against him.

After some ruckus, a new constitution was adopted for New Granada, and General Francisco de Paula Santander returned from exile and became its first president, October 7, 1832.

In Peru, Gamarra and his epileptic wife "Pancha" were ousted in 1833 by the phlegmatic and heavy general, Luís

Obregoso, in turn deposed the following year by dashing young general Felipe Santiago de Salaverry. But in 1835, Santa Cruz (who had served a brief term as president in 1826–27 and was now dictator of Bolivia) marched in with an army and set up the Peru-Bolivian Confederation, assuming the role of "protector," to be inherited by his son on his death. He put in two presidents to govern Peru, the one in the south being Pío Tristán, the last Spanish viceroy, who had survived as the greatest landholder in the country and the wealthiest man in the Americas, brother of Bolívar's old Paris friend, Mariano.

Chile and Argentina invaded the confederation to break it up. The Argentine troops were quickly driven out of Bolivia, but Chile smashed Santa Cruz's forces at Yungay in January, 1839. The "protector" fled to Europe. Gamarra, who had traitorously aided the invaders, took over once more as a Chilean puppet. He tried to recover Bolivia but was killed in battle in 1841.

From the ensuing anarchy, misery, banditry, and nationwide looting by starving demobilized soldiers emerged General Ramón Castilla, who ruled the country until 1862. Aided by the rise of the guano industry, he was able to maintain peace and have revenues to reconstruct the country, promote public works, and extend popular education. His regime ended in vast corruption, but he is the one outstandingly liberal and enlightened ruler Peru has ever had.

Castilla had fought under the Spanish flag in Chile, was captured, and later made his way to Peru where he joined the Independence cause with San Martín; with Bolívar and Sucre he had fought at Ayacucho. He was an earthy soul, and the following vulgar anecdote is told about him.

"My general, the Bolivians believe that they should have half of Lake Titicaca."

"Why not? Anything for peace." He took a pen and ruler and drew it across the lake, bisecting its name. "Titi [teats] for Peru; caca [shit] for Bolivia."

After the driving out of Santa Cruz, Bolivia sank into chaos and was successively ruled by some of the most bloodthirsty and lurid dictators or *caudillos* in the history of the Americas. The strangest and vainest was Mariano Melgarejo, who ruled from 1864–71, a cholo bastard, whose principal talents were drink, women, and wholesale butchery. He drove the Indians off their communal lands, re-establishing the rule of the large landowners. Another anecdote describes his flouting of all law, domestic and international.

During a dispute with the British minister, Melgarejo had him seized and tied head tailward on the back of a donkey and driven around the plaza of La Paz. The minister packed his bags and left. The matter was considered important and humiliating enough to be brought to the attention of Queen Victoria.

"Where is Bolivia?" she asked—so the story goes.

Her ministers brought her a map. One glance told her that the country was mostly out of reach of her Majesty's gunboats. She picked up a pen, drew a crisscross on the territory of the country, said "Bolivia no longer exists," and dismissed her ministers.

vii

Part of Liberator O'Higgins' difficulties in Chile sprang from the heavy burdens imposed by still having to fight the Spaniards and by the tremendous sacrifices necessary to build up a navy and equip the San Martín army against Peru. He drove the Spaniards off the mainland, but they still held the island of Chiloé from which they supported widespread banditry and stirred up the Araucanos.

The intrigues of the Lautaro Lodge and later the intrigues of the reactionary turncoat, Rodríguez Aldea, the struggle with the rich Creole families, his disputes with the Church, still impregnably pro-royalist and allied with the biggest land-holders, the terrible taxes, the uprising by Ramón Freire in part due to the corruption and theft of government supplies by

Rodríguez Aldea, the bitterness of the pro-Carrera elements plus the anger over the killing of resistance leader Manuel Rodríguez created such a welter of instability that O'Higgins was driven step by step toward full dictatorship, often ruthless. His troubles were worsened by drought and earthquake, and, when he re-elected himself for another ten years, the Santiago aristocrats and landholders, in the name of democracy, forced him to resign. He sailed for Peru, where he lived until his death in 1842.

The armed forces of Ramón Freire took over, defied the wealthy Creoles, and set up a loose federal system that was unworkable. After two years, his successor, Francisco Pinto, was driven out by a conservative uprising led by General Joaquín Prieto. A year of bitter civil war gave the Conservatives permanent control of the country for thirty years, following the battle of Lircay in April, 1830. Diego Portales, a trader and speculator who, it is said, overthrew Pinto in order to conceal thefts in the tobacco and other state monopolies he controlled, became the power behind the throne and was largely responsible for the first war with Peru. He was assassinated by the troops he reviewed, who were about to be sent to the campaign abroad.

The anecdote is told that once, attending a fiesta and watching the wild *zamacueca,* a sort of cock-and-hen dance that is the national dance of the country, Portales exclaimed, "I would rather be able to dance the *zamacueca* [he was a portly man] than be president of Chile!" He never achieved either goal.

The story of Argentina is similar to that of Gran Colombia, a process of territorial dismemberment. At the very outset it lost Paraguay; for years the patriots fought to retain the Argentine portions of Bolivia, including Potosí, but were given their final trouncing by Santa Cruz. For years they fought to hang on to the Banda Oriental, but eventually Rio Grande do Sul was incorporated into Brazil and Uruguay became an independent country.

Within Argentina proper, the power struggle went on incessantly between the Gauchos and the municipalities, particularly Buenos Aires; between federalists (the Gaucho *caudillos* of the interior) and centralists (Buenos Aires).

Finally, one of the most ruthless and colossal of South American dictators, Juan Manuel de Rosas, took over full control in 1835 and ruled until 1852. Though born in Buenos Aires, a member of a leading Creole family, he identified himself with the Gauchos of the interior, where he owned and managed thousands of acres. He was a magnificent horseman; expert with the knife, the lasso, the bolero; beloved by Negroes and Indians, for whom he showed respect and for whose rights he often fought. In politics he took the side of the federalists against the ruling oligarchy of Buenos Aires, the *unitarios* or centralists. His slogan became, "Death to the savage *unitarios*," and with his hard-riding Gauchos he rode into power, instituting an era of brutality and progress, in which he abandoned federalist principles entirely and created an ironclad centralized military state, which robbed and killed the people. The slightest suspicion brought his private guards on the scene: household goods were seized, all other property, and the victims were driven into the streets. People were hung in the public market with such signs as "Beef with the hide."

His chief early rival, Facundo Quiroga, the tyrant of La Rioja, a brutal man immortalized in Sarmiento's famous novel, was received with great honor as the dictator's friend and ally; then, riding north, he was assassinated. Rosas ordered an elaborate funeral, wept loudly for his fallen comrade, and put the assassins to death. On hearing that people accused him of having been the author of the crime, he retorted, "Can they prove it?"

He staged campaigns against the Indians, seizing millions of acres of land and turning them over to the richest landholders, to military officers, and to favored politicians—a policy little different from that of his predecessor, President Bernardino

Rivadavia, the Unitarian. Rosas' chief support became, not the Gauchos or the people, but a few great *estancieros* (he was one of the largest), who kept order in the interior and killed with impunity. For years he tried to recover Uruguay but never succeeded in capturing Montevideo; the process cost him twelve years of intermittent war or blockade with France or England, or both, that was not settled until 1850. There was scarcely a whisper about the Monroe Doctrine, though Secretary of State James Buchanan did wish "the Argentine Republic success against foreign interference"; indeed, during part of the period, the United States was too busy taking away half of Mexico's territory to concern itself with the southern end of the continent. It was at this time that England seized (and to this day has kept) the Falkland Islands.

But the long struggle helped unify the country and create patriotism, and it was for this reason that San Martín, who died in exile in 1850, willed his saber that had accompanied him "throughout the entire war of independence . . . to Juan Manuel Rosas, as a token of the satisfaction . . . I have felt for . . . the firmness with which he has sustained the republic's honor against . . . the foreigners who sought to humiliate her."

Uruguay, which finally achieved recognized independence in 1828, soon sank into disorder and misery, further accentuated by foreign interference and the invasions by Rosas.

As early as 1811, José Gervasio Artigas, a thirty-seven-year-old Gaucho, smuggler, and cattle rustler, offered his services to the Buenos Aires junta and led his Gauchos against Montevideo. When the junta signed a truce with the Spanish viceroy in Montevideo, Artigas refused to recognize it. He had to retreat across the river into Entre Rios, at that time Paraguayan territory, but by 1813 was back in the Banda Oriental fighting.

In Paraguay, where the prevailing language is Guaraní, not Spanish, Independence was declared from both Spain and Argentina in 1811. This was recognized by Argentina the following year, and a treaty of alliance was signed on October 12. Relations were broken two years later because of Paraguay's assistance to Artigas of Uruguay.

In 1814, Dr. José Gaspar Tomás Rodríguez Francia, a lawyer-theologian turned Rousseauan and a member of the original revolutionary junta, was voted dictatorial powers for five years. Two years later he was named dictator for life.

His rule was absolute. He forebade all public gatherings except on certain religious holidays. No one could get married without his permission, and Spaniards were required to marry Indians or Negroes. Many Spaniards were imprisoned; monasteries were confiscated. He cultivated close relations with Brazil, but in 1820, because of a border incursion, he cut off all trade with that country, later permitting it only through the single port of Itapúa.

He died in office on September 20, 1840, to be followed by the terrible López dictators, Carlos Antonio (1841–62) and his son Francisco Solano (1862–70). The first López, "a vain, fat, incredibly ugly *estanciero*, named President in 1844," ruled capriciously but did bring Paraguay out of international isolation imposed by the monklike Francia, built a few miles of roads and railways, and opened a few schools. But he seized half the land of Paraguay, owned 300,000 head of cattle and most business enterprises, plus a complete monopoly of the *yerba mate* industry, the most lucrative in the country.

His son was a bloated little man who wore uniforms like those of Napoleon and a replica of his crown. He came back from Europe with a mistress, the Irish girl Eliza Lynch, whom he had picked up in Paris. She became almost the arbiter of Paraguay's destinies. Francisco was shot by the allied troops in the 1864–1870 war, but Eliza escaped to Paris with money and jewels. Between them, Argentina and Brazil annexed 55,000 square miles, levied a staggering indemnity that was never paid, and maintained troops in occupation for six years.

The storm-swept graveyard that was Paraguay after the peace saw either chaos or dictatorship—a state that has continued to this day. From 1870 to 1954, there were thirty-nine presidents, most of whom were jailed, exiled, or murdered.

Following the prolonged Chaco War that may have cost as many as 100,000 lives (though it added 20,000 square miles of the sterile but oil-bearing Chaco to Paraguay), the country has been governed by seven Chaco War generals, fighting for the spoils in the exhausted country. The latest dictator, Alfredo Stroessner, has achieved some progress, chiefly with U.S. aid, but the torture chambers are full and a third of the population has been driven into exile.

Brazil, though caught in the tide of Independence, suffered fewer disorders and less war. When the Queen Mother died in 1816, the regent became João VI of Portugal, Brazil, and Algarve. Though the economic situation had been improved by many of his progressive measures, the costly wars with Argentina and Uruguay drained the country. In 1817, a revolt in Pernambuco had to be put down.

In 1820, the Portuguese overthrew the local regency and demanded that King João bring the court back to Lisbon. He sailed with an entourage of Portuguese nobles, whom Brazilians were glad to see depart, on April 26, 1821, leaving his twenty-one-year-old son, Pedro, to run Brazil.

Pedro had little education except as a soldier, but he was handsome and popular, really a Brazilian since he had few memories of Portugal. When the Portuguese Cortes demanded that he, too, return to the mother country, the Creoles, led by José Bonafácio de Andrada e Silva, a European-educated scientist and leader of the ultra-conservatives, demanded that Pedro remain in Brazil as king. The latter gladly accepted on January 9, 1822, a date celebrated as "I Remain Day." Andrada e Silva headed his government.

Four months later Pedro assumed the title of Perpetual Defender and Protector of Brazil and shortly called for a constitutional assembly.

Portugal sent ships and men to try to recover her colony. On September 7, Pedro announced that henceforth his motto would be Independence or Death—the famous *Grito* or Cry of Ypiranga, for he uttered it on the banks of São Paulo's great river. On October 12, 1822, he was proclaimed constitutional emperor of Brazil and on December 1 was crowned with splendid ceremonies. A constitution was adopted in 1824. That year João died, and Pedro renounced the throne of Portugal but nominated his five-year-old daughter, María da Gloria, and betrothed her to her uncle Miguel, his brother.

The bitter war with Portugal lasted three years. Dom Pedro hired Admiral Cochrane, who organized a navy and defeated the Portuguese roundly. The land forces, under French General Pedro Labatut (who had headed the Independence forces in Cartagena in New Granada when Bolívar was there), soon persuaded the Portuguese that they could never bring back Brazil under the monarchy.

In 1823, Dom Pedro kicked out the more reactionary Creoles from his government, including Andrada e Silva and his two conniving brothers, and instituted liberal reforms: freedom of the press, abolition of the slave traffic, a new criminal code. He promoted education, setting up elementary schools in every city, town, and hamlet.

He pushed war with Argentina over the Banda Oriental most vigorously from 1825–28, but Brazil lost money, men, and prestige—and Uruguay. His extravagances and his infidelity to Queen Leopoldina, a liberal, warm-hearted but uncomely woman who had borne him four children, did not sit well with Brazilians, especially when he took as his mistress Domitila de Castro Canto e Mello and built her a palace near the royal residence, making her the Marchioness of Santos and admitting her to the inner councils of state. When the empress died, the popular fury was so great, he had to banish Domitila. He hastily married seventeen-year-old Princess Amelia de Leuchtenberg.

In April, 1831, he turned his back on the liberal faction, and a revolt forced him to abdicate. He turned over the throne to his five-year-old son and went to Portugal.

Dom Pedro II was proclaimed Emperor, April 13, and a regency set up. It was faced with uprisings all over the country and Andrada e Silva took over once more, only to be driven out a year later. Finally Father Antonio de Feijó became regent in 1835, only to be faced with a slave revolt in Bahía. In this kaleidoscope of shifting government, free provincial legislatures were finally permitted. But a ten-year war of secession in Rio Grande do Sul and a series of revolts in Maranhão kept the country in an uproar.

Dom Pedro was declared of age in 1840 (he was only sixteen) and was crowned emperor in July of the following year. By then he was six feet three, soon able to grow a full-blown golden beard. He ruled with a combination of energy, wisdom, and laziness, which brought him the nickname of "Pedro Banana."

By 1850, Brazil had a population of 7,000,000, made up of 1,200,000 whites, 4,000,000 slaves, 1,000,000 free Negroes, and 500,000 Indians. Rio de Janeiro had a population of 2,500,000 and the entire province 1,400,000, closely followed by Minas Geraes, with 1,100,000. São Paulo and Pernambuco each had 800,000.

viii

South American Independence represented a great step forward, though it failed to bring the freedom or rewards expected by the people. Slavery was abolished, re-established—as in Peru—but finally ended everywhere, though not until much later in Brazil. The Negroes, though becoming free citizens, because of long servitude, lack of education, and poverty, remained an exploited element, though they suffered little of the race bigotry and abuse that have featured and still feature the post-slavery era in the United States. Many Negroes in Brazil became writers, painters, lawyers, statesmen, army generals; some of the most virile and beautiful qualities of Brazilian civilization are of Negro origin.

The Indians also became free citizens, though some were and are still in the head-hunting stage, but most were kept in a condition of abject serfdom, as in Peru, Ecuador, Brazil, and Colombia to this day. Of all the elements of the new societies, the Indians gained the least, though often bearing the worst burdens of the fifteen and more years of struggle. Independence failed entirely to take them into political consideration. Liberty was in sight for the Creoles; the mulattoes and Negroes and mestizos profited, but the Indians hardly at all. The Independence, as had the *Colinaje* (system of Spanish rule), merely exploited them, stole more of their lands (as is still being done in Colombia, Chile and Peru), exploited them, killed them, but otherwise ignored them except as forced army recruits. From time to time, ameliorative laws, mostly inadequate or farcical, have been passed to protect them; laws mostly ignored by their exploiters.

Telling of the colossal burdens of the Independence wars shouldered by the Indians, Oscar Efrén Reyes, Ecuadorian historian, has written, "No caste, no class could escape the torment of the years of struggle for Independence. Even the Indians were subjected to sacrifices of every sort," and with few rewards. "Along with the mules, he carried loads, whatever needed to be carried, over ravines and cliffs the whole length of the *cordillera* or wherever it was impossible to use mules, to wherever the armies camped or fought or halted. He was seized in his villages and off the roads." Sucre—for a time Bolívar—was almost the only leader who tried earnestly to remedy or avoid some of these abuses.

The mestizos reaped considerable advantages during and after the struggle. They moved up in the military, church, and governmental bureaucracies, soon coming to control the national armies and the governments; becoming presidents, cabinet ministers, and wealthy landlords; marrying into the most exclusive Creole clans. Their insatiable ambition for wealth and power, plus their tremendous energy and virility, made them an element of disorder and turbulence. They became the *caudillos,* the authors of palace revolutions and more serious revolutions. In their hands rested the fate of the countries, and they reached power by alliances with this or that faction among the dominant Creole class or sometimes headed up serious popular revolts. But over the years, this brought little benefit to the people or to the countries. Hardly had a mestizo *caudillo* taken over in the name of the people and freedom than he sold his talents to the Creoles and entered the charmed circle of the ruling caste. South American Independence history, picturesque though it often is, is a dreary record of repeated betrayals.

Because of the great gulf between the wealthy and the poor, the impotence of the small middle class, illiteracy and general lack of education, and the absence of an institutionalized political system, the mestizo *caudillos* found little sustained support from the masses they were ostensibly helping. There was no basis for democratic or representative government. The constitutional systems were a fraud, and nearly all elections were (and still are) a fraud. Democracy had no foundations, no roots—and has few roots today.

Nor was there a productive basis for representative and orderly government. A one-crop or one-product country can have only one type of government—a one-man government—dictatorship. So long as that system prevails, an effort to extend democracy or hold elections and install representatives duly chosen by the citizenry is merely so much spitting in the wind; they weaken the real struggle for independence and economic growth and end, as they have for more than a century, in repeated disillusionment.

Everywhere in South America the powerful land-holding class remains in control, though they bicker among themselves on occasion for that control; and their instruments, in any case, are the mestizo militarists. Thus the feudal system that had existed with the Spanish Conquest persisted unchanged to any great extent after Independence, so that the Creole class benefited most.

Independence brought them relief from many burdensome taxes, gave them freedom to grow the crops they desired, opened up to them the highest government posts, the highest posts in the Church and in the army. They merely pushed the Spaniards out of the nest, but kept all the traditional Conquistador methods and ideas.

Thus the revolution in most of the countries was in the hands of the Creoles first, last, and all the time, and if in some of the countries the Creoles who broke Spanish rule were liberal and enlightened men, in others it was more a counterrevolution than a revolution, a counterrevolution to keep out the ideas of the American Revolution, the French Revolution, the Code Napoléon, and to maintain intact the existing system of feudal land ownership and its methods of exploitation.

Where some freedom was introduced and some liberalization of the Spanish absolutist system occurred, the more reactionary Creoles soon gained full control and rolled back much of the progress made. In Chile, the landholders and the Church had to suffer some blows under O'Higgins, Freire and Pinto, but by 1833 they were back in full control and kept it for a century—until the disorderly, modern depression period—and the country is back in their hands today.

The very chaos that Independence unleashed because of so many years of war, everywhere furthered reconquest by the Creoles, however much they suffered from disorder. The demobilized soldiers had to return to *hacendado* serfdom or become bandits and looters. The old unity was rent apart, and in all countries a powerful current of localism and regionalism developed that made central rule more difficult. This, among other things, brought about the break-up of Gran Colombia, Peru, and Argentina—but it represented fierce local pride and demands for self-government, which were alternately granted and torn away again. The Gaucho wars were merely a symptom of a general disintegration. The rivalry between Guayaquil and Quito, which also persists to this day, was another aspect. The even greater division between highland, jungle, and coastal Peru has never been satisfactorily bridged to this day. Northern Chile and southern Chile are more different geographically, culturally, and ethnically than any two countries in Europe.

Transportation and communications were unable to weld even the smallest countries together properly. To this day the roads and railroads have been inadequate. The Araucanians did not permit the Chilean government to put railroads or telegraph lines through their territory until the late eighteen-eighties. It has been less than a decade since the highlands of Bolivia, with the bulk of the population, have been joined by rail or road to the *yungas* and the jungles or the rich plantation regions of Santa Cruz, hence the country has had to import most of its food at high cost from other countries. It is only since the last World War that a few roads have reached from the Peruvian highlands to the rich jungle and river country beyond. Most of Colombia is an impenetrable jungle. Much of the interior of Venezuela is not accessible, nor is that of Brazil. Most of the population of South America still lives within two hundred miles of the coast. Now, of course, the airplane has been revolutionizing the countries more rapidly than at any time in their history.

Soon after Independence came what the Latin Americans call the Second Conquest, the arrival of European and United States immigrants, capital, and enterprise. But mostly this merely accentuated the existing plantation and raw product systems. The new enterprise went into mining and oil production—oil accounts to this day, according to Adolf Berle, Jr., for 80 per cent of United States capital investment in South America. The money from Europe and the United States, quickly drawn out again by large profits, should have been a renovating and transforming force. Actually it merely tied the economies of the local nations to more advanced industrialized economies abroad, and in South America reinforced Creole feudalism rather than undermining it. Indeed the new alliance was and is precisely between foreign capital and the Creole overlords; the latter were the only ones who could maintain a semblance of order, and orderly processes were needed for an uninterrupted supply of raw materials. But for the mass of the population of South America, living conditions have not improved much, if at all, over what they were during the Conquest. In some ways they are worse, for as the original barter economy has broken down and more lands have been enclosed by the big estates, the people have more difficulty in gaining enough to eat and at the same time are beset by cravings for modern civilized gadgets which cannot be satisfied.

Nor can the hacienda modernize itself. To improve farm methods and increase production would merely accumulate commercial crops already in oversupply, which would in turn further reduce standards of living. Nor can those crops pay for modern tools and machinery, which cost three times as much as in the industrialized countries where they are produced. In some of the countries where gasoline and oil must be imported, a prohibitive barrier prevents technical modernization. In the competitive drive of such crops, the only recourse the *hacendado* has is to exploit human labor, to prevent the spread of education, of knowledge, of better living standards. This is the inexorable economic reality, which the new Alliance for Progress, for instance, cannot solve but must only aggravate.

San Martín and Bolívar completed a political revolution of sorts, but the completion of this revolution for independence, now underway, demands economic changes that are not going to be simple or easy, but which inevitably will be carried out. More than a hundred million people in lands as rich or richer than most countries of the world are not going to live indefinitely on an income of less than $100 a year. And their numbers are increasing rapidly.

ix

The twilight of the Gods came quickly after the achievement of Independence. Bolívar and Sucre were dead. As both San Martín and Bolívar foresaw, Independence would bring a new disorderly struggle for power.

It brought trouble first to all the followers of the great leaders. And to no one more than to Manuela. With Bolívar's death her world fell apart; her purpose in life vanished. Boussingault believed that she tried to commit suicide by letting a poisonous fer-de-lance bite her. He found her on a sofa, her right arm hanging down swollen to the shoulder. "How beautiful Manuelita is!"

Within a few months after Bolívar's death she sold her jewels for 1,000 pesos and went with her belongings and her retinue to Guanacas del Arroyo, well outside Bogotá. Even there her home on the Sabana was considered a rendezvous for malcontents.

Santander returned to the country soon after Bolívar died. By 1832 he was president. The following year Manuela was accused of conspiring against his government. It was not a pleasant moment. The enemies real and imagined of the government were being shot right and left.

Her reply to the charges was published. "Santander gives me an unimaginable valor, saying that I have the capacity for the most monstrous deceptions. What I really am is a formidable character, friend of my friends, enemy of my enemies. I have nothing in common with this miserable Santander."

On January 1, 1834, he gave her three days to leave the country. A small army of bailiffs, soldiers, and convicts seized her, trussed her up, and sent her under guard down the Magdalena River. In Cartagena she was thrown into a dungeon in the fortress.

Some months later she was put aboard an English vessel

bound for Jamaica. There Bolívar's old friend of twenty years earlier, Maxwell Hyslop, now assisted Manuela also.

She was unhappy. These people were not her people. The language was not her language. She longed for Ecuador, and on May 6, 1835, she wrote to General Flores, now president of an independent Ecuador, asking for his help so she could get back to her native land. "I always remember with pleasure our old friendship, and in its name I beg you to aid me."

She did not know that at that very hour, her half brother, General José María Sáenz, had been captured and was going before a firing squad.

Her letter contained a veiled threat. "There exists in my hands your intimate correspondence with the Liberator, and I'm going to make full use of it."

Four months later she received an invitation to come to Ecuador, a passport and safe-conduct signed by Flores.

In October she reached Guayaquil and once more started up the Andes. But in the mountain village of Guaranda, under the snows, soldiers burst in at night with naked bayonets and conducted her back to Guayaquil, where she was ordered to leave the country.

She managed to get as far as Paita, Peru, a little burning-hot port on the far northern desert where United States whaling vessels were wont to put in for water and supplies. With what little money she had left she put up a shop, selling tobacco, home-made candies, lace, and embroideries.

With her, still deathlessly loyal, were her two slaves, Jonotás and Natán, her servant, Juana Rosa, and two waifs she had once taken in.

There mostly she sat in a rocking chair or in her hammock, smoked her cigarettes, crocheted, lived with her memories, and perhaps now and then wept a bit.

Over the years she had a few notable visitors. A member of a rebellious whaling crew from New Bedford, Herman Melville, wrote about her, " She was passing into Payta town upon a small ass. . . . She eyed the jointed workings of the beast's armorial cross. . . ."

In 1847 she fell and dislocated her hip. The injury confined her to her hammock for the rest of her life.

In Pativilca, where Bolívar had almost died, a masked gang killed her husband and his mistress, multilating them horribly. He left a huge estate, but his will gave Manuela exactly the 8,000 pesos of her original dowry to him, plus interest. Though she needed the money badly, the court refused to turn it over to her, because she was "a public woman."

A letter came from O'Leary, back in Bogotá as British consul general, asking her for her letters to Bolívar and for her archives, hidden only she knew where. She ordered turned over to him a leather-bound trunk containing all her personal correspondence. After using what he wished, he sent the coffer on to Paita by special messenger.

She was reading them when aged Simón Rodríguez (old Robinson) shuffled into her home. He was eighty but his face, under a fluffy halo of white hair, was still as rosy as a boy's. He had written *Defense of Bolívar*, for which he had been deported from Peru to Ecuador. There he had gotten a teacher's job but was never paid the promised twenty-peso-a-month salary, so he made candles. He had tried to get financing for a grandiose plan to colonize the Amazon and finally put up a powder factory at Latacunga. It blew up just as he completed his first order. He packed his belongings on a mule and set out for Paita, where he found an abandoned hovel in the nearby hamlet of Amotaje.

By this time Manuela was living almost entirely on the charity of her neighbors, and Rodríguez was a great comfort to her. Together they read over Bolívar's letters. He told her of his memories of the Liberator from childhood days on and read and reread Rousseau to her.

In 1851 Giuseppe Garibaldi, liberator of Italy and fighter for Spanish-American Independence—also onetime candlemaker on Staten Island—appeared at her door. His eyes burning with fever, he lay on a couch and asked her about the Liberator. He wrote, "Donna Manuelita was the most gracious and courteous lady I have ever met."

She kept writing O'Leary details of Bolívar's life and of her relations with him. In 1854 he finished his *Memoirs,* three volumes, and twenty-nine volumes of letters and documents, but they were not published until twenty-five years after his death (1879–88). Even then, all but three copies of the volume about Manuela were destroyed. All the Colombian and Venezuelan historians and biographers of Bolívar, in their efforts to recreate him as a demigod, had erased all mention of Manuela from the record of his life. The lost volume was finally republished in 1914. Previously an early compilation, Volume 56 of the National Archives, *Correspondencia y document os relacionadas con la Señora Sáenz* was also destroyed, probably sometime in the seventies. So much for the erudite vandals of Colombia!

O'Leary died that same year of 1854. So did Rodríguez, quoting, *"Comedia finita est."* Manuela was left with a great emptiness, except for her precious letters.

In November, 1856, a sailor from a whaler brought a diphtheria epidemic to Paita that was so terrible everybody who could fled to the interior to the more healthful Andean country. So fast did the dead mount that ships would not touch at the port.

Jonotás and Natán and Juana Rosa died, then Manuela herself.

She was buried in the common pit under Paita's gray cliffs, her grave unmarked. To try to halt the epidemic, the authorities burned everything found in her house, clothes, pictures, medals, battle mementoes, documents, and the leather-bound coffer that held the letters from Bolívar. "The memory of your enchantments dissolves the frost of my years. . . . Come. Come to me. Come now."

x

The political execration of petty men shrouded the memory of Bolívar for many years, and Manuela shared that oblivion. The pendulum swung to the other extreme, and presently he was being deified, which meant that Manuela, more than ever, had to be completely forgotten. Her name, her love, her accomplishments had to be erased from all records.

The sudden revival of Bolívar's fame, his first return to the "glory" of which they had robbed him, came in 1842, when President Páez of Venezuela finally acceded to the years of pleading by his sisters that his body be returned to Caracas.

It was done in style, with great international fanfare. A Venezuelan man-of-war was sent to Santa Marta. A British war vessel accompanied it to add dignity to the occasion.

For the ceremony of reburial, the diplomats of the earth were invited. Many nations sent war vessels in honor of the occasion, and as the Venezuelan vessel with Bolívar's remains and its British escort appeared in La Guayra, the cannon boomed out their salutes.

But uninvited was Manuela, swinging in her Paita hammock quite forgotten, with only her memories. The woman who had defied society to give him her love, who had inspired him in his darkest and most sublime moments, who had nursed him back to health time and again, who had saved his life in the palace of power, was not present. (It would be a hundred years before anything more than brief magazine articles about her would appear: the first full-length biography of her was Alfonso Rumazo González's volume in 1944; and not until 1952 did the beautiful and moving account, *The Four Seasons of Manuela*, by Victor W. Von Hagen, introduce her to English-speaking readers.)

Nor had Manuela been present at what was perhaps the dramatic climax of Bolívar's whole career, a moment of supreme exaltation and glory never surpassed, that occurred in Bolivia.

On October 26, 1825—two days before his saint's day—with O'Leary, Sucre, two Argentine emissaries who had come to offer political union on a continental scale, and various military and civilian bigwigs, he had climbed to the summit of mighty Potosí, the fabulous mountain of silver, and from its highest crest looked out over the majestic south highlands.

Bolívar's most important and beloved companion on that difficult ascent, partly by mule-back, partly on foot past crevices and cliffs, was his old tutor and friend, Simón Rodríguez, thus making this an almost sacred rite, a fulfillment of the pledge he had made years before on the Aventine in Rome, never to rest until all America had been freed from Spanish rule. This was the Aventine of the New World, a much vaster continent, a far wealthier realm, and fifty times as high. It was a fulfillment also of the pledge he had made to himself and to the flamingos of the wet marsh reeds at Barcelona at the start of his last and his successful invasion of Venezuela. His words had sounded like those of a madman. The madman had made them come true.

By this time he had liberated five countries; he was simultaneously acting president of Bolivia, president of Peru, president of Gran Colombia. His head still swirled with dreams of even more grandiose undertakings, possibly permanent union of Gran Colombia with Peru and Bolivia. Ahead of him was the great Amphictyonic Congress soon to be held at Panama, a symbol, a consummation, looking toward the unity of all Hispanic America, of peace and concord in all the world.

He dreamed on the crest of Potosí of new worlds to conquer. He talked grandiloquently of marching his army south to the Straits of Magellan. More seriously, he contemplated invading Paraguay to oblige Dictator Rodríguez Francia—who did not even reply to his requests—to release his old friend, the companion of Humboldt, Aimé Bonpland, being held there against his will.

And so this ascent of the silver mountain was a culmination of all his achievements and his hopes. Bolivia was the pivot of all South America, the heart of the continent. All other countries were within striking distance. From this tableland of the world, this western Tibet, he could look down over the entire continent that had been liberated. Potosí was the eagle's nest of power and wealth—and of universal freedom. This silver mountain, more than anything else, had nourished the wealth and power of Spain in the New World. Now it belonged to the free peoples of the New World.

Bolívar shivered slightly as he looked down at the great black plateau, desolate, empty, not a plant, not a tree, just a vast wind-swept desert, monotonous except that above it rose into the pale blue sky—the pallid blue of all upland regions— the vast snow ridges of the Andes.

And he turned and raised the banners of Peru, of Bolivia, of Colombia, of Argentina, the banners of freedom, just as he had pledged himself to do, above the highest splinter of rock.

"We have come conquering from the coasts of the Atlantic, and in fifteen years of continuous struggle, we have thrown down the edifice of tyranny built without compassion during three centuries of usurpation and violence. . . . They wished to keep us enslaved. With courage and endurance, we have won freedom for millions. Here on this great mass of silver called Potosí, whose rich veins for three hundred years have filled the treasury of Spain, I deem that opulence as nothing compared to the glory of having carried the victorious banners of liberty from the burning shores of the Orinoco to plant them here on the crest of this mountain, whose matrix fires the wonder and envy of the universe."

Bibliography

The readily available literature on the independence of each of the ten countries of South America would require a lifetime to read. These are some of the works found especially useful in the preparation of the present volume.

AMUNÁTEGUI, MIGUEL LUÍS, *La Crónica de 1810*. Santiago de Chile, 1911.

——, *La Dictadura de O'Higgins*. Santiago de Chile, 1914.

——, *La Reconquista Española*. Santiago de Chile, 1912.

ARELLANO MORENO, A., *Guía de Historia de Venezuela, 1492–1945*. Caracas, 1955.

ARGÜEDAS, ALCIDES, *Historia General de Bolivia (1809–1921)*, 3d ed. Santiago de Chile, 1937.

ARIAS, AUGUSTO, *Manuela Sáenz en Paita*. Caracas, 1938.

BAÑADOS ESPINOZA, JULIO, *La Batalla de Rancagua*. Santiago de Chile, 1884.

BARROS ARANA, DIEGO, *Historia General de Chile*, 16 vols. Santiago de Chile, 1884–1902.

——, *Historia General de la Independencia de Chile*. Santiago de Chile, 1854.

BASADRE, JORGE, *Chile, Perú y Bolivia Independientes*. Barcelona, 1948.

BENAVENTE, DIEGO JOSÉ, *Primeras Campañas de la Guerra de Independencia de Chile.* Santiago de Chile, 1856.

BERTLING, HANS, *Documentos Históricos Referentes al Paso de los Andes . . . 1817.* Concepción, 1908.

——, *Estudio Sobre el Paso . . . de los Andes.* Santiago de Chile, 1917.

BLANCO, J. F., ED., *Documentos para la Historia de la Vida Pública del Libertador de Colombia, Perú y Bolivia,* 14 vols. Caracas, 1873–1877.

BLANCO ACEVEDO, PABLO, *Historia de la República Oriental del Uruguay,* 6 vols. Buenos Aires, 1910.

BLANCO-FOMBONA, RUFINO, ED., *Cartas de Bolívar, 1799–1822.* Paris, 1912.

BLEST GANA, ALBERTO, *Durante la Reconquista,* 2 vols. Santiago de Chile, 1942. Second edition, 1946.

BOLÍVAR, SIMÓN, *Obras Completas* (Comp. Vicente Lecuna), 3 vols. Caracas, 1954.

BOUSSINGAULT, JEAN-BAPTISTE, *Mémoires,* 5 vols. Paris, 1899–1903.

BULNES, GONZALO, *Historia de la Expedición Libertadora del Perú, 1817–1822.* Santiago de Chile, 1914.

——, *Ultimas Campañas de la Independencia del Perú.* Santiago de Chile, 1862, 1897.

CABANELLAS, GUILLERMO, *El Dictador del Paraguay, Dr. Francia.* Buenos Aires, 1946.

CADCLEUGH, ALEJANDRO, *Viajes por Sud-América Durante de los Anos 1819, 1820, 1821.* Santiago de Chile, 1914.

CALMÓN, PEDRO, *História da Civilização Brasileira,* 6th ed. São Paulo, 1958.

CARBONELL, DIEGO, *El General O'Leary Intimo.* Caracas, 1937.

COCHRANE, THOMAS, *Narrative of Services in the Liberation of Chile, Peru and Brazil,* 2 vols. London, 1859.

Correo del Orinoco. Angostura, 1818–1821; reprinted, Paris, 1939.

CRUZ, ERNESTO DE LA, ED., *Epistolario de Don Bernardo O'Higgins.* Santiago de Chile, 1916.

CRUZ, ERNESTO DE LA, *La Entrevista de Guayaquil.* Santiago de Chile, 1914.

DAMIRON, A., *Compendio de la Historia de Venezuela.* Caracas, 1840.

DÉLANO, LUÍS ENRIQUE, *Pequeña Historia de Chile.* Mexico, 1944.

DÍAZ, J. D., *Documentos Sobre la Vida de Generalísimo Miranda.* Maracaibo, 1896.

——, *Recuerdos Sobre la Rebelión de Caracas.* Madrid, 1829.

ENCINA, FRANCISCO A., *Bolívar y la Independencia de América Española.* Santiago de Chile, 1954.

ESPEJO, JERÓNIMO, *El Paso de los Andes.* Buenos Aires, 1882.

EYZAGUIRRE, JAIME, *O'Higgins.* Santiago de Chile, 1946.

FINTER, GEORGE DAWSON, *A History of the Revolution in Caracas.* London, 1819.

GÁLVEZ, MANUEL, *Vida de Don Juan Manuel de Rosas.* Buenos Aires, 1942.

GANDÍA, ENRIQUE DE, *Historia de la República Argentina en el Siglo XIX.* Buenos Aires, 1940.

GARCÍA CHUECOS, HÉCTOR, *Siglo Dieciocho Venezolano.* Caracas, 1936.

GARCÍA REYES, ANTONIO, *La Primera Escuadra Nacional.* Santiago de Chile, 1868.

GARIBALDI, GIUSEPPE, *Autobiography.* London, 1889.

GONZÁLEZ, JOAQUÍN VICTOR, *Biografía de José Félix Ribas.* Paris, n.d.

GRAHAM, MARY, *Diario de su Residencia en Chile (1822) y de su Viaje al Brasil (1823).* Madrid, n.d.

HAIGH, SAMUEL, *Viaje a Chile.* Santiago de Chile, 1917.

HALL, BASIL, *Extracts From a Journal Written on the Coast of Chile, Peru, Ecuador,* 2 vols. Mexico, 1826.

——, *Fragments of Voyages . . . ,* 9 vols. London, 1931–1940.

HUMBOLDT, ALEXANDER VON, *Personal Narrative of Travels . . . ,* 7 vols. London, 1821–1829.

IRIARTE, TOMÁS DE, *Memorias.* Buenos Aires, 1944.

JARAMILLO ALVARADO, PÍO, *El Gran Mariscal José de la Mar.* Quito, 1941.

BIBLIOGRAPHY

LARRAZÁBAL, F., *Life of Simón Bolívar*. New York, 1866.

——, *Vida y Correspondencia del Libertador Simón Bolívar*. New York, 1901.

LECUNA, VICENTE, *Bolívar y el Arte Militar*. New York, 1955.

——, *Crónica Razonada de las Guerras de Bolívar*, 3 vols. New York, 1950.

——, *La Entrevista de Guayaquil*. Caracas, 1952.

——, "Papeles de Manuela Sáenz." *Boletín de la Academia Nacional de Historia*, vol. 28. Caracas, October-December, 1945.

——, *Relaciones Diplomáticas de Bolívar con Chile y Buenos Aires*. Caracas, 1954.

LEVENE, RICARDO, *Historia Argentina*. Vols. I–II. Buenos Aires, 1934.

LUGONES, LEOPOLDO, *Historia de Sarmiento*. Buenos Aires, 1911.

LYRA, HEITOR, *Archivo Diplomático de Independencia*. Rio de Janeiro, 1922.

——, *Historia de Dom Pedro II*. Rio de Janeiro, 1939.

MADARIAGA, SALVADOR DE, *Bolívar*. New York, 1952.

MANCINI, JULES, *Bolívar et l'Émancipation des Colonies Espagnoles des Origines à 1815*. Paris, 1912.

MARTÍNEZ, MELCHOR, *Memoria Histórica . . . desde el Cautiverio de Fernando VII Hasta 1814*. Valparaiso, 1848.

MASUR, GERHARD, *Simón Bolívar*. Albuquerque, 1948.

MÉNDEZ, JOSÉ IGNACIO, *El Ocaso de Bolívar*. Bogotá, 1951.

MERINO, LUÍS, *Batalla de Maipú*. Santiago de Chile, 1909.

MILLER, JOHN, *Memoirs of General Miller*, 2 vols. London, 1828.

MIRAMÓN, ALBERTO, *La Vida Ardiente de Manuelita Sáenz*. Bogotá, 1946.

MIRANDA, FRANCISCO, *Archivo*, 15 vols. Caracas, 1929–1938.

——, *Diario*. New York, 1928.

MITRE, BARTOLOMÉ, *Historia de Belgrano y de la Independencia Argentina*, 3 vols. Buenos Aires, 1887.

MITRE, BARTOLOMÉ, *Historia de San Martín y de la Emancipación Sud-Americana*, 3 vols. Buenos Aires, 1887–1888.

MONTAÑER BELLO, RICARDO, *Historia Diplomática de la Independencia de Chile*. Santiago de Chile, 1941.

MORENO, PEDRO ANTONIO, *Argentina-Chile: Las Provincias Unidas de Sud-América*. Buenos Aires, 1944.

NARIÑO, ANTONIO, *Escrito Presentado al Tribunal de Gobierno de Santa Fé de Bogotá*. Bogotá, 1903.

NUCETE-SARDI, JOSÉ, *Aventura y Tragedia de Don Francisco de Miranda*. Caracas, 1935.

O'HIGGINS, BERNARDO, *Epistolario*. Santiago de Chile, 1916.

O'LEARY, DANIEL FLORENCIO, *Documentos*, 29 vols.; *Memorias*, 3 vols. Caracas, 1879–1888; reprint of suppressed vol. 3, Bogotá, 1914.

OLIVEIRA LIMA, MANUEL DE, *Dom João VI do Brasil*, 2 vols. Rio de Janeiro, 1908.

PALACIO FAJARDO, MANUEL, *Outline of the Revolution in Spanish America*. London, 1817; Spanish ed., Caracas, 1953.

PAREJA Y DIEZCANSECO, ALFREDO, *Historia del Ecuador*, 2 vols. Quito, 1958.

PARRA-PÉREZ, CARACCIOLO, *La Monarquía en la Gran Colombia*. Madrid, 1957.

PEÑA, CONCHA, *La Libertadora*, Panamá, 1944.

PEREIRA SALAS, EUGENIO, *La Misión Worthington en Chile, 1818–1819*. Santiago de Chile, 1936.

PEREYRA, CARLOS, *El General Sucre*. Madrid [1917].

PICÓN-FEBRES, GONZALO, *La Literatura Venezolana en el Siglo Diez y Nueve*. Caracas, 1906.

POSADA, PEDRO JOSÉ CARLOS EDUARDO, *Apostillas a la Historia Colombiana*. Madrid, 1908.

——, *Biografía de Córdoba*. Bogotá, 1914.

POSADA GUTIÉRREZ, JOAQUÍN, *Memorias Histórico-políticas*. Bogotá [1847].

POUDEN, J., and MAYER, F., *Mémoires . . . de la Revolution de Caracas*. Paris, 1815.

Recollections of a Service of Three Years in the Colombian Navy. London, 1828.

RESTREPO, JOSÉ MANUEL, *Diario Político y Militar*, vols. 1, 2. Bogotá, 1954.

———, *Historia de la Revolución de la República de Colombia,* 3 vols. Paris, 1827.

REYES, OSCAR EFRÉN, *Breve Historia General del Ecuador,* 6th ed., 3 vols. Quito, 1960.

ROBERTSON, WILLIAM SPENCE, *The Life of Miranda,* 2 vols. Chapel Hill, 1929.

ROBINSON, J. P. and W. P., *Letters on Paraguay.* London, 1839.

ROCHA POMBO, FRANCISCO DA, *Historia do Brasil,* 10 vols. Rio de Janeiro, 1905.

RODRÍGUEZ VELASCO, FRANCISCO DE P., *Biografía del Doctor José Antonio Rodríguez Aldea.* Santiago de Chile, 1862.

ROJAS, ARÍSTIDES, *Estudios Históricos.* Caracas, 1926.

———, *Los Hombres de la Revolución, 1810–1826.* Caracas, 1878.

ROJAS, MARQUÉS DE, *Simón Bolívar.* Paris, 1883.

ROJAS, RICARDO, *El Santo de la Espada.* Buenos Aires, 1933.

RUMAZO GONZÁLEZ, ALFONSO, *Gobernantes del Ecuador (1830–1932).* La Paz, 1933.

———, *Manuela Sáenz.* Buenos Aires, 1944.

———, *O'Leary: Edecán del Libertador.* Caracas, 1956.

———, *Simón Bolívar.* Caracas, 1954.

SALAS, CARLOS I., *Bibliografía del General Don José de San Martín y de la Emancipación Sud-Americana,* 5 vols. Buenos Aires, 1910.

SANFUENTES, SALVADOR, *Chile Desde las Batallas de Chacabuco a la de Maipó.* Santiago de Chile, 1868.

SARMIENTO, DOMINGO FAUSTINO, *La Vida de Juan Facundo.* Santiago de Chile, 1845.

SEMPLE, A., *Sketch of the Present State of Caracas . . . La Victoria and Valencia to Puerto Cabello.* London, 1812.

SHERWELL, GUILLERMO A., *Antonio José de Sucre.* Washington, 1924.

SHERWELL, GUILLERMO A., *Simón Bolívar*. Washington, 1921.

TALAVERA, MANUEL ANTONIO, *Revoluciones de Chile*. Santiago de Chile, 1937.

TAMAYO, JOAQUÍN, *Nuestro Siglo XIX (La Gran Colombia)*. Bogotá, 1941.

TAPAJÓS, VICENTE, *História do Brasil*, 10th ed. São Paolo, 1960.

TEJERA, HUMBERTO, *José de San Martín*. Mexico, 1945.

TEJERA, M., *Vida del General Francisco Miranda*. Caracas, 1877.

TEJERA P., MANUEL DE, *La Historia de Venezuela*. Caracas, 1913.

TORRENTE, MARIANO, *Historia de la Revolución Hispano-Americana*, 3 vols. Madrid, 1829–1830.

URIBE ORREGO, LUÍS, *Los Orígines de Nuestra Marina Militar*. Santiago de Chile, 1892.

URQUINANONA Y PARDO, PEDRO DE, *Memorias. . . .* Madrid, 1917.

VARGAS, PEDRO JOSÉ, *Carlos Soubrette*. Caracas, 1947.

VEJARANO, JORGE RICARDO, ED., *Orígines de la Independencia de las Américas*. Bogotá, 1925.

VICUÑA MACKENNA, BENJAMÍN, *Datos y Documentos . . . [sobre] Don Bernardo O'Higgins*. Santiago de Chile, 1872.

———, *El General Don José de San Martín*. Santiago, 1902.

———, *El General San Martín antes del Maipú*. Santiago, 1877.

———, *El General San Martín después de Chacabuco*. Santiago, 1876.

———, *La Guerra a Muerte (1819–1824)*. Santiago, 1868.

———, *El Ostracismo de los Carreras*. Santiago, 1938.

———, *San Martín en Marcha al Perú*. Santiago, 1878.

———, *Vida de . . . O'Higgins*. Santiago, 1882, 1936.

VILLAMIL, JOSÉ, *Reseña de los Acontecimientos Políticos y Militares de la Provincia de Guayaquil Desde 1813 Hasta 1824*, 2nd ed. Guayaquil, 1937.

VILLANUEVA, CARLOS A., *Historia de Argentina*. Paris, 1914.

———, *La Monarquía en América: Bolívar y San Martín*. Paris, 1911.

VILLANUEVA, LAUREANO, *Vida de . . . Sucre*. Caracas, 1945.

VON HAGEN, VICTOR W., *The Four Seasons of Manuela*. New York, 1952.

WALTON, WILLIAM, *Exposé of the Dissentions of Spanish America*. London, 1814.

ZÚÑIGA, ANTONIO, *La Logia "Lautaro" y la Independencia de América*. Buenos Aires, 1922.

Index

349

About the Author

A veteran writer with thirty-five books to his credit, Carleton Beals has written extensively on the subject of South America. Among his most recent books are *Nomads and Empire Builders* and *Cyclone Carry: The Story of Carry Nation,* also published by Chilton.

Mr. Beals has crossed the Andes four times —by train, by car, on horseback and on foot. Moreover, in 1962 he toured and lectured throughout Latin America.